Special Education in the 21st Century

Special Education in the 21st Century

Issues of Inclusion and Reform

Margret A. Winzer
Kas Mazurek,
Editors

Gallaudet University Press
Washington, D.C.

For our fathers, Jan Mazurek and Leslie Winzer.

Gallaudet University Press
Washington, DC 20002

Library of Congress Cataloging-in-Publication Data

Special education in the 21st century : issues of inclusion and reform / Kas Mazurek
and Margret A. Winzer, editors.
     p.   cm.
Includes bibliographical references and index.
ISBN 1-56368-100-5 (hardcover)
     1. Special education—United States—History—20th century. 2. Inclusive
education—United States—History—20th century. 3. Educational change—United
States—History—20th century. I. Title: Special education in the twenty-first centu
II. Mazurek, Kas. III. Winzer, M.A. (Margret A.), 1940-

LC3981.S594 2000
371.9'973—dc21   00-061705

⊖ The paper used in this publication meets the minimum requirements of American
National Standard of Information Sciences—Permanence of Paper for Printed Library
Materials, ANSI Z39.48-1984.

Contents

General Introduction

Contemporary special education encompasses an extremely complex social and conceptual system that is designed to assist all children and youth with special needs to reach their full potential. Special education is designed to accommodate students who are different from the average in some or many areas of functioning. The children and youth who are served have traits and characteristics that demand unique and often individual programming, although this programming is embedded as far as possible within the general education curriculum.

Philosophies and practices that are seen in today's special education programs are built on a long and honorable history; many of our current philosophies, legislation, techniques, and approaches arise from earlier precedents and activities. And, as special education is an integrative professional area that cuts across a spectrum of services, it makes use of many different fields of knowledge and depends upon the techniques, the concepts, and the practices of several allied disciplines. The myriad of external forces include legislation, politics, medicine, ethics, and economics, to mention only a few.

A field as historically complex and diverse as special education and one influenced by so many different disciplines and fields is bound to reveal a plethora of controversial issues and be open to debate. By extension, the field also tends to reflect major trends and movements, both in the school system and in society in general. For example, today's ongoing debate concerning inclusive schooling is a paramount topic within special education, but it also mirrors a major trend toward inclusive practices throughout the entire education system and a shifting of societal perceptions about individual and educational rights.

In and of themselves, the issues surrounding contemporary special education are inherently interesting for they say a great deal about our society, our schools, and the ways we perceive and treat individuals who are different. More pointedly, as reform initiatives throughout the entire education system (including special education) have shifted the focus toward outcomes, quantifiable data, teacher accountability, and increased teacher responsibilities, both prospective and practicing educators need to broaden their perceptions, their knowledge, and their skills. Whether they specifically provide special education services or whether they are general classroom teachers responsible for including students with special needs, teachers require a thorough understanding of the issues confronting special education. Clear and lucid views of the various issues are essential so that professionals can understand, explain, and take a stance on the issues that are riveting the field.

Our major objective in assembling the papers in this book is to present some of the major issues and debates within the field of special education both to those entering the profession and to experienced educators. The contributing authors write from a number of different stances and philosophical orientations. Although all the papers in the text have inclusion and inclusive practices as their core, the authors address this central issue from a variety of perspectives and disciplines. Readers will, therefore, find diversity in the arguments that will allow them to balance many sides of the debates currently found in the area of special education.

A number of caveats preface our discussion. First of all, a single volume such as this book cannot possibly address every issue in special education. Although discussions of inclusive schooling, legislation, early intervention, technology, and multiculturalism are prominent, readers should be aware that other pressing issues—such as curriculum planning and delivery, consultation and collaboration, transition, and working with paraprofessionals—are not specifically included (although they are touched on by many contributing authors).

Readers should also keep in mind throughout the discussion that education services and the ideas that stimulate and direct the growth of those services are never static; hence, reforms in education are continuous and reflect a society's views of what is important at a given time. This dynamic makes reform in education an open-ended social issue with few definitive solutions. Similarly, this text is a document that is written in a particular place at a particular time. It represents only a snapshot of special education and cannot faithfully reproduce the dynamic shifts that are occurring in the field. Finally, changes in special education are influenced by many external forces—social, legislative, and economic—that influence the progress and practice of the enterprise.

INCLUSIVE SCHOOLING

In historical terms, the question of where children with disabilities went to school and where they sat was a major argument with threads that touched on almost every other aspect of the philosophy and process of special education, such as teacher attitudes, skills, and priorities; personnel; certification standards; and the type and quality of training programs, curricula, and nonbiased assessments. The same central theme continues prominently throughout the enterprise today.

Contemporary special education is no longer a sanctuary for a few children who are removed from the mainstream of education. It is now everybody's concern, from the specialist to the general education teacher. As we see a paradigm shift and a restructuring of special education, the most hotly debated issue of the 1990s concerned inclusion, or inclusive schooling. This ongoing education reform movement has brought numerous other education issues into focus. A broad spectrum of trends and movements, all related in some way to inclusion, are germane to contemporary special education as educators continue their efforts to reform, revamp, and generally improve services for students with special needs.

Few issues have received the attention and have generated the controversy and polarization of perspectives as the movement to include all children with disabilities into regular classrooms. Because inclusion is so central to contemporary special education and because inclusion forms the core of this text, it makes sense to discuss some of the parameters of the movement here.

First, inclusion is not exclusive to special education but, rather, is the adopted child. The call for inclusive education is the outcome of a complex set of discourses about the equality of education that is driven by changing demographics, ideologies, and perceptions of marginalized groups as well as by associated social issues (see Mithaug 1998). During the 1960s, educational institutions at all levels began to respond to the Civil Rights movement in various ways and from different perspectives. Inclusion emerged as a broad notion of social justice that was manifested as an expression of concern for safeguarding the rights of all students. Individuals are not restricted because of some unalterable traits. Rather, an inclusive school is one that is "structured to serve a wide range of students; the environment is flexible and organized to meet the unique needs of all students. In an inclusive school, everyone belongs, is accepted, supports, and is supported while having individual education needs met" (Barnes and Lehr 1993, 82).

In addition to the broad social issue of including marginalized groups, the 1980s and 1990s saw critics take schools to task for a multitude of sins. The whole of public education has come under attack from the media, governments, ad hoc commissions, parent and other interest groups, education critics, and academics. Such an unrelenting assault on the content, processes, and outcomes of schooling has elevated school reform to a major movement for all levels and for all populations.

Many different initiatives that were designed to improve education fall under the rubric of school reform. One wave of reform efforts that brought inclusion to the forefront mirrors the dramatic changes in school populations in the United States and Canada in the past twenty years. An amalgam of different language, ethnic, national, and religious groups and a broad spectrum of physical characteristics (including gender and disabilities) brought enormous diversity to contemporary education. Our public schools are now faced with tremendous linguistic and cultural diversity. Such changing demographics and an increasingly more culturally and linguistically diverse student population has made concerns about equity "desperately more pressing" (Li 1994, 132).

The reform movement did not pass special education by. On the contrary, in the mid-1980s, special education became deeply embroiled in reform efforts that paralleled and reflected reforms in general education. The process of gradual evolutionary change that has traditionally characterized special education was subjected to increasing challenges by a growing legion of critics. The field was faced with enormous pressures for change; widespread criticism came from both within and without the field, and rhetoric demanded new paradigms. Many professionals, parents, and teachers seriously questioned the efficacy and structure of special education, and calls resounded for breaking the mold, for "revolution," for a "paradigm shift," for a "fundamental reconceptualization," and for "radical restructuring" (Kauffman 1993, 10). Central to the issue was the relative value of segregated and integrated settings and whether such separate or integrated classes offered qualitatively different education ecologies. Many held the position that a student's educational experiences should promote membership in a heterogeneous group of students who share primary bonds in their experiences—being children and learning together—as compared to membership in a group that shares a disability classification as the common denominator. Equally important was the development and status of special education as separate from general education—a second system with its own discrete population, specialists, assessments, paradigms, and funding.

The 1980s saw proposals that tried to interest general education in special education concerns. The Regular Education Initiative (REI) called for a restructuring of special education and suggested a dramatic shift in the policies governing the treatment and education of students with special needs (Kauffman 1989). The REI stressed academic competence, and although it applied to many students with disabilities, those with intensive education needs were problematic because their needs extended beyond the normal developmental curriculum that the classroom teacher was responsible for adapting to individual learners (Jenkins, Pious, and Jewell 1990).

Further reforms gained considerable impetus in the mid-1980s from the advocacy of Madeline Will, then assistant secretary of the United States Office of Special Education and Rehabilitative Services, and from other prominent educators. Special educators co-opted the voice of general education reform as they advanced the major prescription for the perceived ailments of contemporary special education, a movement variously referred to as "inclusion," "inclusive schooling," "inclusive education," or occasionally, "progressive inclusion." The overarching objective was to create changes within school communities that coordinated and bridged the programs and services that could transform schools into places where all students could learn together.

Within special education, inclusion can be simplistically viewed as the move to provide education to children with exceptionalities in the school or classroom that they would attend if they were not exceptional. For a program to be fully inclusive requires that children with exceptionalities are taught in the general education classroom for the full day; support services are brought to the child rather than the child removed to a segregated setting. The basic goal is to not leave anyone out of school and classroom communities from the very beginning, and the focus is on the support needs of all students and personnel (Stainback, Stainback, and Jackson 1992).

There is not a single model of inclusion: It is not yet a fully developed structure with a solid base of data. The meanings of inclusion are not uniformly absorbed. Both in concept and in implementation, it defies easy interpretation. The current movement hosts a range of theoretical positions that are related to the underlying philosophy, the relationship of those children who are targeted for inclusion, the nature of the general educational provision, and the manner in which supports are provided.

Different views lie along a continuum. At one end are full inclusionists, those who contend that inclusion should apply to all students with disabilities and who believe that all students belong in regular classrooms all the time. Many of the full inclusionists hold that the desirability of placement options, as represented by a continuum of services, has outlived its usefulness. For this group, no meaningful transformation can occur unless special education and its continuum of placements are eliminated altogether. Some in this group have called for a total restructuring to merge regular education and special education and have argued for an abolishment of the organization and structure of special education.

Further along the spectrum are those who support partial inclusion and hold that only students who meet certain standards should be integrated into regular classrooms full-time. General classrooms, they say, may be the most appropriate placements for many students with disabilities to receive their education, but research clearly does not support the assertion that all students can be managed and taught effectively in general classes (e.g., Braaten et al. 1988; Lundrum 1992; Walker and Bullis 1991). Promoters of full inclusion decry the concept of partial inclusion. Just as *full inclusion* is grammatically redundant, so the phrase *partial inclusion* is contradictory. There is no such thing as partial inclusion; it is only more of what has been done for a long time in the guise of mainstreaming (Idol 1997).

From the 1990s to today, then, the rallying cry has been inclusive schooling. Yesterday's orthodoxy (segregation) has become today's heresy, and the future of the inclusion movement is a prediction we cannot make. Does inclusion work? We do not really know. Current research provides only a crude pointer to the success or appropriateness of inclusion (Thomas 1997), and it cannot tell whether inclusion is good or bad, effective or ineffective—particularly for students with high incidence conditions such as learning disabilities ("Inclusion—where ..." 1996).

While taking into account the fluidity of the inclusion movement, we cannot discount its importance as a major trend in special education. Currently in the United States, nearly five million school-age children with disabilities receive some form of special education services (Vanderwood, McGrew, and Ysseldyke

1998). For these students, inclusion is having a major effect. Although the most significant movement toward general classrooms has occurred in the disability categories that include students with the milder disabilities—learning disabilities, speech and language impairments, orthopedic impairments, and other health problems—in all other categories, including those of children with significant disabilities, there is a trend toward moving students into less restrictive settings (see McLeskey, Henry, and Hodges 1998, 1999). More and more intensive services that are designed to meet children's individualized instructional needs are being delivered within the mainstream of school and society, and children with even the most severe disabilities are receiving their education alongside their nondisabled peers within general schools, classrooms, and community environments.

Since the late 1980s, the number of students with disabilities who are educated in general education classrooms has increased consistently and substantially (McLeskey, Henry, and Hodges 1998). For example, during the 1987–88 school year, 38.8 percent of students aged 6 to 21 with disabilities received services in the regular classroom. By 1992–93, the number was 39.81 percent. In all, between 1990 and 1995, general classroom placements for these students increased by almost 10 percent ("Record number ..." 1995). As the trend continues, larger numbers of students are being taught in general classrooms while the number in resource rooms is declining (McLeskey, Henry, and Hodges 1998). The number of students with disabilities who are served in general education classrooms decreases with the age of the students, and the number who are served in separate classes, separate schools, and residential facilities increases with the age of the students (Hobbs and Westling 1998). The type and severity of disability affects placement: Students with mild disabilities are more likely to be in general classrooms, and those with more severe disabilities are more likely to be in separate classes, schools, or facilities (Hobbs and Westling 1998). Students with deaf-blindness, multiple disabilities, and serious emotional disorders, for example, comprise the categories with the largest proportion in separate schools (McLeskey, Henry, and Hodges 1999). Rural districts serve a greater percentage of students with disabilities in general classrooms than do nonrural districts. In rural areas during 1995, 14.6 percent of students with disabilities were in full-time special education programs, while in nonrural areas, 25.3 percent were in these types of programs (Hanley 1995).

ABOUT THIS BOOK

Special education is currently at a critical juncture—in many ways, in a state of flux. Most parents, educators, allied professionals, and others who are involved in the field share similar ambitions for children who are exceptional. Most would agree that public education should accommodate students with special problems in the least restrictive environment; that service provision should arise from well-trained teachers who collaborate with other service providers and who invite parental participation in decisions to provide special services; that there should be coordination of services; that pre-referral and referral practices, assessment, and categorization and classification procedures be fair and nondiscriminatory; and that teacher training programs reflect reforms and changes in the school system. How these ends are to be achieved remains the subject of intense debate.

The debates, issues, trends, and movements surrounding contemporary special education form the core of this text. To accommodate the diversity of issues and ideas presented by the contributing authors, the text is divided into three parts. Each examines a different, though interrelated, aspect of contemporary special education.

In part 1, "Educational Reform and the Inclusion Movement," we address issues of education reform and the inclusion movement with its emerging discourses of disability and integration. Two of the papers specifically address inclusion and its arguments; the third examines the federal legislation and litigation that surrounds and supports special education. Part 2, "Supporting Education Reform," examines a number of issues that are closely tied to the inclusion movement. Discussions range from the thorny issue of assessing students' abilities to the technological revolution in special education to teacher training. Part 3, "Including Special Populations," addresses, in particular, how ideology can make an easy transition to education practice. It looks at classroom practices for different groups and touches on the technical problems of resources, management, social groupings, instructional design, and the supposition that teachers will automatically change to accommodate an even greater diversity of learners.

Of the many people who contributed to assembling this text, the editors are particularly indebted to Barbara Krushell who, with her usual patience and humor, assisted in the completion of the manuscript. We are also deeply grateful to Ivey Pittle Wallace, of Gallaudet University Press, for her continued support and encouragement.

REFERENCES

Barnes, E., and R. Lehr. 1993. Including everyone: A model preschool program for typical and special needs children. In *Approaches to early childhood education,* ed. J. Roopnarine and J. E. Johnson, 81–96. New York: Merrill.

Braaten, S., J. M. Kauffman, B. Braaten, L. Polsgrove, and C. M. Nelson. 1988. The Regular Education Initiative: Patent medicine for behavioral disorders. *Exceptional Children* 55:21–28.

Hanley, T. V. 1995. The need for technological advances in assessment related to national educational reform. *Exceptional Children* 61:222–29.

Hobbs, T., and D. L. Westling. 1998. Inclusion, inclusion, inclusion: Promoting successful inclusion. *Teaching Exceptional Children* 31:12–19.

Idol, L. 1997. Key questions related to building collaborative and inclusive schools. *Journal of Learning Disabilities* 30:384–94.

Inclusion—Where we are today? 1996. *Council for Exceptional Children Today* 1:1, 5, 15.

Jenkins, J., C. Pious, and M. Jewell. 1990. Special education and the Regular Education Initiative: Basic assumptions. *Exceptional Children* 56:479–91.

Kauffman, J. M. 1989. The Regular Education Initiative as Reagan–Bush educational policy: A trickle-down theory of education of the hard-to-teach. *Journal of Special Education* 23:256–78.

———. 1993. How we might achieve the radical reform of special education. *Exceptional Children* 60:6–16.

Li, A. K. F. 1994. Equity in assessment: From the perspective of new immigrant students. *Canadian Journal of School Psychology* 10:131–37.

Lundrum, T. J. 1992. Teachers as victims: An interactional analysis of the teacher's role in educating atypical learners. *Behavioral Disorders* 17:134–44.

McLeskey, J., D. Henry, and D. Hodges. 1998. Inclusion: Where is it happening? *Teaching Exceptional Children* 31:4–10.

———. 1999. Inclusion: What progress is being made across disability categories? *Teaching Exceptional Children* 31:60–64.

Mithaug, D. E. 1998. The alternative to ideological inclusion. In *Inclusive schooling: National and international perspectives,* ed. S. J. Vitello and D. Mithaug, 1–23. Hillsdale, N.J.: Lawrence Erlbaum Associates.

Record number of special education students served in 1993–94. 1995. *Council for Exceptional Children Today* 2:1, 5.

Stainback, S., W. Stainback, and H. J. Jackson. 1992. Toward inclusive classrooms. In *Curriculum considerations in inclusive classrooms: Facilitating learning for all students,* ed. S. Stainback and W. Stainback, 3–17. Baltimore, Md.: Paul H. Brookes.

Thomas, G. 1997. Inclusive schools for an inclusive society. *British Journal of Special Education* 24:103–7.

Vanderwood, M., K. S. McGrew, and J. E. Ysseldyke. 1998. Why we can't say much about students with disabilities during educational reform. *Exceptional Children* 64:359–70.

Walker, H. M., and M. Bullis. 1991. Behavior disorders and the social context of regular class integration: A conceptual dilemma? In *The Regular Education Initiative: Alternative perspectives on concepts, issues, and models,* ed. J. W. Lloyd, N. N. Singh, and A. C. Repp, 75–93. Sycamore, Ill.: Sycamore.

PART 1

Education Reform and the Inclusion Movement

Introduction

The current atmosphere in the general education system is one that includes reform, restructure, and reinvention. This atmosphere is paralleled in the discrete area of special education where the present reformist climate is making significant differences. The appropriateness of special education as a system is under attack from many constituencies, as is the classification and placement within this system of some students who remain in it for the majority of their educational experiences. Many educators, administrators, politicians, and parents call for reforming and restructuring special education. Today, professionals in law, advocacy, and educational innovation are working together to create a unique environment that is supportive of fundamental changes in the areas of school responsibility, program delivery, and program implementation.

Nevertheless, the varying views of inclusion, as embraced by those concerned with special education, have engendered one of the most divisive debates ever to rivet the field. Few issues have received such attention and have generated such controversy and polarization of perspectives. Some observers contend that the trend toward inclusive classrooms "has garnered enthusiastic and unqualified support in the 1990s from the media and parent organizations" (Lago-Delello 1998, 479). Less sanguine writers note that the manner in which more extensive integration can be achieved remains elusive and that the argument, debate, and counterdebate surrounding the issue remain strikingly prevalent (e.g., Winzer 1995).

Hence, although inclusion has moved from an idea to a conviction, varied and often contradictory discourses remain. A consensus on inclusive schooling is not apparent; rather, a number of philosophies have emerged that appeal to different clusters of ideologically driven advocates and their followers. Current discussions about the inclusion of students with special needs into general classrooms are characterized by widely varied theoretical positions, complex and competing perspectives, unresolved ambiguities that are inherent in the discourse, and a fluidity of ideas. Inclusion means different things to different people, and no interpretation matches the needs of all stakeholders in the process. Definitions and descriptions of inclusion abound. Researchers, policymakers, and practitioners interpret and reinterpret inclusion. They construct, deconstruct, and reconstruct meanings for it. They invent and reinvent the dialogues, and they discuss how inclusion can be implemented. Then, without necessarily reaching consensus, they outline the criteria for successful inclusion, the rela-

3

tionship of those targeted for inclusion, the nature of the general educational provision, and the manner in which supports are to be provided.

Because the meanings of inclusion are not uniformly absorbed, the messages about inclusion are diverse and contradictory. A variety of arguments, both implicit and explicit, are used to promote or reject the legitimacy of the concept. In the opening paper, Winzer teases out the threads of the various arguments to illustrate that a facile interpretation remains elusive because the concept of inclusion involves a family of theories. She shows how reforms in special education are generally proposed in the context of broader education and social issues and, therefore, how one of the most influential of the many impulses underlying today's movement toward inclusion in special education has been the general school reform effort across North America. The paper touches on both the proposals to restructure special education and the spectrum of advocates, and it looks at the placement of choice for many children with disabilities as being with the general education teacher. Ultimately, Winzer argues that we need sensible criteria, not wholesale advocacy, to implement responsible, selective inclusion.

Susan Stainback's paper on restructuring as a goal of education pursues further the theme of reform and restructure. Stainback captures the relationship between policy and research as she argues forcefully for the inclusion of all children in general education. She bolsters her arguments by delving into the historical roots of inclusion and shows that the process of integration is a "well-worn path." In contemporary terms, she speaks to attitudes and values as well as to effective techniques and strategies to promote inclusion. She predicts that school restructuring will continue as the success of inclusion is ensured.

The United States has a long history of relying on legislative and judicial remedies for social issues, including special education. In recent years, the federal government has played an increasingly prominent role in special education. Contemporary special education has been built largely on law; thus, the law defines the special education population to be served in infinite detail and strictly prescribes special education planning and implementation. McLaughlin and Henderson offer a comprehensive examination of special education legislation. They write on recent legislative and judicial development, and they present both a detailed assessment of special education law in the United States and a description of the recent court cases that have affected the inclusionary movement. They discuss the reauthorizations, the content, and the processes of the legislation, and they inform the reader about major changes in the 1997 Individuals with Disabilities Education Act (IDEA) that will affect practice in the next century.

REFERENCES

Lago-Delello, E. 1998. Classroom dynamics and the development of serious emotional disturbance. *Exceptional Children* 64:479–92.

Winzer, M. A. 1995. The inclusive movement in Canada: A critical analysis. Paper presented at the Contemporary Trends Conference, May, in Krakow, Poland.

1

The Inclusion Movement: Review and Reflections on Reform in Special Education

Margret A. Winzer

In the past decade, inclusive schooling has been elevated to a dominant education discourse, the critical orthodoxy in contemporary special education. Increasingly, parents, legislators, educators, and school boards express the desire to follow an inclusive philosophy whereby all children are effectively welcomed into the regular classroom. Spurred on by changing public attitudes, court cases, the work of advocates, and parent pressures, today's inclusion movement likely will continue to grow as more and more jurisdictions break through traditional barriers and forge a strong base for integration and for the education of all students.

Inclusion cannot be described with only a single model; messages about inclusion remain diverse and often contradictory. With the pervasive debates and counterdebates and a paucity of empirical data, inclusion is far from universally accepted among educators and education policymakers (Fox and Ysseldyke 1997). The ideal of full inclusion is not universally shared and is not endorsed by all of those concerned with the education of children with exceptionalities.

This chapter reviews the contemporary literature and reflects on the philosophical and pragmatic bases of the inclusion movement by exploring the discourses that have framed the movement's current thrust. In examining the ideological arguments that surround inclusion, I am neither arguing that the assumptions are incorrect nor denying that a strong trend toward more inclusive schooling is occurring. Rather, by deconstructing the arguments and separating the various strands, I highlight the philosophical underpinnings of the movement, indicate how many arguments are incomplete and open to criticism, and illustrate the diversity of interpretation and method that characterizes the current movement.

THE INCLUSION MOVEMENT

During the 1960s and 1970s, the rallying cry of special education professionals and advocacy groups was greater access to the mainstream. Today, this cry is being replaced by a much more complex cry, one that demands full access to a restructured mainstream (Davis 1989), access that is encapsulated as inclusive schooling.

Many people use the terms *integration, mainstreaming*, and *inclusion* synonymously. But although inclusion is a logical step after mainstreaming, the terms do not mean the same thing at all. Even though both mainstreaming and inclusion describe practices for operationalizing the concept of the least restrictive environment, the terms hold subtle but real differences, with inclusion being more philosophically loaded than mainstreaming.

Integration, the oldest term, simply denotes a physical movement of a child but not necessarily a concomitant change in approach by a school. The term *least restrictive environment* generally refers to placing students in settings that are the most normal and where students can have optimal interaction with their normally developing peers. *Mainstreaming* means providing every student who is exceptional, regardless of type and severity of disability, with an appropriate education, as much as possible, alongside normally developing peers.

Two major characteristics define mainstreaming (as opposed to inclusion). First, it usually only applies to some children, most particularly those with mild disabilities. Second, the target population generally consists of students who are identified as needing special education services and who often move from special classes into regular classrooms. Children have to prove their readiness for an integrated setting, rather than the setting having to prove its readiness to accept a child.

Advocates of inclusive schooling argue that the social–cultural realities of mainstreaming and integration are that one group is viewed as the "mainstream" and one group is not; hence, the members of one group are not full-fledged members of a class but, instead, must "push into" the activities and settings that are occupied by the other group (Salisbury 1991). Under the principles of inclusion, however, children do not push into the mainstream because inclusive programs expect that all children will be based in the schools or classrooms that they would attend if they did not have a disability.

Even so, inclusion defies easy interpretation, and widely varied views surround the concept. A facile interpretation remains elusive because inclusion in special education is not framed within a single paradigm but assumes meaning depending on whether it is viewed from a philosophical, legal, or service-provision perspective (Thousand and Villa 1994).

The very term, inclusion, is problematic. Inclusion means different things to different people, and no one interpretation matches the needs of all stakeholders in the process. The definitions are continually reinterpreted by professionals and advocacy groups to fit the needs of a particular constituency (Bassett et al. 1996). Often, different perspectives reflect the working agenda of people within different disability areas, so the rifts that have developed over these perceptions and education issues are a function of disability boundaries (see Fuchs and Fuchs 1994).

Some people see inclusion as an emerging education paradigm with broad implications for the services that are provided to all students; others view it as yet another placement option that can be added to the continuum of services traditionally found in special education (Bassett et al. 1996). Advocates for people with severe and profound disabilities see inclusion as an issue of access to education and other opportunities; those advocating for students with mild disabilities often focus on whether inclusion represents another way to enhance academic and social achievement (Peck et al. 1993).

THE DEBATE ABOUT INCLUSION

A general perception has been created by the literature and, perhaps, by the media that inclusion is a fully accepted movement in special education. This is not true; debate still abounds. The discussions of the inclusionary movement cannot discount the fluidity of the ideas. Whether it is considered philosophically or carried out in practice, the construct of inclusive education has little consistency (Zigmond and Baker 1996). The present inclusion movement tells a tale of ambivalent goals and muddied outcomes, a tale of confusion between the philosophic and the pragmatic as well as between intention and implementation. So far, the debate on inclusion has been largely at the philosophical rather than at the practical level, at the university level rather than at the level of teacher and parent participation, on the highly visible dimension of placement rather than on the level of curriculum, and about conceptual needs rather than about practical needs.

The contemporary movement toward the inclusion of all children in general schools or classrooms, regardless of degree and type of disability, is founded on a number of superimposed and ever shifting layers. Each single layer weaves into and builds on others. Attempting to isolate specific threads is arbitrary. Nevertheless, to lend clarity to the debate, the following sections discuss the dominating arguments (and counterarguments) separately.

General School Reform: The Argument

The outcomes of education became a key concern of education reform during the l980s. Contributing factors to this concern included dissatisfaction with the current education system, public concern over the costs and outcomes of education, changing lifestyles and family structures, new and diverse needs in the marketplace, changing demographics in North American society, an increasingly linguistically and culturally diverse student population, and high failure and dropout rates among students from diverse cultural backgrounds (Winzer and Mazurek 1998).

As reform efforts accelerated, the literature was flooded with a rash of new terms and phrases that were associated with a growing concern over the quality and delivery of education in contemporary schools (Treffinger 1991). Buzzwords included education reform, accountability, parent participation, collaborative schools, and "back to the basics." Operationalized, education reforms have generally focused on six policy areas: standards, assessment, accountability, governance, teachers, and finance (Goertz and Friedman 1996).

Inclusive schooling is one of the terms that emerged. It grew from the wave of school reform that addressed the structural causes of inequity in terms of the massive student diversity characterizing contemporary classrooms and from the wave of reform that emphasized the special learning needs of some students (for example, students who were disadvantaged, dropouts, minority children, and students with disabilities). Hence, the inclusive reform movement embraces diversity and sets out to deal with new social demands on education. Inclusion applies to cultural, social, linguistic, racial, gender, mental, and physical differences. Advocates contend that "all children with learning problems, whether they be 'special education' students, 'at-risk' students, or otherwise regarded as disadvantaged in schooling, belong in regular classroom environments" (Laski 1991, 412).

While general education was seeking reform, special education passed through a crisis of confidence in the 1980s and embarked on a period of self-flagellation. "Unless major structural changes are made," cried critics, "the field of special education is destined to become more of a problem, and less of a solution in providing education for children who have special needs" (Reynolds, Wang, and Walberg 1987, 391).

Once it was accepted that special education was in such desperate straits and that the need for fundamental change was self-evident, many (researchers, advocates, and academics rather than teachers) demanded radical change and co-opted the voice of general school reform. Rhetoric called for special education to "break the mold." It called for "revolution," a "paradigm shift," a "fundamental reconceptualization," and a "radical restructuring" (Kauffman 1993, 10).

The "inclusion revolution" (Rogers 1993, 10) built on a complex of perceived historical and contemporary problems within special education. Critics drew energy from negative research findings and marshaled evidence of the failure of special education. They complained about the reliability of the instruction of students with disabilities, the efficacy of pull-out programs, the misalignment of curriculum, and the cost-effectiveness of a dual system (Manset and Semmel 1997). Further, the manner in which special education classes could be made more effective was not solved (Vergason and Anderegg 1989) and the outcomes for youth with disabilities who were exiting special education had not improved. Few students, for example, actually exited the special education system, a fact that, critics suggested, pointed to both a failure of the interventions offered to these children and the presence of a stable and increasing population of students who may be the education equivalent of a permanent underclass (Walker et al. 1988).

General School Reform: The Counterargument

The concept of inclusion in special education flowered in a climate of criticism of education services in general. This climate of criticism evolved both as a part of and as an extension of the effective schools movement to include more groups in general education. Hence, the popularity of inclusion in special education rests, at least in part, on its concordance with wider social notions; it "chimes with the philosophy of a liberal political system and a pluralistic culture" (Thomas 1997, 106). Whereas, in the past, reform in special education has tended to parallel rather than converge with the efforts of general education, today, special education is trying to redefine itself to fit within the broader education context. In pursuing reform, we have collapsed the special education conundrum into the general mission of school improvement (see Slee 1997). The restructuring and reinventing of special education stakes us a strong claim in this so-called era of inclusion.

Pursuing this thread, inclusion in special education is not a minor reform; rather, it is a fundamental conceptual shift that involves the way in which both people with disabilities and their place in society are seen and how education rights are provided. When operationalized, inclusive schooling equates with school restructuring. In this way, it cannot be treated as a new program or innovation but must be seen as part of the fabric of a school's restructuring efforts. The focus cannot be on only all students but, also, must be on all teachers, all curricular reforms, all support personnel, all policies, all strategies for student assessment, and so on (see Ferguson 1998).

Moral Imperative: The Argument

Inclusion addresses how we, those able and those disabled, are going to live together. In the schools, inclusion becomes a philosophical value that is manifested in the way the education and development of children is promoted and conceptualized. The desired end is the creation of socially just and democratic communities.

Full inclusion is "often presented as a moral imperative" (Bricker 1995, 180), as a value judgment, and as an ethical issue. The conviction is that inclusion is a morally defensible ideal; the imperative, that everyone must champion the cause of full inclusion and accept the underlying premises as well as the practical implications for programming because it is simply the right thing to do.

Because the issue of what constitutes the best education can only be answered by moral inquiry, questions of location and equal rights are elevated above scientific authority. When characterizing programming as a moral imperative, proponents of full inclusion contend that the practice does not require research support. In the general classroom, a quest for proof of success is not only unnecessary but also hurtful (Shaw 1990), and full inclusionists often reject the need to empirically test the effects of inclusion (MacMillan, Gresham, and Forness 1996; Manset and Semmel 1997). As Shaw observes, "Being [included] in an ordinary school no more requires a guarantee of success than does participation in any of the ordinary life experiences. [Inclusion] reflects ... the sort of society schools are aiming to build" (Shaw 1990, 1).

What we know or believe is shaped by how we interpret the narratives we hear. Anecdotal reports of successful inclusion, particularly for children with severe and profound disabilities, are emerging consistently in the literature (e.g., Giangreco et al. 1993; Janney et al. 1995; Kozleski and Jackson 1993; Ruiter 1997; Salisbury, Palambaro, and Hollowood 1993).

Moral Imperative: The Counterargument

Moral imperatives, most prominent in the voices of those promoting full inclusion, particularly of students with severe disabilities, too often shed more ideological heat than educational light. In the sea of moral rhetoric, the most dangerous of its many shoals are the increasing stridency of some advocates, the uncritical advancement of a single point of view, and the reconceptualization of disability as a complex form of social oppression.

Too often, inclusion has become an emotional debate, and advocates have moved from proposing an education approach to advocating a cause. Diane Bricker, a potent advocate for the inclusionary movement, observes that "during the past ten years, the rhetoric for full inclusion has grown increasingly strident" while "the call to arms emanating from full-inclusion camps" has grown "too dogmatic, simplistic, and value laden" (1995, 180).

In presenting inclusion as the only moral answer, some advocates paint the issue in simple, either–or terms. In other words, "You can have any color you want, as long as it's black" (Smelter, Rasch, and Yudewitz 1994, 38). Inclusion and segregation are not opposite sides of the same, most appropriate education coin. They are diametrically opposed, with inclusion as the sole moral choice.

Those of the moral persuasion bring to the debate unyielding commitment and stalwart faith that are joined to preconceived notions of right and wrong. They divide the world into villains and heroes, and they frame the controversies surrounding the inclusive movement as a debate between abolitionists and conservatives. As Bricker observes, "The right thinking 'good guys' support and work for full inclusion whereas those who are opposed to it or who suggest cautious implementation are placed on the wrong side of the fence" (Bricker 1995, 180). In the face of this dynamic, others become increasingly reluctant to question the movement because they fear censorship. To debate or question the movement's premises and philosophical base is to ally oneself with education critics and conservatives. Those who are skeptical about a radical restructuring of special education are marked as conservative and as preservative, defenders of the status quo (see Fuchs and Fuchs 1994).

Full inclusionists often use rhetoric that is designed to convey appealing images, but just as often, they use the language of oppression and metaphors of symbolic violence. Such expressions create a forceful effect, particularly when inclusion is used in counterpoint to an evil opposite—exclusion. When children with special needs are segregated, they can be characterized as "humiliated, cast out, or neglected" (Befring 1997, 185). In stressing the dynamics of oppression and domination, some draw parallels between the labeling and segregation in special classes and the negative connotations in American society and history. Oppression is highlighted and paralleled with, for example, race and apartheid, and it is seen as an ethical issue much like school desegregation (see Stainback and Stainback 1992, xv). Forest and Pearpoint, for example, liken the label "disabled" to the "yellow star pinned on people labeled Jewish and the pink triangle pinned on people labeled homosexual during World War II" (1992, 81). Others equate our current system with South Africa's apartheid (e.g., Hahn 1987).

When interpreted from the moral point of view, inclusive schooling becomes a superficial argument over what is right, characterized by ambiguity and inconsistency and accented by simplistic and naive declarations of how to achieve the goal. Empirical research cedes to a reliance on narratives. But partisan research that consists of single anecdotal reports cannot confirm universals. Some critics decry the contention that the new paradigm has outdated the scientific study of education as we have known it (Kauffman 1996). They argue, instead, that doubts about inclusion will be removed in direct proportion to demonstrations that inclusion can work. An inadequate research base exists to document the effects of a radical change such as inclusion, and as education research has produced trustworthy results that underlie past effective practices, these critics demand empirical analysis of policy change.

We must primarily rely on robust scientific methods. As MacMillan and his colleagues stress, "Approaches designed to meet the needs of children with disabilities should be adopted on the basis of empirical validation, and not based on ideology, persuasive slogans, or on the nature and stridency of the voices advocating a particular treatment or position" (MacMillan, Gresham, and Forness 1996, 146).

Civil Rights: The Argument

Special education is intimately connected to common views of social justice. The provision of less restrictive, more natural, integrated environments for students with disabilities is an outgrowth of a social philosophy about individual civil rights. As the many threads of inclusive reform are grounded in democratic themes, advocates juxtapose social justice and injustice with civil rights arguments.

Central to the issue is physical place, which, as James Kauffman observed, is pervasive and highly emotional and "has been the hub of controversy because it clearly defines proximity to age peers with certain characteristics" (1993, 7). Those who hold that the right to be educated with one's peers is a civil right (e.g., Wang, Reynolds, and Walberg 1989) reject pull-out programs and segregated classes. They see such arrangements as indefensible, as discriminatory and unequal, and as in violation of the democratic ethos that allows equal access to education for all students. Segregated classes, they argue, are often more benefit to the people who do not attend them than to the people who do. For children with special needs, segregation highlights their disabilities, disrupts their education, and teaches them to be dependent.

We are more enlightened when we alter the classroom and school structure to allow all children to gain an education there than when we segregate them in special settings. Rather than segregate them, we must recognize that all children belong in heterogeneous classrooms where the learning-teaching bond is forged in normalized ways instead of in segregated settings where the disability classification is the common denominator (Bassett et al. 1996).

Civil Rights: The Counterargument

The civil rights discourse suggests that separate programs are a violation of civil rights and that all children learn best in regular classrooms. As equity is popularly seen to mean access to the same schools and instructional programs for all students, inclusionists argue that, for children with special needs, separate but equal is unequal. All children have the right to education with other children and these rights are founded in general education programs.

Equity equates with the belief that the education of normally developing students is universally desirable and is the best way for all students to learn. This idea—that instruction that is effective for mainstream students will benefit all students, whatever their backgrounds—has dominated North American education. As special education adopts this notion, program advocacy dominates child advocacy, and placement is confused with equity. In contrast to mainstreaming philosophy, place is more important than learning; success in the regular classroom is not a prerequisite for regular class placement in the inclusionary model (McGregor 1997). The general education setting is more desirable than a special setting whether it meets the needs of children with disabilities or not because the goals of social equity that are met by keeping children mixed with their peers are of greater importance than how much children learn (Smelter, Rasch, and Yudewitz 1994).

The concept of equitable opportunity rests on the legal and education criteria of access, participation, and benefit (Thompson 1994). When these criteria are considered, then sameness of opportunity and open access to all schools for all students are equated with educational equality, which seems a biased pursuit of justice. These legal and educational criteria ignore some of the more fundamental issues of equality of opportunity and access to the process of schooling. Equity does not mean the same treatment for all; it means equitable treatment despite individual differences and treatment that takes such differences into account (see Kauffman 1993). Similarly, substance does not equate with mere placement. Equal education treatment does not necessarily result in equal opportunity to learn.

The underlying philosophy of special education is rooted in the principle that all humans have equal value and that every child should receive an appropriate and relevant education. When education services are equated with placement, we deny the essence of individualization. Such a fixing of "attention on sameness and shying away from confronting differences extracts a dear price" (Kauffman 1997, 130) as we attempt to provide students the maximum chance to reach their full potential.

Dual System: The Argument

Critics speak to the manner in which special education and regular education have developed historically as dual systems. They chide that special education is built to serve the lowest achieving children who are then maintained through a complex interaction of professional beliefs, pedagogy, and legislation. Many people question the necessity for this dual system, particularly the high proportion of education funding that is directed toward special education and the fragmentary nature of so much of special education service delivery.

Reformers hold that special education and regular education can no longer exist as separate entities; they must join forces to provide the most appropriate education for every child, whether exceptional or normally developing. The aim is "an educational model for all students—supple, variegated, and individualized—in an integrated setting" (Gartner and Lipsky 1987, 368).

Although a merger of regular and special education was first mentioned in the early 1980s (e.g., Stainback and Stainback 1984, 1985; Will 1986), it was a distinctly minority viewpoint (Mesinger 1985). However, in 1987, writers called for "the joining of demonstrably effective practices from special, compensatory, and general education to establish a general educational system that is more *inclusive*, and better serves all students, particularly those who require greater-than-usual educational support" (Reynolds, Wang, and Walberg 1987, 394, emphasis added). Rather than perpetuate special education, educators needed to fundamentally change the general education teaching and learning processes so that school programs would be responsive to fast, average, and slow learners alike (see Fuchs and Fuchs 1994).

A reconfiguration to unite a balkanized system calls for a total restructuring to merge regular education and special education and to abolish the organization and structure of contemporary special education. Allies of full inclusion challenge educators to identify where supports will be provided to students with disabilities, and they present full inclusion as a contrast to providing a continuum of placements. Promoters of full inclusion hold that the desirability of placement options, represented by a continuum of services, has outlived its usefulness and that no meaningful transformation can occur unless special education and its continuum of placements are eliminated altogether (see Fuchs and

Fuchs 1994; Kauffman 1993; Porter 1994; Pugach 1992; Sindelar, Pugach, Griffin, and Seidl 1995).

Two broad and generally nonallied factions adhere to the notion that education would be best served by the elimination of a dual system. The left faction questions the assumptions that underly the practice of special education, stresses moral imperatives, and mobilizes the discourse of equality. From the fiscal right, critics point to duplicative, inefficient, and fragmented programs in special education. Today's schools are at the intersection of political and social ideals as well as economic realities. As public education policies attempt to reconcile more expectations with fewer resources, special education represents a problem of resource management. Fiscal considerations promote inclusion because it is politically correct and may even be cost effective.

Dual System: The Counterargument

At the classroom level, inclusion may not be a merger but a collision of two systems (see Kauffman 1993). Enthusiasts for inclusion have advocated for radical changes in teacher responsibility without showing that regular educators can actually support these changes (Minke, Bear, Deiner, and Griffin 1996). Teachers themselves have articulated the weaknesses in the shifting propositions.

Many teachers support the philosophy of inclusion, but many identify critical problems in its implementation. A recent national study of 1,492 Canadian teachers found that more than two-thirds of teachers believed that inclusion was academically beneficial to children with special needs and to their peers in regular classrooms. In addition, 90 percent of teachers cited social benefits to both groups of students (Galt 1997; "Resistance ..." 1997). Nevertheless, although a majority of teachers support the philosophical underpinnings of inclusion, many express a deep concern that in too many cases the inclusive process is not working and is, in fact, creating educationally unsound situations (e.g., Alberta Teachers' Association 1993; Buski 1997; "Report ..." 1997).

Teachers regard students with disabilities in the context of procedural classroom concerns and have definite opinions about the types of disabilities they are most willing to accept (Margolis and McGettigan 1988). Generally, the more severe the disability, the more negative the attitudes teachers have toward inclusion (Wisniewski and Alper 1994). Both prospective and experienced teachers report more positive attitudes toward students who can learn and who do not inhibit the learning of their peers (Wilczenski 1992). Many general education teachers specifically disagree with the placement of students who have intellectual disabilities and behavioral or emotional difficulties in the general classroom (Taylor et al. 1997). They prefer including students with sensory and physical disabilities as compared to students with behavioral disorders and cognitive difficulties (Johnson 1987). Findings show a tendency of secondary level teachers to be less accepting than other teachers of students with special needs in regular classrooms (Savage and Wienke 1989).

When targeting the students with disabilities and the extent of their inclusion, the two groups who present the greatest challenges are those with significant disabilities and those with serious behavioral disorders. The term *severely disabled*, however defined, has always indicated a boundary condition that determines the success of any reform. Even if schools become relatively comfortable with or, at least, resigned to children functioning below the norm in intellectual, physical, or social domains, they remain resistant to accepting students with severe behavioral or intellectual disabilities.

One of the great fears of teachers is increased behavioral problems from special education students in general. In particular, there is considerable resistance among teachers to including students with behavioral disorders. Hence, for students with serious and violent behavior, there is "a murky picture as to the future of inclusive education" (Bassett et al. 1996, 365). The literature continues to highlight the limitations of general settings for these students.

Some writers (e.g., Fuchs and Fuchs 1994; Lundrum 1992; MacMillan, Gresham, and Forness 1996) argue that it is deleterious to the child with behavioral disorders, to the teacher, and to other students to retain that child in the general education classroom if he or she cannot conform to the basic expectations of the classroom. They contend that expecting general education teachers to welcome, successfully teach and manage, and tolerate the most disruptive students is extremely naive and illogical, both from the viewpoint of common sense and from the perspective of available research (Fuchs et al. 1991). Timothy Lundrum goes so far as to argue that "regular education teachers may be considered victims in that they are subject to the idealistic expectation that all teachers should accommodate difficult-to-teach students, particularly on the grand scale proposed by many reform advocates" (1992, 142).

Others contend that there is a population of students—those with severe and multiple disabilities—who, despite any currently popular instruction, will not be capable of functioning in the general classroom, will not be completely self-sufficient, and will not live independently within our society (Link 1991). They argue that children with severe and multiple disabilities may be at odds with a system that has few resources and little inclination to meet their needs. The intense needs of such children challenge the boundaries of practitioner knowledge and organizational supports, and they extend beyond the normal developmental curriculum that the classroom teacher is responsible for delivering and adapting for individual learners.

All Teachers Can Teach All Children: The Argument

Instructionally, advocates hold that when children with disabilities are included in regular classrooms, only minor accommodations will be needed. They argue that special education is really nothing more than a thoroughly good, ordinary education; that regular classroom teachers are already prepared to teach children with disabilities; that fundamentally different instructional techniques are not necessary; and that children who are identified as disabled do not differ significantly in educationally relevant ways from those not so identified (e.g.,

Stainback and Stainback 1984). Advocates also assume that the same sort of generic teaching skills, attitudes, and beliefs will be effective regardless of students' characteristics, and they maintain that if general education teachers would engage in more successful teaching behaviors—providing positive feedback, asking questions to ensure high response rates, and using punitive interventions infrequently—they could teach many of the students with disabilities who usually go to special education (Reynolds and Lakin 1987; Wang, Reynolds, and Walberg 1986).

The belief is that all students can learn skills that they value, even though these skills will differ from one student to the next (Raynes, Snell, and Sailor 1991). Although the basic education goals for all students may remain the same, the specific curricular learning objectives may be individualized in some instances to fit the unique needs, skills, interests, and abilities of students (Stainback, Stainback, and Stefanich 1996). Advocates propose that students work in flexible learning environments with flexible curricula, where they receive the instruction they need, not that of a specific grade level. Students work toward appropriate goals, rather than common or unattainable goals. Even if the academic competencies of general education are not within the purview of children with severe and profound disabilities, students for whom traditional task requirements are not relevant can still learn social skills and can learn that they are full class members, not inferior to others.

Inclusion implicitly acknowledges and accepts the value of what regular schooling provides, and it demands that all teachers be prepared to teach all children. Advocates of inclusion hold that good teachers can teach all students because only minor adjustments need to be made to accommodate special learners. Teachers will find that the strategies, techniques, modifications, and inspirations that have always produced effective instruction and management in their classrooms work equally well in integrated settings (Weber 1994).

All Teachers Can Teach All Children: The Counterargument

Although enthusiasts for inclusion have advocated for radical changes in teacher responsibility and many hold that all general education teachers can and should accommodate students with disabilities, other observers are more cautious within the current reality of teacher responsibilities and accountability. Skeptics counter that inclusion requires extensive retraining of both regular and special education teachers in personal-communication, team-teaching, problem-solving, and curricula frameworks (Hueffner 1988). They question whether regular educators can actually support these changes, whether general education can transform itself into a more responsive, resourceful, and humane system to deal with children it has avoided in the past (see Fuchs and Fuchs 1994), and whether regular education teachers will accept the loss of the safety valve called special education. More pointedly, they ask, Can special educators teach teachers to teach the children they have failed in the past? Can we expect classroom teachers to welcome as well as successfully teach and manage students who are disruptive or who have severe and profound disabilities? How likely is it that teachers can change their techniques to accommodate children with special needs? Will teachers be able take on additional workloads and anxieties, devote extra time to assessment and referral, and find time to work on teams to develop, implement, and evaluate programs? Will the needs of special children completely eclipse the needs of teachers? What consideration should be given to other students whose educational programs may be disrupted by the presence of children with serious behavioral disorders (Winzer 1998)?

To many researchers and policymakers, inclusive schooling is a paradigm shift. In contrast, for many general classroom teachers, the essential core of the old and traditional paradigms remains the same. Even though an increasingly rich literature addresses not only the moral and ethical importance but also the practical value of, at least, partial inclusion, many classroom teachers remain unconvinced.

Inclusion means that the paradigms providing frameworks for teaching must change. Yet many teachers reject the demands that all teachers be prepared to teach all children. They dispute that inclusion can be used as a universal template to provide the one and only solution to the various challenges faced by children with special needs. They are unwilling to lose the safety valve of special education. In fact, they prefer the present system. Although pull-out programs are sometimes perceived as nonpreferred, stigmatizing, disruptive, and not leading to long-term academic gains for students, studies indicate that both regular and special education teachers are not dissatisfied with the pull-out model. In fact, the majority of teachers in one study (Semmel et al. 1991) perceived special education classrooms as more effective and more preferred than regular classrooms for students with mild disabilities.

Within the regular classroom, special education students "are educationally starved by the standard instructional diet" (Kauffman 1996, 205). Many students, particularly those with mild disabilities or those at risk, do not respond to the traditional teaching techniques that are used in general education such as recitation, lecturing, rote learning, and so on (Boyle and Yeager 1997). These students can experience success only when the teacher is able to meet their individual learning needs through appropriate curriculum modifications (Haman, Issacson, and Powell 1985).

Although successful inclusion demands social and instructional scaffolds to ensure full access, perhaps the most commonly cited source of resistance from teachers is a lack of skills necessary to teach students with disabilities (Minke et al. 1996). In addition to lacking the required skills, teachers are often not willing to make the pilgrimage toward meeting the needs of special learners. Fuchs and colleagues (1997), among others, argue that many teachers cannot or will not adjust their instruction to meet each student's education needs. In general, the planning frame of regular classroom teachers is the whole class. They teach to single large groups and incorporate little or no differentiation based on student need (Baker and Zigmond 1995; Fuchs and Fuchs 1995b). Individualization rarely occurs in general education classrooms, and curriculum adaptations are not a part of classroom life. In fact, evidence documents the inability or unwillingness of regular educators to incorporate strategies for learners with special needs into general education approaches (Fuchs and Fuchs 1995a).

Many veteran teachers broadly resist mandates to differentiate curriculum and instruction for a wide range of learners (Behar and George 1994); they make few modifications in general classrooms for learners who are gifted (Archambault et al. 1993) and those who qualify for special education (Bateman 1993). When students with behavioral disorders are integrated into regular classrooms, teachers provide little academic support or modifications and almost no behavioral support and adaptations (Meadows et al. 1994). Indeed, chided Kauffman, "it is only with great effort that teachers are induced to learn and practice the positive, supportive procedures emanating from three decades of scientific research on behavior management" (1999, 455).

General educators lack the necessary skills to adapt instruction, to meet the needs of students with disabilities, or to integrate specific strategies (Scanlon, Deshler, and Schumaker 1996). Hence, changed delivery models necessitate training personnel to adapt to new roles. Yet there is little evidence that general educators are receiving the kind of training they need to comfortably support students with disabilities (Heumann 1994; Reiff, Evans, and Cass 1991). Even when teachers are offered specialized training and ongoing support, that training and support varies substantially in the extent to which it prepares regular educators to implement inclusive programs and in the extent to which it results in the progress that students with disabilities achieve (see MacMillan, Gresham, and Forness 1996).

Although good general education programs should prepare teachers to work with all students effectively, explicit efforts to prepare teachers in training to work with students with exceptionalities are a relatively recent phenomenon, and teacher education programs are not yet providing adequate preparation (Kearney and Durant 1992; Maheady, Mallette, and Harper 1996). Many potential general educators receive limited preparation (Patton and Braithwaite 1990). In the United States, less than 5 percent of all general education teachers have been formally prepared to work with students with special needs in inclusive settings (Smith and Luckasson 1995). In one study (George et al. 1995), two-thirds of teachers of children with behavioral disorders reported that their college course work was poor preparation for their teaching environments. Jack and colleagues (1996) found that only 5 percent of the teachers in their study indicated that they learned about the management strategies they used in their classrooms from course work; most learned them from other teachers. Likewise, the traditional special education courses do not work very well. Goodlad and Field (1993) found in a national U.S. study that preservice general education teachers rated their own abilities to teach children with disabilities as the lowest of twelve domains of perceived instructional competence.

Special Education Is Not Special: The Argument

This argument intertwines with the one above, that is, with the notion that all teachers can teach all children. However, if all teachers can teach all children, then it follows that not much is really special about special education. Inclusionists hold that special education can become general and can establish programs that serve the needs of all problem learners. So special education is not special at all; it is no more than good general education, and all teachers must be prepared to teach all children effectively.

Special Education Is Not Special: The Counterargument

Critics of the argument that special education is not special contend that something is, indeed, ascertainably different about special education. By denying the essence of special education and by inappropriately including students with disabilities, we denigrate the quality of instruction for normally developing students and deny students with disabilities instruction that is tailored to their needs.

There are many areas of convergence between regular and special education; observational studies have confirmed numerous instructional similarities. Nevertheless, differences are seen in programming and implementation. The focus of general and special education teachers tends to be dissimilar in terms of instructing students, curriculum, materials, teaching styles, and expectations (see Ryan and Paterna 1997).

The backbone of special education is intensive, goal-directed, individualized instruction. As Kauffman observes, "Compared to the general practice of education, special education is instruction that is more urgent, more intensive, more relentless, more precisely delivered, more highly structured and direct, and more carefully monitored for procedural fidelity and effects" (1996, 206). The techniques are different because if these children not treated differently, they will not succeed (Lieberman 1991). Reviews of the effects of placement do not suggest that location in the mainstream is the key to improvement in special education outcomes (Kauffman 1993). Special classes and resource rooms contribute more to the academic achievement of some types of students with special needs, especially those who are learning disabled or emotionally disturbed, than do regular classrooms (see Fuchs and Fuchs 1995b).

CURRENT STATUS

Some people speak of inclusion as though it were a universally accepted movement in special education and not as something that is evolving. Yet as the delineations of the various arguments show, considerable controversy remains about the nature and extent of reform as it relates to inclusion. Moreover, inclusion seems to be a continuous cycle of change in terms of its proponents, the policies for its implementation, the call for empirical research, its targeted students, and the criteria for its success.

Despite ideological and philosophical contradictions, inclusion is better accepted in concept than in practice. The efforts to forge a fundamentally different education framework for students with special needs are ambitious, but school restructuring and reform efforts have failed to have a great effect on traditional school structures. So far, reform efforts have been piecemeal, fragmented, and clearly less effective than anticipated (Lupart 1998).

Moreover, in the past four years, the emancipatory powers of inclusion have come under heavy attack and the goal of inclusion for all students has become inconsistent with the views expressed by many both within and without the special education community. Many parent and advocacy groups as well as professional groups—groups primarily representing students with mild disabilities—speak against the elimination of a continuum of special education services. In addition, as previously mentioned, teachers are often resistant to inclusion. As special education groups press for an inclusive agenda, they expect all teachers to transform their conceptual knowledge and their teaching roles and to use that transformation as a basis for making decisions. They also expect all teachers to be more instructionally diverse and use a broader repertoire of effective teaching practices. However, many classroom teachers are minimally equipped to provide for the needs of those who are not responding to group instruction. Although acceptance of all students is the responsibility of every teacher, not all have the skills needed for successful inclusion nor are all receptive to the principles and demands of inclusion (Winzer 1998).

In conjunction, the reformist message has changed recently and the debate has taken a new turn. In many areas, inclusion is now regarded as an organizational rather than an educational intervention; it is not a place where students with disabilities receive services but a way to deliver services effectively. Hence, the opportunities made available by the setting, rather than the setting itself, become important. The critical issue is not where children sit; rather, the major placement objective is where students can receive the most effective education.

Thus, many educators support inclusionary philosophies but dispute inclusion as a universal template that assumes only one solution exists to the various challenges faced by children with special needs. They hold that we do not need to retreat from the principles that support a continuum, but we need to thoughtfully deploy the ideas (Marston 1996). Rather than follow the traditional tendency in special education to focus on restructuring the instructional setting, we need to emphasize interventions that are applicable to varied settings.

With a full continuum of services, educators faced with placement decisions will base their decisions on student outcomes—on which setting will help the child succeed and be prepared to become a productive and active citizen ("Inclusion—where ..." 1996). Whether this decision leads to the child receiving educational services in the general classroom; moving out of the classroom for short periods of time to get remedial help; or working in a resource room, self-contained classroom, or even a separate setting must be determined individually. Similarly, each school must be examined individually to determine what works best for it and its overall population ("Inclusion—where ..." 1996).

CONCLUSION

The inclusion of exceptional students into general education settings has been the dominant discourse among special educators for the past decade. For many educators, advocacy groups, and parents, inclusion is the clarion call of education orthodoxy. For others, it is a radical reform to be approached cautiously. A single, unifying argument does not support the contemporary inclusionary movement. Rather, a group of complex and interwoven arguments confronts issues such as civil rights, a merger of regular and special education, and the responsibilities of regular classroom teachers.

If students with disabilities are placed in general age-appropriate classes, the very assumptions of education as well as the goals and strategies of instruction must be reexamined and adapted. When schools reform to accommodate the diverse needs of students, then the roles of teachers change and the circumstances of regular education personnel take on substantial significance. When students with exceptionalities are placed into regular classrooms where general classroom teachers are expected to duplicate the results of special education and the treatments associated with them, then inclusion represents a basic shift that changes who does what, to whom it is done, where it is done, and how resources support what is done. Although much that is positive is emerging in the literature, negative findings about classroom adaptations that should cause alarm are also emerging. If teachers are reluctant, resistant, or unable to provide adaptations for students with special needs, then a child's academic career is seriously at risk. Lacking adaptations, inclusion becomes only a matter of where students sit, not where they are provided optimal opportunities to learn.

We cannot predict the future course of the inclusionary movement. Relatively speaking, inclusion is a youthful field. Just as yesterday's orthodoxy (segregation) has become today's heresy, the future course of inclusion could also change. Educators may have designed an ark, but they have placed it on an uncharted sea. On the one hand, inclusive schooling may, indeed, prove to be the social and academic prescription for children with special needs. On the other hand, it could remain a vague philosophy that will be disconcerting if not dangerous to students with disabilities.

REFERENCES

Alberta Teachers' Association. 1993. *Trying to teach.* Edmonton: Alberta Teachers' Association.

Archambault, F., K. Westberg, S. Brown, B. Hallmark, W. Zhang, and C. Emmons. 1993. Classroom practices used with gifted third and fourth grade students. *Journal for the Education of the Gifted* 16:103–19.

Baker, J. M., and N. Zigmond. 1995. The meaning and practice of inclusion for students with learning disabilities: Theories and implications from five cases. *Journal of Special Education* 29:163–80.

Bassett, D. S., L. Jackson, K. Ferrel, J. Luckner, P. Hagerty, T. Bussen, and D. MacIsan. 1996. Multiple perspectives on inclusive education: Reflections of a university faculty. *Teacher Education and Special Education* 19:355–86.

Bateman, B. 1993. Learning disabilities: The changing landscape. *Journal of Learning Disabilities* 25:29–63.

Befring, E. 1997. The enrichment perspective: A special educational approach to an inclusive school. *Remedial and Special Education* 18:182–87.

Behar, L., and P. George. 1994. Teachers as change agents: Implications for how teachers use curriculum knowledge. *Educational Researcher Quarterly* 16:8–11.

Boyle, R., and N. Yeager. 1997. Blueprints for learning: Using cognitive frameworks for understanding. *Teaching Exceptional Children* 29:26–31.

Bricker, D. D. 1995. The challenge of inclusion. *Journal of Early Intervention* 19:179–94.

Buski, J. 1997. Education reform—what you've told us. Part 2. *ATA [Alberta Teachers' Association] Magazine* 7 (4):34–35.

Davis, W. 1989. The Regular Education Initiative debate: Its promises and problems. *Exceptional Children* 55:440–46.

Ferguson, D. L. 1998. Changing tactics: Embedding inclusion reforms within general education restructuring efforts. In *Inclusive schooling: National and international perspectives*, ed. S. Vitello and D. Mithaug, 35–53. Hillsdale, N.J.: Lawrence Erlbaum Associates.

Forest, M., and J. Pearpoint. 1992. Putting all kids on the MAP. *Educational Leadership* 50:81–86.

Fox, N. E., and J. E. Ysseldyke. 1997. Implementing inclusion at the middle school level: Lessons from a negative example. *Exceptional Children* 64:81–98.

Fuchs, D., and L. S. Fuchs. 1994. Inclusive schools movement and radicalization of special education reform. *Exceptional Children* 60:294–309.

———. 1995a. Counterpoint—special education—ineffective? Immoral? *Exceptional Children* 61:303–5.

———. 1995b. Special education can work. In *Issues in educational placement*, ed. J. M. Kauffman, J. W. Lloyd, D. P. Hallahan, and T. A. Astuto, 363–77. Hillsdale, N.J.: Lawrence Erlbaum Associates.

Fuchs, D., L. S. Fuchs, P. Fernstrom, and M. Hohn. 1991. Toward a responsible reintegration of behaviorally disordered students. *Behavioral Disorders* 16:133–47.

Fuchs, L. S., D. Fuchs, K. Karms, C. L. Hamlett, M. Katzaroff, and S. Dutka. 1997. Effects of task-focused goals on low-achieving students with and without learning disabilities. *American Educational Research Journal* 34:513–43.

Galt, V. 1997. Teachers support disabled in classes: Fiscal, social realities prevent student integration. *Globe and Mail* 28 (August):A1, A10.

Gartner, A., and D. K. Lipsky. 1987. Beyond special education: Toward a quality system for all students. *Harvard Educational Review* 57:367–95.

George, N. L., M. P. George, R. Gersten, and J. K. Grasenick. 1995. To leave or to stay? An exploratory study of teachers of students with emotional and behavioral disorders. *Remedial and Special Education* 16:227–36.

Giangreco, M. F., R. Denis, C. Cloninger, S. Edelman, and R. Schattman. 1993. "I've counted Jon": Transformational experiences of teachers educating students with disabilities. *Exceptional Children* 59:359–72.

Goertz, M., and D. Friedman. 1996. *State education reform and students with disabilities: A preliminary analysis.* New Brunswick, N.J.: Rutgers University Consortium on Policy Research in Education and Center for Policy Research on the Impact of General and Special Education Reform.

Goodlad, J. I., and S. Field. 1993. Teaching for renewing schools. In *Integrating general and special education*, ed. J. I. Goodlad and T. C. Lovitt, 229–52. New York: Merrill Macmillan.

Hahn, T. 1987. Civil rights for disabled Americans: The foundation of a political agenda. In *Images of the disabled/Disabling images*, ed. A. Gartner and T. Joe, 181–203. New York: Praeger.

Haman, T. A., D. K. Issacson, and O. H. Powell. 1985. Insuring classroom success for the learning disabled adolescent. *Academic Therapy* 20:517–24.

Heumann, J. 1994, Februrary. *A message for the Assistant Secretary.* Denver, Colo.: Strategies for Inclusive Education.

Hueffner, D. S. 1988. The consulting teacher model: Risks and opportunities. *Exceptional Children* 54:404–13.

Inclusion—Where we are today? 1996. *Council for Exceptional Children Today* 1:1, 5, 15.

Jack, S. L., R. E. Shores, R. K. Denny, P. L. Gunter, T. DeBriere, and P. DePaepem. 1996. An analysis of the relationship of teachers' reported use of classroom management strategies and types of classroom interactions. *Journal of Behavioral Education* 6:67–87.

Janney, R. E., M. E. Snell, M. K. Beers, and M. Raynes. 1995. Integrating students with moderate and severe disabilities: Classroom teachers' beliefs and attitudes about implementing an educational change. *Education Administration Quarterly* 31:86–114.

Johnson, A. B. 1987. Attitudes toward mainstreaming: Implications for in-service training and teaching the handicapped. *Education* 107:229–33.

Kauffman, J. M. 1993. How we might achieve the radical reform of special education. *Exceptional Children* 60:6–16.

———. 1996. The challenge of nihilism. *Teacher Education and Special Education* 19:205–06.

———. 1997. Caricature, science, and exceptionality. *Remedial and Special Education* 18:130–32.

———. 1999. How we prevent the prevention of emotional and behavioral disorders. *Exceptional Children* 65:338–468.

Kearney, C. A., and V. M. Durant. 1992. How prepared are our teachers for mainstreaming? A survey of postsecondary schools of education in New York state. *Exceptional Children* 59:6–11.

Kozleski, E. B., and L. Jackson. 1993. Taylor's story: Full inclusion in the neighborhood elementary school. *Exceptionality* 4:153–75.

Laski, F. J. 1991. Achieving integration during the second revolution. In *Critical issues in the lives of people with severe disabilities*, ed. L. H. Meyer, C. A. Peck, and L. Brown, 409–21. Baltimore, Md.: Paul H. Brookes.

Lieberman, L. 1991. REI revisited . . . again. *Exceptional Children* 56:561–566.

Link, M. P. 1991. Is integration really the least restrictive environment? *Teaching Exceptional Children* 23:63–64.

Lundrum, T. J. 1992. Teachers as victims: An interactional analysis of the teacher's role in educating atypical learners. *Behavioral Disorders* 17:134–44.

Lupart, J. 1998. Setting right the delusion of inclusion: Implications for Canadian schools. *Canadian Journal of Education* 23:251–64.

MacMillan, D. L., F. M. Gresham, and S. R. Forness. 1996. Full inclusion: An empirical perspective. *Behavioral Disorders* 21:145–59.

Maheady, L., B. Mallette, and G. F. Harper. 1996. The pair tutoring program: An early field-based experience to prepare preservice general educators to work with students with special needs. *Teacher Education and Special Education* 19:277–97.

Manset, G., and M. I. Semmel. 1997. Are inclusive programs for students with mild disabilities effective? A comparative review of program models. *Journal of Special Education* 31:155–80.

Margolis, H., and J. McGettigan. 1988. Managing resistance to instructional modification in mainstreamed environments. *Remedial and Special Education* 9 (4):15–21.

Marston, D. 1996. A comparison of inclusive only, pull-out only, and combined service models for students with mild disabilities. *Journal of Special Education* 30:121–32.

McGregor, G. 1997. Introduction to special issue on inclusion. *Education and Treatment of Children* 20:1–6.

Meadows, N. B., R. S. Neel, C. M. Scott, and G. Parker. 1994. Academic performance, social competence, and mainstreaming: A look at mainstreamed and nonmainstreamed students with serious behavior disorders. *Behavioral Disorders* 19:170–80.

Mesinger, J. F. 1985. Commentary on "A rationale for the merger of special and regular education" or is it now time for the lamb to lie down with the lion? *Exceptional Children* 51:510–12.

Minke, K. M., G. G. Bear, S. A. Deiner, and S. M. Griffin. 1996. Teachers' experiences with inclusive classrooms: Implications for special education reform. *Journal of Special Education* 30:152–86.

Patton, J. M., and R. Braithwaite. 1990. Special education certification/recertification for regular educators. *Journal of Special Education* 24:117–24.

Peck, C. A., I. Schwartz, F. Billingsley, and O. White. 1993. *What research tells us about inclusive education.* Vancouver: Washington State University.

Porter, G. L. 1994. Equity and excellence in education: An update. *Abilities,* 33–35.

Pugach, M. C. 1992. Unifying the preservice preparation of teachers. In *Controversial issues confronting special education: Divergent perspectives,* ed. W. Stainback and S. Stainback, 255–69. Boston: Allyn and Bacon.

Raynes, M., M. Snell, and W. Sailor. 1991. A fresh look at categorical programs for children with special needs. *Phi Delta Kappan* 73:326–31.

Reiff, H. B., E. D. Evans, and M. Cass. 1991. Special education requirements for general education certification: A national survey of current practices. *Remedial and Special Education* 12:56–60.

Report of the Blue Ribbon Panel on Special Education. 1997. Edmonton: Alberta Teachers' Association.

Resistance and acceptance: Educator attitudes to inclusion of students with disabilities. 1997. *Keeping in Touch* (fall):1, 4.

Reynolds, M. C., and K. C. Lakin. 1987. Noncategorical special education: Models for research and practice. In *Handbook of special and remedial education: Research and practice.* Vol. 1, *Learner characteristics and adaptive education,* ed. M. C. Wang, M. C. Reynolds, and H. J. Walberg, 331–56. New York: Pergamon.

Reynolds, M. C., M. Wang, and H. J. Walberg. 1987. The necessary restructuring of special and regular education. *Exceptional Children* 53:391–98.

Rogers, J. 1993. The inclusion revolution. *Research Bulletin of PDK [Phi Delta Kappan]* (May):1–6.

Ruiter, L. 1997. Celebrating friendship. *ATA [Alberta Teachers' Association] Magazine* 7 (4):31.

Ryan, S., and L. Paterna. 1997. Junior high can be inclusive: Using natural supports and cooperative learning. *Teaching Exceptional Children* 30:36–41.

Salisbury, C. L. 1991. Mainstreaming during the early childhood years. *Exceptional Children* 58:146–55.

Salisbury, C. L., M. M. Palambaro, and T. M. Hollowood. 1993. On the nature and change of an inclusive elementary school. *Journal of the Association for Persons with Severe Handicaps* 18:75–84.

Savage, L. B., and W. D. Wienke. 1989. Attitudes of secondary teachers toward mainstreaming. *High School Journal* 73:70–73.

Scanlon, D., D. Deshler, and J. B. Schumaker. 1996. Can a strategy be taught and learned in secondary inclusive classrooms? *Learning Disability Research and Practice* 11:41–57.

Semmel, M. I., T. V. Abernathy, G. Butera, and S. Lesar. 1991. Teacher perception of the Regular Education Initiative. *Exceptional Children* 58:9–23.

Shaw, L. 1990. *Each belongs: Integrated education in Canada.* Montreal: Centre for Studies on Inclusion in Education.

Sindelar, P. T., M. C. Pugach, C. C. Griffin, and B. L. Seidl. 1995. Reforming teacher education: Challenging the philosophy and practices of educating regular and special educators. In *Integrating school restructuring and special education reform,* ed. J. L. Paul, H. Rosselli, and D. Evans. New York: Harcourt Brace.

Slee, R. 1997. Inclusion or assimilation? Sociological explorations of the foundations of theories of special education. *Educational Foundations* 11:55–71.

Smelter, R. W., B. W. Rasch, and G. J. Yudewitz. 1994. Thinking of inclusion for all special needs students? Better think again. *Phi Delta Kappan* 75:35–38.

Smith, D. D., and R. Luckasson. 1995. *Introduction to special education: Teaching in an age of challenge.* 2d. ed. Needham Heights, Mass.: Allyn and Bacon.

Stainback, S., and W. Stainback. 1985. The merger of special and regular education: Can it be done? *Exceptional Children* 51:517–21.

———. 1992. *Curriculum considerations in inclusive schools: Facilitating learning for all students.* Baltimore: Paul H. Brookes.

Stainback, W., and S. Stainback. 1984. A rationale for the merger of special and regular education. *Exceptional Children* 51:102–11.

Stainback, W., S. Stainback, and G. Stefanich. 1996. Learning together in inclusive classrooms: What about the curriculum? *Teaching Exceptional Children* 28:14–19.

Taylor, R. L., S. B. Richards, P. A. Goldstein, and J. Schilit. 1997. Teacher perceptions of inclusive settings. *Teaching Exceptional Children* 29:50–54.

Thomas, G. 1997. Inclusive schools for an inclusive society. *British Journal of Special Education* 24:103–7.

Thompson, K. 1994. *A child's right to English language instruction in Alberta.* Calgary: Alberta Civil Liberties Research Centre.

Thousand, J. S., and R. A. Villa. 1994. Including students with moderate and severe learning and behavioral challenges. Denver: Council for Exceptional Children.

Treffinger, D. J. 1991. School reform and gifted education—Opportunities and issues. *Gifted Child Quarterly* 35:6–25.

Vergason, G. A., and M. L. Anderegg. 1989. Save the baby! A response to "Integrating the children of the second system." *Phi Delta Kappan* 71:61–63.

Walker, D. K., J. D. Singer, J. S. Palfrey, M. Orza, M. Wenger, and J. A. Butler. 1988. Who leaves and who stays in special education? A 2 year follow-up study. *Exceptional Children* 54:393–402.

Wang, M. C., M. C. Reynolds, and H. J. Walberg. 1986. Rethinking special education. *Educational Leadership* 44:26–31.

———. 1989. Who benefits from segregation and murky water? *Phi Delta Kappan* 71:64–67.

Weber, K. 1994. *Special education in Canadian schools.* Ontario: Highland Press.

Wilczenski, F. L. 1992. Measuring attitudes toward inclusion. *Psychology in the Schools* 29:306–12.

Will, M. 1986. Educating students with learning problems: A shared responsibility. *Exceptional Children* 52:405–11.

Winzer, M. A. 1998. The inclusion movement and teacher change: Where are the limits? *McGill Journal of Education* 33:229–51.

Winzer, M. A., and K. Mazurek. 1998. *Special education in multicultural contexts.* Columbus, Ohio: Merrill.

Wisniewski, L., and S. Alper. 1994. Including students with severe disabilities in general education settings. *Remedial and Special Education* 15:4–13.

Zigmond, N., and J. M. Baker. 1996. Concluding comments: Current and future practices in inclusive schooling. *The Journal of Special Education* 29:245–50.

2

The Inclusion Movement: A Goal for Restructuring Special Education

Susan Bray Stainback

Educational inclusion "is the process of allowing all children, regardless of disability, race, or any other difference the opportunity to remain a member of the regular classroom" (Encarta Encyclopedia 1998). Educational inclusion involves practices that include everyone in all aspects of school and community life. Within these practices, steps are taken to make everyone a respected, successful, contributing part of the whole, regardless of individual differences. Given this broad definition of inclusion, evaluation of the success in the movement becomes more apparent: If a child, teacher, or other member of the school community is not respected, successful, and contributing to the group, success has not been achieved.

HISTORICAL PERSPECTIVE

The integration of previously excluded students into the mainstream of our education system is not a new concept. Throughout history, there has been a movement toward greater integration of more students into the mainstream. Reynolds and Birch (1982) refer to this trend as "progressive inclusion."

The movement to integrate students into the education mainstream did not begin with the students who had disabilities. In 1779, Thomas Jefferson began the struggle to include students from poor families in the education system. He proposed the first state-supported education plan in Virginia in an attempt to allow children, other than those from wealthy families, an opportunity to receive educational services. Although the plan did not pass because the middle class and the wealthy did not want to pay taxes for the poor to go to school (Sigmon 1983), it was a start in considering greater inclusion of students in our schools. Not until approximately one hundred years later did publicly supported education in America become commonplace, allowing students into schools regardless of their ability to pay.

Still, even with public education, many students were excluded in one way or another. For instance, although most students were educated, education for students who were African American, Native American, or disabled was typically provided in separate schools. Many children with more pronounced disabilities were placed in institutions, often receiving no education at all. Even with the passage of compulsory attendance laws in the early 1900s, children in wheelchairs, those who were not toilet trained, or those who were considered "uneducable" were excluded from the public school system (Sigmon 1983). Asylums and residential institutions were a strong force in keeping children with disabilities out of the education mainstream.

In the 1950s, students with moderate disabilities (called trainable) received what education their parents could arrange, often in church basements. These programs were often taught by parents. At that time, students with severe and profound disabilities were still generally housed in institutions without education (Chaves 1977).

The advent of the Civil Rights movement in the 1950s and 1960s brought increased recognition and respect for human dignity. Public education began to scrutinize its most blatant exclusionary policies. The landmark case for integration was the 1954 *Brown v. the Board of Education of Topeka, Kansas* decision that "separate was not equal." This decision had an almost immediate effect of recognizing and supporting the breaking down of education exclusionary policies toward students who were African American or considered to be a minority. In addition, it led the way toward examining the exclusion of students considered disabled. John Davis, chief advocate for the defense in the *Brown* case, stated that if segregation for African American children is unconstitutional, surely the segregation of children with disabilities is also unacceptable (Gilhool 1976).

From the late 1950s to the early 1970s, a number of prominent professionals—including Isaac Goldberg and William Cruickshank (1958), Lloyd Dunn (1968), Gunnar Dybwad (1964), Wolf Wolfensburger (1972), Burton Blatt (1969), Nicholas Hobbs (1966), Maynard Reynolds (1962), and Steven Lilly (1970)—began advocating for more normalized experiences and less exclusion for students who were considered handicapped. Just as important was the landmark for integration, the 1975 passage of PL 94–142, the *Education for All Handi-*

capped Children Act, reauthorized as the *Individuals with Disabilities Education Act* (IDEA) in 1990. This legislation required that all students with disabilities be provided an appropriate education in the least restrictive environment (LRE). It spurred individual states to pass laws subsidizing public school programs for students with disabilities, with all states passing such laws by 1976.

However, throughout the history of education and community integration of all groups, the notions inherent in equality and integration that direct change in common practice initially were never overwhelmingly popular, not even with some of the people that the changes were intended to help, such as African Americans and women. But gradually, a steady trend toward acceptance and equality for all people within the mainstream, regardless of their differences, has been and can be expected to continue (Karagiannis, Stainback, and Stainback 1996). For example, the inclusion of students with severe disabilities in the public school systems and the inclusion of increasing numbers of students with mild to severe disabilities in regular education classes and activities soon followed PL 94–142 and continues today (see *Oberti v. Clementon,* 1993, as discussed in chapter three of this volume).

FINDINGS FROM RESEARCH AND EXPERIENCE

Edmonds, a leading researcher in the effective schools movement, concluded nearly two decades ago that "we can whenever and wherever we choose, successfully teach all children whose schooling is of interest to us. We already know more than we need to do that [but] whether we do it or not must finally depend on how we feel about the fact that we haven't done it so far" (1979, 23). More recent research and practice substantiate the position that educational inclusion can be done successfully (e.g., Hunt et al. 1994; Jenkins et al. 1994; Meyer 1992; S. Stainback and W. Stainback 1996; Thousand and Villa 1994). Just a few examples are included in this chapter.

The 1982 report of the Disability Rights, Education, and Defense Fund stated "that regardless of race, class, gender, type of disability, or age of onset, the more time spent in integrated public school classes as children, the more people achieved educationally and occupationally as adults" (Ferguson and Asch 1989, 124). To be accepted in the workplace and the community, all people, including people with disabilities, need to learn how to perform and function in the "regular" world and to interact with their peers. Equally important, people without disabilities need to learn to function and interact with their peers who have disabilities because "to be excluded from an ordinary educational career and placed in a special education system probably means the person is destined for a special life style and special employment" (Flynn and Kowalczyk-McPhee 1989, 30). According to a person who was labeled disabled and who was segregated during her school years, "I graduated ... completely unprepared for the real world. So I just stayed in the house all day a shut-in, believing a job was out of the question.... Believe me, a segregated environment just will not do as preparation for an integrated life" (Massachusetts Advocacy Center 1987, 4).

Brinker and Thorpe (1984) indicated that when provided appropriate learning opportunities, students labeled as disabled achieve more of their Individualized Education Program (IEP) in integrated regular classroom settings than in segregated settings. In a study by Cole and Meyer (1991) on measures of the social competence of students with severe disabilities, the findings indicated that integrated children progressed, whereas segregated children regressed. Further studies have confirmed these findings (Hunt et al. 1990; Hunt et al. 1994; Kennedy and Itkonen 1994; York et al. 1990). For example, findings from an investigation by Hunt and her colleagues (1994) indicated that not only were more objectives achieved in an inclusive classroom, but also the objectives were of a higher level and the included students showed greater active participation, involvement, and more positive, student-initiated interactions.

Although researchers have consistently found that when appropriate educational experiences and supports are provided, students with various disabilities and at various levels do learn more in integrated settings than they do in segregated settings (e.g., Brinker and Thorpe 1984; Epps and Tindal 1987), the key to success in these studies is that the students were provided appropriate programs and educational opportunities in integrated settings. The point has been made that simply including students with disabilities in regular education classes does not ensure learning benefits (e.g., Marston 1987/1988).

Parents have also noted that their children demonstrate more achievement in integrated settings than in segregated settings. A Massachusetts parent whose son has been labeled autistic said:

> While taking nothing away from the dedication and quality of his teachers, my child can talk. And there's one reason why he can. It's because of the other children. The typical children kept coming up to him and demanding that he talk. They knew how to get an answer from him, and they wouldn't let him get away with a single-syllable response. Now I ask you, what teacher or teachers could do that for my son, much less for a whole class of kids with autism? They simply do not have the time. That's just not realistic. (Massachusetts Advocacy Center 1987, 6)

From an educator's perspective, we look to a regular junior high teacher who works in a school in which students with a variety of learning needs are integrated into regular classes. This teacher noted the reasons for these students' gains:

> When we create integration programs we open up educational possibilities. How better to teach a student who is blind to get to the cafeteria than to practice with her seeing classmates in the hubbub of everyday school life? How better for a student with severe retardation to learn when to laugh, how to dress, and how to walk, than to observe his so-called nondisabled peers? (Massachusetts Advocacy Center 1987, 6)

Benefits occur not only for students who experience learning, physical, or behavioral difficulties but also for students who are already in regular classrooms. Vandercook and her colleagues noted that "Inclusion has an effect on the other children's academic learning by increasing awareness of their own capabilities and respect for themselves and others, which affects the learning climate and susceptibility to learning" (1991, 1). Likewise, as a result of these students' inclusion, greater attention and resources can be directed at evaluating and addressing the unique needs of every student in the regular classroom.

Inclusion can also produce benefits in attitude development. Both research and experience have found that, with proper guidance from adults and with the opportunity to interact in an integrated setting, students can develop more positive attitudes toward and relationships with students who have exceptionalities (Murray-Seegert 1989). Several studies indicate that a critical factor in understanding and accepting individual differences is being around students who exhibit various individual differences (e.g., Voeltz 1980, 1982). This finding is not that surprising when considering the words of the education scholar, Seymour Sarason, who stated, "It is not good teaching strategy to attempt to teach a value but implement practices in direct opposition to that value. For instance, it is not logical to divide and segregate students in their school years, yet try to teach them the value of integration, respect for individual differences, and how to live and work together in an integrated society" (1982, 56).

Attitude changes among educators are also influenced by inclusion. Research has indicated that, when involved in the planning process and when given choices about the design and type of support and assistance they will receive, general educators are willing to join special educators to make general education classes more flexible and conducive for all students, including those labeled disabled (Giangreco et al. 1993; Myles and Simpson 1989). Further, for those teachers who are initially reluctant to include students with disabilities in their classes, participation in an inclusive arrangement frequently changes the attitudes. According to one teacher, "Until you are in the classroom experiencing it, you kind of imagine it being more difficult than it is" (Stainback et al. 1992, 309). Another teacher stated, "I made the full swing of fighting against having Bobbi Sue placed in my room to fighting for her to be in a mainstream classroom ... I'm a perfect example of how you have to have an open mind" (Giangreco et al. 1993, 365).

PRACTICES AND PERSPECTIVES

As noted by Sage, "Inclusive schooling cannot spontaneously occur, regardless of what any one individual does. However, it is a goal toward which systems can evolve" (1996, 105). Pursuing this goal, numerous effective techniques and strategies have been and continue to be developed that can be used to promote the successful inclusion of all students. These include Circle of Friends (Forest, Pearpoint, and O'Brien 1996); Choosing Options and Accommodations for Children, or COACH (Giangreco 1996); Student and Adult Collaboration (Villa and Thousand 1996); Support Networking (Stainback and Stainback 1990); Friendship Facilitation (Bishop et al. 1996; Strully and Strully 1996). Underlying these approaches are principles, practices, or perspectives that can guide educators in addressing the concept of educational inclusion. The following sections explore three of the underlying practices or perspectives that are inherent in the understanding and evolution of an increasingly inclusive setting.

The Way Educators View Students

A standardized definition of a category, based on the results of a battery of tests, is applied to a student. Hence, students with varied learning needs are psychologically separated and segregated because they are grouped in predefined categories such as emotionally disturbed, behaviorally disordered, mentally retarded, culturally deprived, learning disabled, normal, gifted, at-risk, visually impaired, deaf or hard of hearing, and so on (Wehman 1997).

For instance, if a student is categorized as having a learning disability, then the most commonly used definition of the category also is typically assigned, by default. In the case of learning disabilities, the typically assigned definition is the 1990 updated definition by the National Joint Committee on Learning Disabilities (NJCLD), which reads, "learning disabilities is a general term that refers to a heterogeneous group of disorders manifested by significant difficulties in the acquisition and use of listening, speaking, reading, writing, reasoning, or mathematical abilities. These disorders are intrinsic to the individual" (Bender, Marshall, and Wehman 1997, 182). If a student is diagnosed as mentally retarded (even at a mild level), the American Association on Mental Retardation definition is most popular and is assigned. That definition is, "Mental retardation refers to substantial limitations in present functioning. It is characterized by significantly subaverage intellectual functioning, existing concurrently with related limitations" (1992, 5).

These categorization efforts attempt to provide some helpful ideas: Just as a predetermined definition is associated with the category, predetermined characteristics and interventions are accepted and typically constitute an education prescription (see Wehman 1997). However, for the labeled student, such definitions would not appear very flattering. They would not build confidence in those individuals who have been assigned them, nor would they serve to foster positive expectations among peers or teachers.

Further, categories do nothing to enhance the likelihood of inclusive education and, in fact, actually serve as roadblocks. These practices not only are a financial and personnel drain on the education system but also do not provide any instructionally relevant data or improvement (Stainback, Stainback, and Forest 1989). Instead, these practices tend to mask both the abilities and humanness of the child and interfere with the recognition of the child as a unique person. As described by Harlan Hahn (1989), a political scientist from the University of Southern California, when a model of functional limitations operates, disabilities are viewed as a personal misfortune that requires the individual to acquire skills to adapt to environments that do not meet their needs. This adaptation causes others to see the individual as different or apart from other group members and also as less valued.

A premise or perspective of inclusive education is that, to be successfully included and for positive learning opportunities to occur, each student must be viewed as an equally worthy and welcomed member of the class, not different, devalued, or somehow apart from other members. Every student, as a member of the group, may need some support to be successful in the classroom, but every student also has something to offer and can be a provider of support to other class members.

School environments should be adaptable so the needs of all who are to be included can be addressed. In this way, no one is being left out. One example that shows this adaptation is the story of John, a student with cerebral palsy. In his earlier educational career, John was labeled severely disabled and assigned to a special classroom. With the advent of computer assisted instruction that made communication for and with John easier, with the unflinching advocacy of his mother, and through his own hard work to make up for the learning he had lost out on earlier, John was admitted to a general school classroom. When he was in high school, John could not do his English assignments like other class members because the plays that the teacher required the students to review were in a nonaccessible building. John was given different assignments. He went to the student council and a boycott of assignments requiring work in nonaccessible buildings was organized. As a result, assignments were subsequently arranged in accessible buildings so everyone, including John, could participate successfully. This simple, concrete example shows that when the educators shifted their focus from expecting an adaptation of John to making an adaptation to the environment, they fostered John's inclusion rather than his exclusion.

The Way Educators View Heterogeneity among Students in a Classroom

Too often in education, heterogeneity in a classroom has been viewed as a "liability" that needs to be handled, fixed, or, if possible, eliminated (Snow and Forest 1987). However, diversity among students, if properly organized, can promote rather than impede learning for all class members. Differences among students can be an asset: Differences can constitute positive learning capital that can enhance opportunities for learning in classrooms. To reiterate what parent and educator Robert Barth stated, "Differences hold great opportunities for learning. Differences offer a free, abundant and renewable resource.... What is important about people—and about schools—is what is different, not what is the same" (1990, 515).

Visits to two elementary classrooms illustrate how diversity among students can be used for either the detriment or the benefit of the students. During a visit to a second grade class, two children were sitting at a table at the back of the room coloring mimeographed pictures while their classmates were involved in a group science activity. When a child sitting close by was asked by the observer for an explanation, he said, "Those kids are from Thailand and don't speak English very good so no one can understand them. The teacher gives them stuff to do so they don't make noise and bother us" (personal communication to Stainback 1989).

In another classroom, kindergartners were, over a period of time, involved in a group, a play, and a snack activity. During these activities, the teacher would say a key word and then follow it with the sign for the word. The children would practice saying and signing the words in their conversations in a playful way with their peers. Repeatedly, the children used the signs the teacher had taught them throughout the observation period. When questioned, the teacher noted that one of the children in the classroom had a significant hearing loss and was relatively fluent in sign language, so everyone was learning to better communicate with her. At the same time, the interaction was giving the child an opportunity to practice and improve her speechreading skills.

The Way Values Are Instilled in Children during Learning Experiences

Alfie Kohn stated it this way:

> Our society's current infatuation with the word "competitiveness" which has leached into discussions about education encourages a confusion between two very different ideas: excellence and the desperate quest to triumph over other people.... At a tender age, children learn not to be tender. A dozen years of schooling often do nothing to promote generosity or a commitment to the welfare of others. To the contrary, students are graduated who think that being smart means looking out for number one. (1991, 498)

In response to this concern, education researchers have undertaken studies to determine how to combat the development of such attitudes. It is beginning to be recognized that all students can excel without necessarily triumphing over others. Students can excel in academic and other areas and still learn to care about and assist each other.

A number of strategies have been developed along this line. Daniel Solomon and his colleagues (Solomon et al. 1992) in San Ramon, California, have been studying how to foster cooperation and support among all school members that leads to caring schools and classroom communities. Another example is the well-known work on cooperative learning done by Johnson and Johnson (1987, 1994) in Minnesota and by Robert Slavin (1989) at Johns Hopkins in Baltimore. Action research method work by Marsha Forest, Jack Pearpoint, and their colleagues (Forest, Pearpoint, and O'Brien 1996) in Canada and throughout the United States is involving peers in mutual support for social and personal activities as well as for sharing in academic program mapping.

The role of student collaboration has also been an important variable in developing positive attitudes among students (Villa and Thousand 1992, 1996). These practices involve classrooms and schools where students and educators learn to assist and support each other through peer tutoring, buddy systems, teacher assistance teams, team teaching, and circles of friends. Such supportive, community-oriented educational procedures that foster positive understandings of self and peers are very successful in fostering the inclusion of students with disabilities in the mainstream of general education.

ARGUMENTS AND POSITIONS ON THE ISSUE OF INCLUSION

In addition to research and experiential evidence regarding the benefits and ability to successfully develop inclusive educational settings, other reasons also support this movement. One is that inclusive education avoids the ill effect of segregation. In the United States, Chief Justice Warren in the *Brown v. The Board of Education* (1954) decision stated that separateness in education can "generate a feeling of inferiority as to [children's] status in the community that may affect their hearts and minds in a way unlikely ever to be undone." A student who was educated in a special class confirms Justice Warren's statement as he describes his school experience:

> The only contact we had with the "normal" children was visual. We stared at each other. On those occasions, I can report my own feelings: embarrassment.... I can also report their feelings: Yech! We, the children in the "handicapped" class, were internalizing the "yech" message—plus a couple of others. We were in school because children go to school, but we were outcasts, with no future and no expectation of one. (Massachusetts Advocacy Center 1987, 4–5)

From a regular-class adolescent student who was placed in a "low-track" class when entering junior high school, we hear the same message: "I felt good when I was with my [elementary] class, but when they went and separated us that changed us. That changed our ideas, the way we thought about each other, and turned us to enemies toward each other because they said I was dumb and they were smart" (Schafer and Olexa 1971, 96).

Every day that a student remains in a segregated setting, he or she is being denied opportunities to learn with and from his or her peers. In addition, a lack of self-confidence, a lack of motivation, and a lack of positive expectations for achievement are all results of a segregated learning environment. These results all operate to promote education failure rather than education success.

However, although all the previous material can be used to support inclusive schooling, there is a more fundamental reason for providing all students the right to be educated with their peers in regular classrooms. This reason is based on a moral or value of equality: "The ultimate rationale for quality education of students in an inclusionary setting is not based on research, law, or pedagogy, but on values. What kind of society do we wish to develop? What values do we honor?" (Gartner and Lipsky 1987, 389).

As the intent was described in the 1954 *Brown* case and reiterated repeatedly over the past several decades in documents—such as the Canadian Commission on Emotional and Learning Disorders report of 1970s; the 1978 Warnock report in England; the 1984 report by the Ministry of Education in Victoria, Australia; and the 1991 policy statement of the New Mexico Department of

Education—separate is not equal. That is, all children should be provided rather than denied the opportunity to grow and learn with and from their peers regardless of any individual differences they may have. All children should have an equal right to be a part of the education and community mainstream. In addition, it is inherently unfair and discriminatory that some students must earn the right or be gotten ready to be in the regular education mainstream while other students who are not labeled disabled or different are allowed unrestricted access to the education and community mainstream. If we want an integrated society in which all people, including those labeled disabled or having learning differences, are considered to have equal worth and equal rights, we need to reevaluate how we operate our schools. Finally, if we truly want integration in our community, segregation in our schools cannot be justified.

THE CHALLENGE

Historically, we have made strong and steady gains toward the progressive inclusion of all students in the mainstream of public education. We can be proud of the educational and social opportunities that have been created for all students. In the past several decades, students who were previously excluded are now receiving a public education. Curriculum and teaching procedures as well as techniques that allow for increased diversity among students have been developed and refined. More importantly, an increasingly positive perspective toward respecting the individuality among students and toward teaching attitudes that can better address student needs have received much attention. As a result, society has become more tolerant of diversity, and the community has become more accessible for all children and adults. Further, inclusive education has progressed past being just an issue in special education. Educational inclusion within the present decade is now being recognized in a broader context.

However, these strong gains cannot justify complacency. Education reform must continue to move forward because much remains to be done. Many students are still excluded from the schools and classrooms of their neighborhood peers. Educators continue to use and propose standardized, graded, lockstep, curricular requirements and standards that do not fit the educational needs of students (e.g., reference to Clinton's State of the Union message in Dahl 1997), requirements and standards that are out of reach for some and not challenging for others. As educators and advocates for children, we must be ever vigilant and critically aware of the influence that new policies and procedures may have on fostering mutual respect among individuals, on the opportunities being made available by promoting diversity, and on the development of a caring community.

We as educators and community members are in key positions to help these reforms continue to happen in our schools. Although sometimes we feel impotent in our attempts to change the established routine, we can have an effect. John Kennedy pointed out this dynamic many years ago. He stated, and it was reiterated more recently by his brother Ted:

Let no one be discouraged by the belief that there is nothing that one man, or one woman can do against the enormous array of the world's ills; against misery and ignorance; injustice, and violence. Few will have the greatness to bend history itself, but each of us can work to change a small portion of the events, and in the total of all those acts, will be written the history of this generation. It is from numberless diverse acts of courage and belief that human history is shaped. Each time a man stands up for an ideal, or acts to improve the lot of others, or strikes out against injustice, he sends forth a tiny ripple of hope; and crossing each other from a million different centers of energy and daring, those ripples build a current which can sweep down the mightiest walls of oppression and resistance. (Kennedy 1986, 7)

REFERENCES

American Association on Mental Retardation. 1992. *News and Notes* 5:1–8.

Barth, R. 1990. A personal vision of a good school. *Phi Delta Kappan* 71:512–71.

Bender, W., R. Marshall, and P. Wehman. 1997. Learning disabilities. In *Exceptional individuals in school, community, and work,* ed. P. Wehman, 175–205. Austin: Pro-Ed.

Bishop, B., K. Jubala, W. Stainback, and S. Stainback. 1996. Facilitating friendships. In *Inclusion: A guide for educators,* ed. S. Stainback and W. Stainback, 155–60. Baltimore: Paul H. Brookes.

Blatt, B. 1969. *Exodus from pandemonium*. Boston: Allyn and Bacon.

Brinker, R., and M. Thorpe. 1984. Integration of severely handicapped students and proportion of IEP objectives achieved. *Exceptional Children* 51:168–75.

Brown v. Board of Education of Topeka, Kansas 347 US 483, 493 (1954).

Chaves, I. 1977. Historical overview of special education in the United States. In *Mainstreaming: Problems, potentials, and perspectives,* ed. P. Bates, T. West, and R. Schmerl, 25–41. Minneapolis: National Support Systems Project.

Cole, D., and L. Meyer. 1991. Social integration and severe disabilities: A longitudinal analysis of child outcomes. *Journal of Special Education* 25:340–51.

Dahl, D. 1997. Clinton calls for big rise in spending on education. *St. Petersburg Times* (February 5):1A, 10A.

Dunn, L. 1968. Special education for the mildly retarded—is much of it justifiable? *Exceptional Children* 35:5–22.

Dybwad, G. 1964. *Challenges in mental retardation*. New York: Columbia University Press.

Edmonds, R. 1979. Some schools work and more can. *Social Policy* 2:28–32.

Encarta Encyclopedia. 1998. Educational inclusion. *Microsoft Encarta Encyclopedia*. Redmond, Wash.: Microsoft Corporation.

Epps, S., and G. Tindal. 1987. The effectiveness of differential programming in serving students with mild handicaps: Placement options and instructional programming. In *Handbook of special and remedial education: Research and practice*. Vol. 1, *Learner characteristics and adaptive education,* ed. M. C. Wang, M. C. Reynolds, and H. J. Walberg, 213–48. New York: Pergamon.

Ferguson, P., and A. Asch. 1989. Lessons from life: Personal and parental perspectives on school, childhood, and disability. In *Disability and society,* ed. D. Biklen, A. Ford, and D. Ferguson, 108–40. Chicago: National Society for the Study of Education.

Flynn, G., and B. Kowalczyk-McPhee. 1989. A school system in transition. In *Educating all students in the mainstream of regular education,* ed. S. Stainback, W. Stainback, and M. Forest, 29–42. Baltimore: Paul H. Brookes.

Forest, M., J. Pearpoint, and J. O'Brien. 1996. MAPS, Circles of Friends, and PATH: Powerful tools to help build caring communities. In *Inclusion: A guide for educators,* ed. S. Stainback and W. Stainback, 67–86. Baltimore: Paul H. Brookes.

Gartner, A., and D. Lipsky. 1987. Beyond special education. *Harvard Educational Review* 57:367–95.

Giangreco, M. 1996. Choosing options and accommodations for children (COACH): Curriculum planning for students with disabilities in education. In *Inclusion: A guide for educators,* ed. S. Stainback and W. Stainback, 237–54. Baltimore: Paul H. Brookes.

Giangreco, M., R. Dennis, C. Cloninger, S. Edelman, and R. Schattman. 1993. "I've counted Jon": Transformational experiences of teachers educating students with disabilities. *Exceptional Children* 59:359–72.

Gilhool, T. 1976. Changing public policies: Roots and forces. In *Mainstreaming: Origins and implications,* ed. M. Reynolds, 8–13. Reston, Va.: Council for Exceptional Children.

Goldberg, I., and W. Cruickshank. 1958. The trainable but not educable: Whose responsibility? *National Education Association Journal* 47:622.

Hahn, H. 1989. The politics of special education. In *Beyond special education,* ed. D. Lipsky and A. Gartner, 225–42. Baltimore: Paul H. Brookes.

Hobbs, N. 1966. Helping the disturbed child: Psychological and ecological strategies. *American Psychologist* 21:1105–15.

Hunt, P., M. Alwell, L. Goetz, and W. Sailor. 1990. Generalized effects of conversation skills training. *Journal of the Association for Persons with Severe Handicaps* 15:250–60.

Hunt, P., F. Farron-Davis, S. Beckstead, D. Curtis, and L. Goetz. 1994. Evaluating the effects of placement of students with severe disabilities in general education versus special classes. *Journal of the Association for Persons with Severe Handicaps* 19:200–214.

Jenkins, J., M. Jewell, N. Leicester, R. O'Connor, L. Jenkins, and N. Troutner. 1994. Accommodations for individual differences without classroom ability groups: An experiment in school restructuring. *Exceptional Children* 60:344–58.

Johnson, D., and R. Johnson. 1987. *Learning together and alone: Cooperation, competition, and individualization.* 2d ed. Englewood Cliffs, N.J.: Prentice Hall.

Johnson, R., and D. Johnson. 1994. An overview of cooperative learning. In *Creativity and collaborative learning: A practical guide to empowering students and teachers,* ed. J. Thousand, R. Villa, and A. Nevin, 31–45. Baltimore: Paul H. Brookes.

Karagiannis, A., S. Stainback, and W. Stainback. 1996. Historical overview of inclusion. In *Inclusion: A guide for educators,* ed. S. Stainback and W. Stainback, 17–28. Baltimore: Paul H. Brookes.

Kennedy, C., and T. Itkonen. 1994. Some effects of regular class placement on the social contacts and social networks of high school students with severe disabilities. *Journal of the Association for Persons with Severe Handicaps* 19:1–10.

Kennedy, T. 1986. Our right to independence. *Parade Magazine* 23 (November):4–7.

Kohn, A. 1991. Caring kids: The role of the schools. *Phi Delta Kappan* 72:496–506.

Lilly, S. 1970. Special education: A tempest in a teapot. *Exceptional Children* 32:43–49.

Marston, D. 1987/1988. The effectiveness of special education. *Journal of Special Education* 21:13–27.

Massachusetts Advocacy Center. 1987. *Out of the mainstream*. Boston: Massachusetts Advocacy Center.

Meyer, C. 1992. What's the difference between authentic and performance assessment? *Educational Leadership* 49:39–40.

Murray-Seegert, C. 1989. *Nasty girls, thugs, and humans like us: Social relations between severely disabled and nondisabled students in high school*. Baltimore: Paul H. Brookes.

Myles, B., and R. Simpson. 1989. Regular educators' modification preferences for mainstreaming mildly handicapped children. *Journal of Special Education* 22:479–89.

Rafael Oberti v. Board of Education of Clementon, New Jersey (3d Cir 1993).

Reynolds, M. 1962. Framework for considering some issues in special education. *Exceptional Children* 28:367–70.

Reynolds, M., and J. Birch. 1982. *Teaching exceptional children in all America's schools*. 2d ed. Reston, Va.: Council for Exceptional Children.

Sage, D. 1996. Administrative strategies for achieving inclusive schooling. In *Inclusion: A guide for educators*, ed. S. Stainback and W. Stainback, 105–16. Baltimore: Paul H. Brookes.

Sarason, S. 1982. *The culture of the school and the problem of change*. Boston: Allyn and Bacon.

Schafer, W., and C. Olexa. 1971. *Tracking and opportunity*. Scranton, Penn.: Chandler.

Sigmon, S. 1983. The history and future of educational segregation. *Journal for Special Educators* 19:1–13.

Slavin, R. 1989. Review of cooperative learning: Consensus and controversy. *Educational Leadership* 47:52–54.

Snow, J., and M. Forest. 1987. Circles. In *More education integration: A further collection of readings on the integration of children with mental handicaps into regular school systems*, ed. M. Forest. Downsview, Ontario: G. Allan Roeher Institute.

Solomon, D., E. Schaps, M. Watson, and V. Battistich. 1992. Creating caring school and classroom communities for all students. In *Restructuring for caring and effective education: An administrative guide to creating heterogeneous schools*, ed. R. Villa, J. Thousand, W. Stainback, and S. Stainback, 41–60. Baltimore: Paul H. Brookes.

Stainback, S., and W. Stainback. 1990. Facilitating support networks. In *Support networks for inclusive schooling*, ed. W. Stainback and S. Stainback, 25–36. Baltimore: Paul H. Brookes.

———, eds. 1996. *Inclusion: A guide for educators*. Baltimore: Paul H. Brookes.

Stainback, S., W. Stainback, and M. Forest. 1989. *Educating all students in the mainstream of regular education*. Baltimore: Paul H. Brookes.

Stainback, W., and S. Stainback. 1996. Contemplating inclusive education from a historical perspective. In *Inclusion for all*, ed. R. Villa and J. Thousand, 15–23. Reston, Va.: Association for Supervision and Curriculum Development.

Stainback, W., and S. Stainback, J. Moravec, and J. Jackson. 1992. Concerns about full inclusion: An ethnographic investigation. In *Restructuring for caring and effective education: An administrative guide to creating heterogeneous schools*, ed. R. Villa, J. Thousand, W. Stainback, and S. Stainback, 305–24. Baltimore: Paul H. Brookes.

Strully, J., and C. Strully. 1996. Friendships as an educational goal: What have we learned and where are we headed? In *Inclusion: A guide for educators*, ed. S. Stainback and W. Stainback, 141–54. Baltimore: Paul H. Brookes.

Thousand, J. S., and R. A. Villa. 1994. Strategies to create inclusive schools and classrooms. Paper presented at the Excellence and Equity in Education International Conference, August, Toronto, Ontario.

Vandercook, T., J. York, M. Sharpe, J. Knight, C. Salisbury, B. LeRoy, and E. Kozleski. 1991. The million dollar question . . . *Impact* 4:20–21.

Villa, R., and J. Thousand. 1992. Student collaboration: An essential for curriculum delivery in the 21st century. In *Curriculum considerations in inclusive classrooms: Facilitating learning for all students*, ed. S. Stainback and W. Stainback, 117–42. Baltimore: Paul H. Brookes.

Villa, R., and J. Thousand. 1996. Student collaboration: An essential for curriculum delivery in the 21st century. In *Inclusion: A guide for educators*, ed. S. Stainback and W. Stainback, 193–202. Baltimore: Paul H. Brookes.

Voeltz, L. 1980. Children's attitudes toward handicapped peers. *American Journal for Mental Deficiency* 84:455–64.

———. 1982. Effects of structural interactions with severely handicapped peers on children's attitudes. *American Journal for Mental Deficiency* 86:380–90.

Wehman, P. 1997. *Exceptional individuals in school, community and work.* Austin: Pro-Ed.

Wolfensburger, W. 1972. *The principle of normalization in human services.* Toronto: National Institute on Mental Retardation.

York, J., T. Vandercook, E. Caughey, and C. Heise-Neff. 1990. Regular class integration: Beyond socialization. *TASH [The Association for Persons with Severe Handicaps] Newsletter* 16:3.

3

Defining U.S. Special Education into the Twenty-first Century

Margaret J. McLaughlin   *Kelly Henderson*

M any forces are shaping modern special education in the United States. Although numerous factors have influenced the system as it exists today, few have had as significant an effect as federal legislation and litigation. The foundations that undergird the field are reflected in the turbulent and triumphant history of special education and civil rights law. This chapter provides a brief review of the critical federal legislation and court decisions that have affected education of students with disabilities in the United States. It also provides an overview of recent policy changes that are altering the way in which special education is defined, measured, and improved.

FOUNDATIONS OF SPECIAL EDUCATION IN THE UNITED STATES

The initial legal efforts to improve educational opportunities on behalf of children and youth with disabilities focused on gaining access to public education. Early special education litigation was grounded in federal civil rights cases in the

The authors are grateful to the preservice teachers in 1998 and 1999 who allowed the use of their portfolios for this study.

1950s and 1960s. Several landmark cases provided the foundation for a constitutionally established right to an education for all children in the United States. In addition to its findings that desegregation of students by race was unconstitutional, *Brown v. Board of Education of Topeka, Kansas* in 1954 set a legal precedent in establishing education as a right that must be available to all on equal terms.

In 1972, two federal court cases established the "zero-reject" principle for special groups of students with disabilities by ordering public school officials to provide these students with a free, appropriate public education (FAPE). Additionally, court rulings established, for the first time, several procedural safeguards for parents and families of children with disabilities to formally challenge schools that did not comply with court orders regarding special education. The Pennsylvania Association for Retarded Citizens brought suit against the state education department for failure to provide access to education for students with mental retardation. *Pennsylvania ARC v. the Commonwealth of Pennsylvania* (1971) established that schools in the state must provide a free public education to all school-age children with mental retardation.

Mills v. the Board of Education of the District of Columbia (1972) found that exclusion of children with disabilities from free, appropriate public education is a violation of the due process and equal protection clauses of the Fourteenth amendment to the Constitution, and it expanded the class of students with disabilities beyond mental retardation to include all types of disability. Public schools in Washington, D.C., were required to provide a free education to all children with disabilities regardless of the children's functional level or their ability to adapt to the present education system.

These landmark court cases reinforced the need for what many disability advocates and parents of children with disabilities had been urging for decades—federal support for a mandate that all children with disabilities be educated in public schools. In 1975, the Education for All Handicapped Children Act (PL 94–142, renamed the Individuals with Disabilities Education Act, or IDEA, in 1990) was established as U.S. law, guaranteeing a free, appropriate public education to all children and youth with disabilities. This law, however, does not function in isolation.

Two other sweeping federal mandates have made significant contributions to expanding the opportunities for persons with disabilities. Together with IDEA, Section 504 of the Rehabilitation Act of 1973 and the Americans with Disabilities Act (ADA; 1990) form the solid foundation on which today's U.S. special education system is built. The Rehabilitation Act of 1973 established a system of vocational rehabilitation programs and services that were designed to increase opportunities for individuals with disabilities to prepare for, secure, maintain, and regain employment. In addition, it prohibits discrimination on the basis of disability in programs and activities, both public and private, that receive federal financial assistance. The ADA extends these antidiscrimination provisions to private-sector employment and to all public services, programs, and telecommunications as well as guarantees access to privately owned establishments.

Over the years, these three pieces of legislation have shaped school policy and our knowledge regarding who may be considered students with disabilities and how best to educate them. The rest of this chapter will focus specifically on some of the most critical issues facing U.S. special education policy and practice.

SPECIAL EDUCATION POLICY

The various pieces of federal legislation have been amended over the years to reflect both litigation and changing notions about how to educate students. A summary of the current major special education provisions in Section 504 of the Rehabilitation Act, the ADA, and IDEA is provided in table 1.

During the twenty-three years since the initial enactment of federal special education policy, several issues have been identified as areas for concern and further policy consideration in the provision of special education services. The primary issues that have driven many of the efforts to reform special education are (1) determining eligibility for special education services, (2) disciplining children with disabilities, (3) interpreting "least restrictive environment" (LRE) and the degree to which students with disabilities will be included in general education programs, and (4) providing accountability for the outcomes of special education. Each will be discussed briefly below.

Eligibility for Special Education

According to recent national data, approximately 4.8 million youths between the ages of six and seventeen qualified for special education during the 1995–96 school year (U.S. Department of Education 1997). This number represents 10.6 percent of the school-age population. The current federal and state special education laws employ an all-or-none system of determining eligibility for special education services in that a student is either determined disabled and eligible for all services or determined eligible for no services whatsoever. The statute requires that only those students whose learning problems are attributed to a disability—and not those students whose problems are caused by environmental, cultural, or economic disadvantage—can be found eligible for special education. This system is somewhat at odds with professional practice that generally conceives of a continuum of disabilities and recognizes the limitations of the current research base to reliably distinguish students with high incidence disabilities, such as learning disabilities, from students referred to as low achieving or educationally disadvantaged (Keogh and MacMillen 1996; Lyon 1996; McDonnell, McLaughlin, and Morison 1997).

The eligibility process is further complicated by a federal statutory scheme that requires that students be further classified as fitting into one of thirteen disability categories (such as learning disability, emotional disturbance, and mental retardation) to be found eligible. This requirement of categorical eligibility has proven to be problematic because current assessment procedures are not able to

Table 1.

The Major Special Education Provisions in U.S. Federal Law.

	Section 504 of the Rehabilitation Act	Americans with Disabilities Act	Individuals with Disabilities Education Act
Structure	The Rehabilitation Act of 1973 establishes a variety of federal and state-based services, centers, agencies and programs. Title V, Section 504, has the greatest impact on the education of children who have disabilities. Section 504 prohibits discrimination against people with disabilities in federally-funded programs, such as "a local education agency, system of vocational education, or other school system." Implementation is the responsibility of the Office of Civil Rights, U.S. Department of Education.	The ADA has five titles, which cover employment, public accommodations, and telecommunications. Title II mandates accessibility of all services, programs, and activities of state and local governments, addressing both physical facility and program accessibility. The U.S. Department of Education enforces Title II in public elementary and secondary school systems, public institutions of higher education, many public vocational education schools, and public libraries.	The Individuals with Disabilities Education Act guarantees educational rights to children and youth with disabilities. The Office of Special Education Programs, U.S. Department of Education is responsible for developing and enforcing regulations. Part B requires each state to develop a plan clarifying special education policies and related services to eligible children and youth with disabilities. Parts C and D fund research, training, and early intervention services.
Who is protected?	Under Section 504, a qualified "individual with a disability" is any person who (1) has a physical or mental impairment that substantially limits one or more major life activities, (2) has a record of such impairment, or (3) is regarded as having such an impairment.	The ADA protects an individual with a disability who (1) has a physical or mental impairment that substantially limits one or more life activities, (2) has a record of such impairment, or (3) is regarded as having such impairment. Further, the person must be qualified for the program or service.	IDEA's Part B makes eligible all children ages 3–21 years who fall within one or more of the 13 specific categories of disability and who are in need of special education and related services. Part C makes infants and toddlers with disabilities eligible for early intervention services if they are at risk of experiencing a developmental delay.

(continued)

reliably differentiate among high-incidence disability populations (Gajar 1979; Hallahan and Kauffman 1977; MacMillan and Hendrick 1993; Reschly 1988). Even though assessments are not reliable for this purpose, states have expended

Table 1. *(continued)*

The Major Special Education Provisions in U.S. Federal Law.

	Section 504 of the Rehabilitation Act	*Americans with Disabilities Act*	*Individuals with Disabilities Education Act*
Responsibility to provide a free, appropriate, public education (FAPE)	Section 504 requires provision of a FAPE, including individually designed instruction, to eligible students. This may be defined as regular or special education services and related aids and services. Students can receive related services even if they are not provided any special education.	The ADA makes no direct requirement to provide a FAPE to eligible students. However, the ADA contains two provisions that may impact the education of children and youth with disabilities. First, the ADA applies its protections to non-sectarian private schools. Second, the ADA provides an additional layer of protection in combination with actions brought under Section 504 and IDEA.	IDEA requires the provision of a FAPE to eligible students. Related services are provided if required for the students to benefit from instruction. States are required to ensure the provision of "full educational opportunity" to all children with disabilities. IDEA requires an Individualized Education Program (IEP) for each eligible student.
Setting in which services can be delivered	Section 504 requires that students be educated with their nondisabled peers to the maximum extent appropriate. Reasonable accommodations must be made for students with disabilities so that they may be afforded "an opportunity to participate in or benefit from the aid, benefit, or service" that is provided to other students.	The ADA requires that goods, services, facilities, privileges, advantages, and accommodations are to be provided to individuals with disabilities in the most integrated setting appropriate to the needs of the individual.	The IEP team's placement decision should ensure that the child is served in the least restrictive environment. A full continuum of placement alternatives must be available for providing special education and related services.

significant resources on assessments that were relevant primarily for classification rather than for educational or treatment purposes (McDonnell, McLaughlin, and Morison 1997; Merrill 1990; Shinn, Tindall, and Stein 1988; Slate and Jones, this volume).

Because states have always been allowed some freedom to define the exact parameters of the federal disability categories, a great deal of variability has developed in both the state definitions of various disabilities and the local (i.e., school district level) implementation of those definitions (MacMillan and

Hendrick 1993). Concerns arise about the equity of a system where a student can be eligible to receive special education in one state or district but not in another. Concerns have been raised about the validity of the categories (e.g., learning disabilities) themselves and about the overrepresentation of minority males in special education. This overrepresentation has been ascribed to problems and biases that are inherent in the assessment instruments, such as IQ tests, and to a system of referral and assessment that is biased against those whose language and behaviors do not match the White, middle-class norms of classrooms.

Discipline

The issues of eligibility for special education and related services are further complicated by questions about if and when the right to a free, appropriate public education ends for an identified child with a disability. In no other area have these questions stirred more controversy and publicity than in the area of student discipline. The Supreme Court's *Honig v. Doe* decision in 1988 addressed the extent to which the free, appropriate public education principle applies in cases of student discipline. The Court's interpretation barred schools from unilaterally changing placements for more than ten days. In the Court's view, IDEA does not include or imply a "dangerousness" exception to the guarantee of procedural safeguards regarding any change of student placements, even for students with disabilities who engage in disruptive behavior. If, in response to a school's disciplinary action, parents of a child with a disability initiate procedural safeguard actions, such as a due process hearing, the child is to remain in his or her then-current placement. This "stay-put" provision was amended by Congress in 1997 (see section on discipline of students with disabilities).

The *Honig* decision also affirmed that a manifestation determination must be made to determine the relationship of the child's behavior to his or her disability. If the misconduct is a manifestation of a disability, the student may not be suspended for more than ten days. Disciplinary reactions toward misconduct that is unrelated to the disability may be like those toward children who are not disabled. However, subsequent interpretations by the U.S. Department of Education clarify that, even in those cases where a special education student is disciplined for a behavior that is unrelated to his or her disability, a discontinuation of special education services would be a violation of the student's right to a free and appropriate public education. The 1997 amendments to IDEA reinforce this "no cessation" requirement in law.

Least Restrictive Environment

The question of what constitutes education in the least restrictive environment is one of the more controversial issues in special education and is subject to much litigation. Much of the conflict has arisen from the inherent tension between two requirements. On the one hand, IDEA requires that each student have available a full continuum of placements to meet his or her needs (including such restrictive settings as residential schools), with the placement determination resting on an individualized determination of each student's educational needs. On the other hand, IDEA requires that the general education classroom be the preferred placement. Although courts have generally held that the LRE mandate is secondary to the determination of an appropriate instructional program, they have also made clear that the preference for placement in general education classrooms is to be given great weight (McDonnell, McLaughlin, and Morison 1997).

Large numbers of students with disabilities are already being educated within general education classrooms for much if not all of each day. Data from the 1993–94 school year indicate that 44.5 percent of all students with disabilities are educated at least 80 percent of the day in general education classrooms while another 29 percent are in those classrooms 40–79 percent of the day (U.S. Department of Education 1997). For these students, the issue of LRE is not whether they can have access to regular education classrooms but whether sufficient levels of support will be provided in that setting instead of in more specialized environments such as resource rooms or pullouts. Beginning with a 1986 paper issued by Madeline Will, former assistant secretary for the Office of Special Education and Rehabilitative Services, many have called for a restructured special education system that would no longer use pull-out services to educate students with disabilities but would merge special education programs and funding with general education to promote inclusion for disabled students (see, for example, Gartner and Lipsky 1987; Stainback and Stainback 1984; Wang, Reynolds, and Walberg 1986).

Much of the subsequent debate about inclusion is split along lines that are demarcated by differing views of the purpose of special education. Those who focus on using special education to provide severely disabled individuals with an opportunity to develop social networks and the social skills that will allow them to integrate more fully into the mainstream of society often reject the notion of preserving a continuum of placements outside of the regular classroom. Others who focus on using the special education system to allow students with disabilities to meet the demands of the general education curriculum and attain increased academic competence advocate for maintaining a continuum of placements in which separate and specialized support services can be provided.

Several major court cases that were appealed to the U.S. Circuit Courts of Appeals hold significant implications for the placement of students with disabilities in the least restrictive environment (Osborne and DiMattia 1994; Yell 1995). In 1993, the *Oberti v. Board of Education of the Borough of Clementon (N.J.) School District* was brought before the Third Circuit Court of Appeals on behalf of Rafael Oberti, an eight-year-old with Down syndrome, whose parents were seeking an inclusionary setting for their child.

A district court ruled for Oberti, and the U.S. Court of Appeals for the Third Circuit affirmed the district court's decision. The opinion of the Court of Appeals was based on a two-pronged test, originally cited in another Circuit

Court of Appeals case, *Daniel R. R. v. State Board of Education*, in 1989. First, the court had to determine whether a child with a disability could be educated satisfactorily in a regular class with supplemental aids and services. Several factors had to be considered in making that determination, including the efforts, if any, made by the school district to accommodate the child in a regular classroom; the educational benefits available to the child in a regular class as compared to the benefits provided in a special education class; and the possible negative effects on the education of other students in the class resulting from the inclusion of the child.

The second recent Court of Appeals case to influence the application of the least restrictive environment principle was the 1994 *Sacramento City Unified School District v. Rachel H.* The case involved a dispute over the appropriate educational placement of eleven-year-old Rachel Holland, who was described as having significant retardation and an IQ of 44. Her parents requested that Rachel be placed in a full-day regular education class. The school district proposed that she be placed in a separate special education classroom for at least half the school day and receive nonacademic activities with the regular education class.

The district court examined four factors: (1) the educational benefits to Rachel of a regular class, (2) the nonacademic benefits to Rachel of the regular class placement, (3) the potential detrimental effect on others in her regular classroom, and (4) the cost of serving Rachel in a regular classroom with appropriate services. The district court determined that the appropriate placement was full-time in the regular classroom with supplemental aids and services. The Ninth Circuit Court affirmed the district court's decision, including the four-factor test. Legal and special education scholars have used these landmark cases as models for developing some core principles for determining the least restrictive environment.

Accountability for Outcomes of Special Education

Every student receiving special education services is entitled, as required by IDEA, to an appropriate education as defined in the document known as the Individualized Education Program (IEP). The IEP spells out the degree to which a student will participate in regular education programs, the long- and short-term goals for the student, and the objective criteria as well as the evaluation schedule for determining, at least annually, whether the student's goals have been met. The IEP and the process that leads to its development for each student have become the primary tools to carry out the concept of an "appropriate education" for students with disabilities (McDonnell, McLaughlin, and Morison 1997; Smith 1990).

A number of court cases, including one Supreme Court decision, have interpreted the appropriateness of standards. In 1982, *Board of Education of the Hendrick Hudson Central School District v. Rowley* (458 U.S. 176) defined free, appropriate public education and determined that the access to FAPE was met if the education that was provided conferred some educational benefit upon the child. The court further established that appropriateness is defined in accordance with an IEP that is "reasonably calculated to enable" the child to receive educational benefits. The suggestion in the *Rowley* case that FAPE is defined by an intent standard rather than an effect standard may complicate efforts by school personnel to reconcile FAPE compliance with the efforts made to meet content standards for students with disabilities (Gallegos 1989).

In the past, discussions and research regarding IEPs have generally focused on determining local levels of compliance and on the development and carrying out of IEPs, including issues relating to parental participation (e.g., Harry, Allen, and McLaughlin 1995) and to the degree of instructional usefulness of the documents (e.g., Smith 1990). In recent years, however, the focus has shifted to how the IEP can better function to ensure school district accountability for student outcomes (e.g., meeting certain performance standards or attaining a job after graduation) rather than for only school inputs, namely, the provision of particular services (McDonnell, McLaughlin, and Morison 1997).

One issue related to accountability for special education is the effect that state and federal funding mechanisms have on the ability of local school districts to provide a free, appropriate public education to children with disabilities. Since 1989, the constitutionality of school finance systems in twenty-one states has been questioned in state courts. Issues of adequacy and inequalities between poor and wealthy districts have been the basis of these court challenges. Of the eleven high court decisions since 1989 in which finance systems have been invalidated, three have included challenges to both the states' special education and general education finance systems. Specific findings included (1) that state finance systems discriminated against both general and special education students in poor districts by failing to recognize the justifiable additional costs of educating children with special needs and (2) that special and general education funding systems are inextricably intertwined. When special education is inadequately financed, it encroaches on revenues for necessary general education expenses.

EFFECT OF EDUCATION REFORM ON
SPECIAL EDUCATION POLICY

Federally mandated access to a free, appropriate public education was a pivotal turning point in the history of special education. More than two decades of efforts were dedicated to enforcing this access and to increasing educational opportunities in the least restrictive environment. During this time, however, American public education as a whole has been undergoing many transformations, and the U.S. schools have been buffeted by changes.

One of the principal forces behind the move to reform U.S. schools has been a desire to improve student education outcomes and to raise levels of achievement for all students regardless of economics, race, or culture. The shift to a focus on outcomes began almost two decades ago, in part because of press reports of declines in student test scores on traditional assessment measures. For example, the publication *A Nation at Risk: The Imperative for Education* (National Commission on Excellence in Education 1983), along with other reports that were critical of the education system, created a sense that the current U.S. education system was deeply flawed, encouraged mediocrity, and threatened the nation's economic viability (Toch 1991).

Business leaders and politicians became deeply involved in the education reform movement of the 1980s and 1990s because of the concerns about the effects of poor education outcomes on the national and state economies. Groups such as the National Governors' Association, the Business Roundtable, and the Center for Education and the Economy focused on education as it relates to global competitiveness and to the creation of a highly skilled workforce for the twenty-first century (Toch 1991). These national groups wanted to refocus the education system so that it would produce workers who could engage in cooperative problem solving as well as critical thinking and who could adapt to changing job demands. American business was also very concerned about those students who exit high school directly into the labor market, a group representing slightly more than half of all young people.

The legislation known as Goals 2000: Educate America Act (PL 103–227), which was enacted in 1994 under the Clinton administration, represents the national vision for education reform. The legislation enumerates eight national education goals. In addition to clarifying the national goals, Goals 2000 encourages states to adopt two types of voluntary standards:

1. Content standards, defined as "broad descriptions of the knowledge and skills students should acquire in a particular subject area" (PL 103–227, sec 3[4])
2. Performance standards, defined as "concrete examples and explicit definitions of what students have to know and be able to do to demonstrate that such students are proficient in the skills and knowledge framed by the content standards" (PL 103–227, sec 3[9])

The adoption of Goals 2000 provides a general concept of reform. However, state participation in Goals 2000 is voluntary, and its passage has created numerous concerns. As an inducement to states to adopt the national vision of standards-based education reform, the statute offered modest federal grants to states that agreed to develop education improvement plans that adopted both content standards and performance standards. In accordance with the U.S. emphasis on local control of education, however, Goals 2000 leaves each state free to set its own content and performance standards and to choose its own means of assessing progress toward its goals. In addition, federal oversight of state compliance with the statute is minimal. The statute has no implementing regulations, and states are no longer required even to submit their plans to the U.S. Department of Education for review (McDonnell, McLaughlin, and Morison 1997).

From its inception, Goals 2000 was intended to embody an ideal of high-quality, equitable schooling based on voluntary standards. Goals 2000 offered states a small amount of funding to help them implement their own approaches to that vision without imposing significant federal mandates on them. The original legislation encouraged states to address issues of fiscal equity. Fiscal equity between students in different districts and in different states became a critical issue in education reform. Lawsuits challenged the manner in which states distributed education funding. For example, in 1989 the Kentucky Supreme Court invalidated the entire state system of public education in response to a lawsuit challenging the existing funding system (Schofield 1996). Public reports such as Kozol's *Savage Inequalities* (1992) brought wide public attention to the extreme disparities in funding and resources between the nation's highest and lowest spending districts. The need to reduce these disparities has been a recurrent theme in the education reform movement (McDonnell, McLaughlin, and Morison 1997).

The original Goals 2000 legislation encouraged states to adopt opportunity-to-learn (OTL) standards. These were defined as "the criteria for and the basis of assessing the sufficiency or quality of the resources, practices, and conditions necessary at each level of the education system (schools, local agencies, and states) to provide all students with an opportunity to learn the material in the voluntary national content standards or state content standards" (PL 103–227, sec 3[7]). The OTL standards were intended to ensure that disadvantaged students would be provided with the curricular resources to meet the new content and performance standards by which they would be judged. However, because of concerns that the OTL standards could lead to mandated equalization of funding or other intrusions on state and local autonomy, the original OTL standards were specifically stated to be voluntary and nonbinding. Even these watered-down OTL standards were removed, however, when the Goals 2000 legislation was reauthorized in 1996.

The concern for equitable access to a demanding curriculum found expression in two statements in the Goals 2000 legislation. The act stated that "all children can learn and achieve to high standards and must realize their potential if the United States is to prosper" (PL 103–227, sec 301[1]) and that "all students are entitled to participate in a broad and challenging curriculum and to have access to resources sufficient to address other education needs" (PL 103–227, sec 301[15]). The legislation is also clear that "all students" and "all children" include those with disabilities (PL 103–227, sec 3[1]).

Other Federal Legislation

Although direct federal influence is limited under Goals 2000, the Improving America's Schools Act (IASA), which is the reauthorization of the 1994 Elementary and Secondary Education Act, contains major new requirements for obtaining funds under Title I, the largest federal school-aid program that serves poor, underachieving students. The purpose of the new legislation is "to enable schools to provide opportunities for children served to acquire the knowledge and skills contained in challenging state content standards and to meet the challenging state performance standards developed for all children" (PL 103–328, sec 1001[d]).

To receive Title I grants, states are now required to submit state plans that provide for challenging content and performance standards, state assessments, yearly reports on meeting standards, and provisions for teacher support and learning that are aligned with the new curriculum standards and assessments. Assessments and reports must be aligned with the content standards. Tests at three separate grade levels must be based on "multiple, up-to-date measures that assess higher order thinking skills and understanding" and must "provide individual student interpretive and descriptive reports" as well as aggregated results that are broken down to the local school level by race, gender, English proficiency, migrant status, disability, and economic status (PL 103–328, sec 1111).

Because Title I provides much more than $7 billion a year in federal funding and includes a detailed set of mandates that local districts must meet as a condition for funding, it is likely that the federal government's influence over the standards and assessments in individual states will be greater through Title I than through Goals 2000 (McDonnell, McLaughlin, and Morison 1997). As with Goals 2000, Title I acknowledges students with disabilities and specifies that they are to be included in the state standards for teaching and assessment.

The 1997 Amendments to IDEA: Key Provisions

Congress reauthorized IDEA for the seventh time in 1997. The revised law contains a number of new provisions that significantly affect children with disabilities, their families, and the schools that provide special education and related services. Several of these provisions are new and attempt to align the special education legislation with federal education reform policies. Other changes are designed to remove barriers to LRE, promote greater flexibility, or address issues related to discipline. Only some of the more significant changes are described below.

Least Restrictive Environment

Educational placement of children with disabilities is linked to funding, to personnel certification and workload, as well as to education reform initiatives that effect all students. The 1997 IDEA includes language designed to address several aspects of the law that had been considered barriers to providing inclusive educational environments.

The formula used to distribute federal funds to states is based on the number of students identified and served in special education. After the federal appropriation reaches $4.9 billion, a base amount will be distributed through child count. However, amounts above the $4.9 billion mark are to be distributed based on the relative population of children aged three to twenty-one, with an adjustment for the relative number of children who are living in poverty. In addition, the 1997 IDEA removes the "incidental benefit rule" by permitting federal funds to be used for costs of special education and related services that are provided in a regular class to a child with a disability in accordance with a student's IEP, even if that funding benefits one or more children without a disability. Also, for the first time, the revised IDEA allows for a limited coordination of funds between its grants to states and the funds provided under other federal education programs, such as Title I of the Elementary and Secondary Education Act. These three provisions signal the change to using some federal special education funds more flexibly to promote prevention and other school improvement programs, which may diminish the need to formally identify children as disabled to receive supports or accommodations.

To ensure placements that are consistent with the principle of least restrictive environment, state education agencies must revise any funding mechanisms so they are based on the type of setting in which a child is served. All funding mechanisms must, in effect, be placement neutral.

Assessment and Accountability

The revised law addresses, for the first time, the inclusion of children with disabilities in state and local school accountability measures that have been adopted for all students. Students with disabilities are to be included, with necessary accommodations, in general state- and districtwide assessment programs. Some students with significant disabilities may participate in alternate assessments. Guidelines for these assessments are to be developed and students are to be participating in these assessments by July 1, 2001. Rates of participation and performance of students with disabilities on general and alternate assessments must be reported.

States are also required to establish formal goals for the performance of children with disabilities that are consistent with goals and standards for other students. The state educational agency (SEA) is also to establish indicators to assess progress toward goals. At a minimum, these are to include graduation and dropout rates. However, the indicators are expected to include student assessment data as more students move into these systems. Data that are relative to student progress on the performance goals must also be publicly reported.

A state can now grant authority to local districts to select individual schools to design and implement a schoolwide improvement plan for students with disabilities and other students. The plans include full participation of all members of that school community and are grounded in schoolwide goals as well as in indicators and sound assessments of how students with disabilities are meeting those schoolwide goals.

Changes to the Individualized Education Program

Consistent with the efforts to encourage opportunities for children with disabilities to participate in general education settings and in the general curriculum, the IEP has been expanded and now includes the following requirements:

- Records of recent levels of education performance, including how the disability affects the child's involvement and progress in the general curriculum

- A statement of measurable annual goals, including benchmarks or short-term objectives to enable the child to be involved in and to progress in the general curriculum

- A statement of the special education and related supplementary aids and services

- A statement of the program modifications or supports for school personnel that will be provided for the child to advance appropriately toward attaining the annual goals, to be involved and progress in the general curriculum, to participate in extracurricular and other nonacademic activities, and to be educated and participate with other children both with and without disabilities

- An explanation of the extent, if any, to which the child will not participate in the regular class and in activities with children who do not have disabilities

- A statement of any modifications that are needed to state- or districtwide achievement assessments for the child to participate in such assessment

- A statement explaining—if the IEP team determines that the child will not participate in a particular statewide or districtwide assessment—why that assessment is not appropriate for the child and how the child will be assessed

- The projected beginning for the services to be provided; the instructional modifications to be made; and the anticipated frequency, location, and duration of the services and modifications

- A statement explaining needed transition services for the child, beginning at age fourteen, under the applicable components of the child's IEP, that focuses on the child's courses of study (e.g., participation in advanced-placement courses or a vocational education program)

- A statement explaining needed transition services for the child, beginning at age sixteen, including, when appropriate, a statement of the interagency responsibilities or any needed linkages

- A statement, beginning at least one year before the child reaches the age of majority, that the child has been informed of his or her rights, if any, under this title that will transfer to the child on reaching the age of majority

- A statement explaining how the child's progress toward the annual goals will be measured

- A statement explaining how the child's parents will be regularly informed of their child's progress toward the annual goals and the extent to which that progress is sufficient to enable the child to achieve the goals by the end of the year

The required IEP team members have also been expanded, and now include the parents; at least one regular education teacher of the child (if the child is or may be participating in regular education); at least one special education teacher; a knowledgeable representative of the local education authority (LEA); an individual who can interpret the instructional implications of evaluation results; other individuals, at the discretion of the parent or the agency, who have knowledge or special expertise regarding the child, including related services personnel as appropriate; and whenever appropriate, the child himself or herself.

The IEP team shall consider certain factors for specific types of children. In the case of a child whose behavior impedes him- or herself or others, the team must consider positive behavioral interventions, strategies, and supports to address that behavior. In the case of a child with limited English proficiency, the team must consider the language needs. In the case of a child who is blind or visually impaired, it must provide for instruction in braille and the use of braille. In the case of a child who is deaf or hard of hearing, it should consider the child's language and communication needs and opportunities for direct communication. The team must also consider whether the child requires assistive technology devices and services. Although IEPs must be reviewed and monitored annually, the mandatory three-year evaluation of each student is voluntary. Its purpose is to focus on whether additions or modifications to the special education and related services are needed to enable the child to meet the measurable annual IEP goals and to participate in the general curriculum.

Discipline of Students with Disabilities

During the extensive deliberations around the 1997 reauthorization of IDEA, one of the most divisive issues was that of discipline procedures for students with disabilities who violate school rules. The new law includes several additions that are designed to clarify the guarantees and rights of students with disabilities consistent with the need to maintain safe school environments.

A key and much-debated issue is that states must provide free, appropriate public education to all children aged three to twenty-one who have disabilities, including those who have been suspended or expelled from school; however, states now have an option to not provide special education and related services to incarcerated youth from eighteen to twenty-one years old who, prior to their incarceration in an adult correctional facility, were not identified as eligible for special education or did not have IEPs. A state may also require local school districts to include a record of any current or previous disciplinary action in the records of a child with a disability and to transmit that record to the same extent that similar disciplinary information is transmitted with records of students who do not have disabilities.

A number of revisions in the 1997 IDEA pertain to the procedures that are used to change the educational placements of students with disabilities who have violated school rules regarding the use or sale of drugs or the carrying of a weapon. School personnel may order a change in placement to an appropriate interim alternative educational setting (IAES), a change to another kind of setting, or suspension. A suspension cannot be ordered to last for more than ten school days (to the extent such alternatives would be applied to children without disabilities). A change to an appropriate IAES can be ordered only for the same amount of time that a child without a disability would be subject to discipline; however, if the child carries a weapon to school or to a school function or if the child knowingly possesses, uses, sells, or solicits illegal drugs while at school or a school function, then the change in placement can be ordered for not more than forty-five days. During this time, the school district must conduct an initial functional behavioral assessment and must carry out a behavioral intervention plan. If a plan is in place, the plan must be reviewed and modified to address the problem behavior. In a situation in which maintaining the current placement of a given child is substantially likely to result in injury to the child or others, a contingency is made, on the authority of a hearing officer, for placement in an interim alternative educational setting for not more than forty-five days.

Encouraging Parent Participation

Several additions to the law address new mechanisms for encouraging and supporting participation of parents in the identification process, the placement process, and the delivery of special education and related services for their children with disabilities.

School districts must obtain permission from parents prior to initial evaluation. If parents refuse consent for evaluation, the school district may pursue their consent through mediation and due process procedures. Evaluations must include a variety of assessment tools that have been selected and administered in a nondiscriminatory manner and in a child's native language. For the first time, parents are required to be part of the team that makes the determination of eligibility based on evaluation results. Determination of eligibility must not be made based on lack of instruction in math or reading or on limited English proficiency.

Several new procedural safeguards were added, including an opportunity for mediation, a notice to school districts by parents or their attorney of complaint and a proposed resolution of the problem, and a requirement that the state develop a model form to assist parents in filing complaints. The contents of the written notice of proposal or refusal to initiate or change student placement and the contents of the procedural safeguards notice are spelled out.

Mediation

A new section requires states and local districts to establish and carry out voluntary mediation procedures. One of these requirements states that, if parents choose not to use mediation, districts may require them to meet with a disinterested party to discuss the use of mediation. The states are responsible for the cost of mediation, and written mediation agreements are required if mediation is successful.

PREDICTIONS AND CHALLENGES FOR FUTURE U.S. SPECIAL EDUCATION POLICY

The l997 IDEA amendments, though relatively modest, signal the beginning of a number of changes to federal special education policy that will emphasize a new emphasis on accountability for student performance as well as new paradigms for school organization and governance. It is important to note, however, that federal-level changes do not represent individual state policies that have far exceeded the federal law in some areas. Nonetheless, the pressures for additional change that will drive further federal-level policy changes are similar to those faced by states and local school districts. Many of these pressures for additional change will also be driven by the need to address issues of adequacy and efficiency in the allocation of finite education resources. We believe that, based on these factors, U.S. special education policy and practice will be marked by three key characteristics: increased flexibility and collaboration, increased "high-stakes" accountability, and continued litigation.

Increased Flexibility and Collaboration

The strengthened mandate for LRE, coming from the judiciary and from the slightly greater acknowledgment within federal policy, will certainly increase the need for more collaboration between special and general education teachers. However, more significant are the provisions that call for the inclusion of students with disabilities in general education curriculum and assessments. As school systems increasingly become accountable for each student, schools and individual teachers must focus on ensuring that all students are making progress in the curriculum. A student with a disability is no longer only special education's responsibility: that student is the system's responsibility. Indeed, some research (McLaughlin, Henderson, and Rhim 1997) has already indicated that, in selected districts with experience carrying out new curricular standards and assessments and enhanced accountability, schools and teachers are seeking new ways to work together to provide the array of supports and services that many students need to progress in the curriculum.

As collaboration shifts from a focus on the setting to a focus on progress or achievement, the accountability for results may run up against the desire to promote heterogeneous classrooms. Some students will need more intensive and specialized instruction to help them progress, and this fact may require that schools offer a variety of settings and alternatives for extended practice for an array of students. Some special education teachers have expressed concern that this required variety may result in less "inclusive" classrooms. An alternative option is that the concept of the classroom will also change, and schools will be organized in more flexible and fluid instructional groupings that are more inclusive and responsive to diverse learners.

These efforts to help all students achieve are aided by governance changes that seek greater flexibility in how resources are used and how instruction is organized at the school level. School improvement plans and provisions to participate in schoolwide Title I programs that attempt to more flexibly use funds from multiple funding streams are evident in both state and federal policy.

Within special education, census-based funding and the removal of the incidental benefit rule are important ways to ensure that schools can provide an array of services and avoid the costly and often meaningless activity of trying to determine who is eligible for a service. These efforts are particularly critical given the overlap in characteristics between many students with disabilities and other high-risk or academically underachieving students. To date, at least one state, Vermont, which has experience with such funding flexibility, has demonstrated that the approach does not result in lowered achievement for any student with a disability (Parrish 1997). Yet there are a number of concerns about overall loss of funds and loss of program identity in such blended approaches (McLaughlin and Verstegen 1998; Verstegen 1996).

Increased Accountability

Within this same vein, as accountability becomes more "high stakes" (i.e., more consequences, such as school reconstitution or linking assessment results to high school diplomas), many wonder if some students, particularly low-achieving students and students with disabilities, will be harmed. Although these high-stakes accountability concerns have not been a particular problem within states that have minimum competency high school tests, it is a potential issue as the assessments and curricula linked to such competency tests are increasingly academic and require higher levels of knowledge and skills (McDonnell, McLaughlin, and Morison 1997).

The larger reforms are driven by the challenge of improving the performance of all students within the same challenging curriculum. Only through experience with assessments and through increased opportunities for students with disabilities to access the general education curriculum will we be able to ground our expectations. For this reason, a recent committee of the National Academy of Sciences (McDonnell, McLaughlin, and Morison 1997) recommended that students with disabilities be part of a universal accountability system based on performance of all students. However, the committee recommended that the data be carefully monitored until there is more data on the actual performances of these and other low-achieving students.

Continued Litigation

Undoubtedly, many of the critical factors that will drive changes in special education policy are still to be defined through the judicial process. An overreliance on the courts for the resolution of special education due process issues may be stemmed somewhat by the increasing use of mediation. By 1994, thirty-nine states had adopted some type of special education mediation system (Ahearn 1994). The 1997 IDEA amendments require states to provide mediation as an alternative procedure to resolve disputes. Mediation approaches that incorporate principles of good-faith conflict resolution strategies—including confidentiality, flexible structure, and mutual problem solving—have been effective at reducing the emotional, financial, and administrative costs of due process hearings and subsequent court proceedings (Schrag 1996). Nevertheless, litigation will continue to play a major role in shaping national special education policy.

Among the concepts that are likely to be influenced and further refined by litigation is the "appropriateness" standard. Although the concept of individually referenced decision making through the IEP process will likely remain a cornerstone of a student's right to an appropriate education, the standards for determining what is appropriate will become more consistent. As states develop standards, the legality of determinations about appropriateness must be considered.

Despite some disagreement among legal observers, the *Rowley* Supreme Court decision may provide clear guidance for defining an appropriate education for students with disabilities under standards-based reform (McDonnell, McLaughlin, and Morison 1997). Under the *Rowley* standards, a free and appropriate public education should be defined by state standards and should be designed to provide educational benefit. The new educational environment that is defined by content and performance standards and high-stakes assessments may provide fertile legal ground for those advocating on behalf of special education students who are not making progress toward the standards.

Contributing to these definitions of appropriateness are the recent fiscal equity cases in general education that are attempting to establish an adequacy standard to equity, meaning that districts are entitled to enough resources to ensure that all students or some proportion of them are meeting state performance standards. Although far from definitive, these cases are pointing to new concepts of what will be considered an appropriate education for a student with disability.

Discipline is one final area that will likely continue to be heavily influenced by decisions made in the courts rather than in the classroom. Effects of the *Honig* Supreme Court decision have long scared school administrators who see the mandates to serve all students with disabilities and to maintain procedural safeguards, even in situations involving school discipline, as infringing on their ability to maintain safe school environments. Although the 1997 IDEA amendments do address some of these concerns, putting them into effect will present further challenges for school personnel who struggle to establish new procedures for conducting functional behavioral assessments and developing behavioral intervention plans. Identification and development of appropriate interim alternative educational settings for students with disabilities who need to be removed from their current settings will be an additional challenge.

With these frustrations, however, come new opportunities for change. These changes regarding student discipline are rooted in research about effective prevention and behavioral intervention. New requirements may encourage schools and districts to adopt empirically proven, proactive, schoolwide behavior management systems that are designed to promote safe, healthy school environments for all students. Indeed, special education policy may be the unlikely impetus for far-reaching reform toward sound student discipline and comprehensive management of safe schools.

REFERENCES

Ahearn, E. 1994. *Mediation and due process procedures in special education: An analysis of state policies.* Alexandria, Va.: National Association of State Directors of Special Education.

Gajar, A. 1979. Educable mentally retarded, learning disabled, and emotionally disturbed: Similarities and differences. *Exceptional Children* 45:470–72.

Gallegos, E. M. 1989. Beyond *Board of Education v. Rowley*: Educational benefit for the handicapped? *American Journal of Education* 97 (May):258–85.

Gartner, A., and D. K. Lipsky. 1987. Beyond special education: Toward a quality system for all students. *Harvard Educational Review* 57:367–95.

Goals 2000: Educate America Act of 1994. PL 103–227, 103d Congress.

Gostin, L. O., and H. A. Beyer, eds. 1993. *Implementing the Americans with Disabilities Act: Rights and responsibilities of all Americans.* Baltimore: Paul H. Brookes.

Hallahan, D. P., and J. M. Kauffman. 1977. Labels, categories, and behaviors: ED, LED, and EMR reconsidered. *Journal of Special Education* 11:139–49.

Harry, B., N. Allen, and M. J. McLaughlin. 1995. Communication versus compliance: African American parents' involvement in special education. *Exceptional Children* 61:364–77.

Keogh, B. K., and D. L. MacMillen. 1996. Exceptionality. In *Handbook of educational psychology,* ed. D. Berliner and R. Calfee. Washington, D.C.: American Psychological Association.

Kozol, J. 1992. *Savage inequalities.* New York: Crown.

Lyon, G. R. 1996. Learning disabilities. *The Future of Children: Special Education for Students with Disabilities* 6:54–76.

MacMillan, D. L., and J. G. Hendrick. 1993. Evolution and legacies. In *Integrating general and special education,* ed. J. I. Goodlad and T. C. Lovitt. Columbus, Ohio: Merrill.

McDonnell, L. M., M. J. McLaughlin, and P. Morison, eds. 1997. *Educating one and all: Students with disabilities and standards-based reform.* Washington, D.C.: National Research Council, National Academy Press.

McLaughlin, M. J., K. Henderson, and L. M. Rhim. 1997. Reform for all? General and special education reforms in five local school districts. Paper presented at the American Educational Research Association annual meeting, March 24–28, Chicago, Illinois.

McLaughlin, M. J., and D. A. Verstegen. 1998. Increasing regulatory flexibility of special education programs: Problems and promising strategies. *Exceptional Children* 64:371–84.

Merrill, K. W. 1990. Differentiating low achieving students and students with learning disabilities: An examination of performances on the Woodcock-Johnson Psycho-Educational Battery. *Journal of Special Education* 24:296–305.

National Commission on Excellence in Education. 1983. *A nation at risk: The imperative for educational reform.* Washington, D.C.: National Commission on Excellence in Education.

Osborne, A. G., and P. DiMattia. 1994. The IDEA's least restrictive environment mandate: Legal implications. *Exceptional Children* 61:6–14.

Parrish, T. 1997. *Special education in an era of school reform: Special education finance.* Washington, D.C.: Federal Resource Center, Academy for Educational Development.

Reschly, D. J. 1988. Minority MMR overrepresentation and special education reform. *Exceptional Children* 54 (4):316–23.

Schofield, P. 1996. *School-based decision making: Perceived effects on students in special education.* Ph.D. diss., University of Maryland, College Park.

Schrag, J. A. 1996. *Mediation and other alternative dispute resolution procedures in special education.* Alexandria, Va.: National Association of State Directors of Special Education.

Shinn, M. R., G. A. Tindall, and S. Stein. 1988. Curriculum-based measurement and the identification of mildly handicapped students: A research review. *Professional School Psychology* 3:69–85.

Smith, S. W. 1990. Individualized Education Programs (IEPs) in special education: From intent to acquiescence. *Exceptional Children* 57:6–14.

Stainback, S., and W. Stainback. 1984. A rationale for the merger of special and regular education. *Exceptional Children* 51:102–11.

Toch, T. 1991. *In the name of excellence: The struggle to reform the nation's schools, why it's failing, and what should be done.* New York: Oxford University Press.

U.S. Department of Education. 1997. *To assure the free appropriate public education of all children with disabilities: Nineteenth annual report to Congress on the implementation of the Individuals with Disabilities Education Act.* Washington, D.C.: Office of Special Education Programs.

Verstegen, D. A. 1996. Integrating services and resources for children under the Individuals with Disabilities Education Act: Federal perspectives and issues. *Journal of Educational Finance* 21:477–505.

Wang, M. C., M. C. Reynolds, and H. J. Walberg. 1986. Rethinking special education. *Educational Leadership* 44:26–31.

Yell, M. L. 1995. Least restrictive environment, inclusion, and students with disabilities: A legal analysis. *Journal of Special Education* 28:389–404.

PART 2

Supporting Educational Reform

Introduction

The ongoing education reform movement has brought numerous education issues into sharp focus. As we have seen, few issues have received the attention and generated the controversy and polarization of perspectives as has the movement to include all children with disabilities in general classrooms. This section examines a range of supports that are necessary if inclusion is to be successful.

Ongoing assessment of student learning is an essential aspect of effective teaching. School-based assessment involves collecting and synthesizing information about a problem. It is "an ongoing process which involves a wide array of materials, techniques, and tests across a variety of time periods and situations" (Witt, Elliott, Kramer, and Gresham 1994, 5). The primary purpose of classroom assessment is to inform teachers and to improve learning, not to sort and select students or to justify a grade.

In the opening chapter of this section, John Slate and Craig Jones address the controversial issue of assessment. They outline the parameters of current assessment practices in special education, indicate how assessment complies with statutory mandates, and then review documented criticisms of the current system, which include the technical inadequacy of many instruments, the lack of a link between assessment and pupil performance, and the categorical diagnoses. The authors then outline more appropriate and adequate procedures, such as curriculum-based measurement.

It is probably trite to observe that technology is changing not only the world in which we all live and work but also classroom experiences for normally developing students and for those with special needs. However, the reality is that students today use word processors to prepare written assignments, and teachers maintain databases of their students' achievements.

As with many innovations in both general and special education, battles are raging—in this case, as to whether technology actually improves teaching and learning. Some critics, for example, contend that "There is no good evidence that most uses of computers significantly improve teaching and learning" (Oppenheimer 1997). Nevertheless, technology has been a boon to individuals with disabilities in many ways that extend beyond computers and the Internet, such as the enormous range of adaptive equipment and augmentative communication devices.

Maddux's informative and comprehensive paper examines the technological revolution within special education. He examines the early but overly optimistic claims of education computing advocates and the problems that occurred at the outset. Maddux then takes the reader on a journey that touches on the potential of information technology in special education and an examination of various applications. He looks at trends in technology, their long-term effect, and a variety of tools and applications. Finally, he makes predictions about the future of technology in special education.

In the past decade, both general and special education have responded in various ways to the clarion calls to restructure, reform, and reinvent. New paradigms and innovative practices have not passed teacher education by; indeed, the discourse on school reform very often includes references to reform in teacher education. New conceptual orientations and theories are giving fresh direction to teacher preparation as reformers seek to establish more coherent and effective programs. In the context of inclusive classrooms, many bold critics of teacher education reform have proposed both macro- and microeducation reforms (see Winzer, Altieri, and Larson, in press).

One area of teacher education restructuring revolves around the entire question of increasing cultural, ethnic, and linguistic diversity in North American society. At the moment, ethnic minorities constitute approximately one-third of the U.S. population and, with increased birth rates and immigration trends, minority group numbers are increasing at a faster rate than those of the Anglo majority (see Delgado and Rogers-Adkinson 1999).

As demographic trends shift, education practices will shape the futures of communities. Schools must accommodate all learners by developing programs and environments that enhance academic and social skills and that promote equity of education opportunities. Such needs have spawned an increasing interest in the topic of multicultural special education.

Addressing diversity within the context of special education, the field has examined many aspects of the school population to be served (see chapter 12 of this text). But although scrutiny of the education outcomes of minority students has been prominent for several years, disturbing statistics remain on children's achievement, and we have made little progress in disentangling cultural and linguistic differences from other attributes. At the same time, the area of special education has articulated competencies for teachers. The field is recognizing that model programs in teacher education should assist both in-service and preservice teachers to better identify the needs of culturally and linguistically diverse students (Obiakor and Utley 1997).

In the third chapter of this section, Sileo and Prater provide links between theory and practice as they discuss how to repair and elaborate teacher training. They are specific and cogent in their details of the needs for teachers from diverse cultural and linguistic backgrounds in the field of special education, and they are equally as specific in their suggestions for improvements in preparing teacher candidates.

REFERENCES

Delgado, B. M., and D. Rogers-Adkinson. 1999. Educating the Hispanic-American exceptional learner. In *Advances in special education: Multicultural education for learners with exceptionalities,* ed. F. E Obiokor, J. O. Schwenn, and A. F. Rotatori. Stanford, Conn.: JAI Press.

Obiakor, F. E., and C. A. Utley. 1997. Rethinking preservice preparation for teachers—the learning disabilities field: Workable multicultural strategies. *Learning Disabilities and Practice* 12:100–106.

Oppenheimer, T. 1997. The computer delusion. *Atlantic Monthly* July:45–48, 50–56, 61–66.

Winzer, M., E. Altieri, and V. Larson. In press. Portfolios as a tool for attitude change. *Rural and Special Education*.

Witt, J. C., S. N. Elliott, J. J. Kramer, and F. Gresham. 1994. *Assessment of children: Fundamental methods and practices.* Madison, Wis.: Brown and Benchmark.

4

Assessment Issues in Special Education

John R. Slate *Craig H. Jones*

T he purpose of special education, in its simplest terms, is to meet the educational needs of students whose disabilities interfere with learning under typical instructional arrangements (Deno 1989). Given this purpose, any assessment system in special education is defensible only when the measurement practices involved can demonstrate treatment utility (Hayes, Nelson, and Jarrett 1987). That is, assessment can be justified only to the extent that its results are directly applied to the planning of effective modifications in the instruction that students receive. Indeed, assessment results "are quite useless and potentially harmful if the context of their use does not emphasize interventions" (Reschly and Wilson 1990, 444).

DEFINITION AND CURRENT PARAMETERS OF ASSESSMENT IN SPECIAL EDUCATION

Special education assessment is currently based on an approach that mixes standard psychometric practices with a diagnostic classification system rooted in the medical model (Kratochwill and McGivern, 1996). The use of standard psychometric practices to deal with instructional problems dates to 1905 when the first version of the Binet intelligence test was used to determine which children in the

Paris school system were sent to special schools (Hilgard 1987). The use of norm-referenced tests ultimately became mixed with a diagnostic classification system, reflective of the medical model, which places students in categories on the basis of overt symptoms. The merging of psychometrics with the medical model as we now know it in special education became legally entrenched in 1975 with passage of PL 94–142, the Education for All Handicapped Children Act (U.S. Department of Health, Education, and Welfare 1977). The resulting classification scheme was reinforced and extended in 1990 when PL 94–142 was reauthorized as the Individuals with Disabilities Education Act, or IDEA (PL 101–476).

A basic assumption behind the diagnostic categories in IDEA is that they increase treatment utility. That is, the standard practice of placing special education students into diagnostic categories reflects the intuitively appealing assumption that, if students can be sorted into disability categories and teachers can be trained to work with specific disability groupings, then special education students will receive appropriate instruction. More than two decades of experience, however, have clearly demonstrated that this approach does not work (Reschly and Ysseldyke 1995). Although misdiagnosis of students certainly contributes to the failure of current assessment practices (e.g., Algozzine and Korinek 1985), misdiagnosis alone is not the problem. Rather, empirical evidence clearly and convincingly demonstrates that the assumption underlying the diagnosis–treatment approach to instruction is simply wrong. Furthermore, the use of syndrome-based, categorical approaches to deal with behavior problems has also failed to demonstrate treatment utility (Kratochwill and McGivern 1996). As Haywood, Brown, and Wingenfeld noted nearly a decade ago, "The hope that proper classification leads to proper treatment has not been realized" (1990, 413).

The argument presented in this chapter is that assessment as currently practiced in special education is indefensible because it lacks treatment utility. Although technical problems with assessment instruments certainly play a role in the problems that currently plague special education, we contend that today's assessment system is fundamentally flawed and cannot be saved, even with drastic modifications. That is, the difficulties arise primarily from the use of an inappropriate conceptual framework. Current assessment simply provides the wrong information about students (Haywood, Brown, and Wingenfeld 1990). The wrong information is useless no matter how technically adequate it is. Therefore, making the current practices more technically adequate cannot resolve existing assessment problems. As a result, we recommend that current assessment practices in special education be discontinued and replaced with practices that have direct relevance to instructional planning.

ARGUMENTS AGAINST CURRENT PRACTICES

Current practices in special education assessment do not have treatment utility (Kratochwill and McGivern 1996; Reschly and Ysseldyke 1995). The fundamental issue thus becomes whether or not treatment utility can be established through refinements of these practices. A number of lines of research and argument indicate that current practices cannot be satisfactorily linked to treatment utility.

Diagnosis–Treatment Linkage

Although the diagnosis–treatment approach is based on the assumption that students who are placed in different categories need and will receive different instruction, research clearly shows that special education diagnosis is not currently linked to the type of instruction that students receive (Edgar and Hayden 1984/1985; Reynolds and Lakin 1987; Reynolds, Wang, and Walberg 1987). In other words, special education students typically receive the same instruction regardless of their specific disability category. Howell argued that assessment and intervention are not linked because current assessment practices "are indirect, nomothetic, narrowly applied, and environmentally insensitive" (1986, 325). As a result, special education assessment is linked to a search for pathology rather than to the identification of appropriate interventions (Sarason and Doris 1979). Under these circumstances, assessment can serve only the administrative purpose of categorical identification (Batsche and Knoff 1995) and cannot result in increased student competence (Ysseldyke and Christenson 1988).

More important, however, is the fact that research does not support the need for any such linkage to be made. That is, there is no evidence to support the contention that students with one disability should be taught differently from students with another disability (Reynolds 1979). Across specific disability categories, special education students are generally most in need of remediation in reading, math, and written expression (Reynolds and Lakin 1987). Furthermore, similar instructional practices are effective in promoting student learning regardless of diagnostic category (Heller, Holtzman, and Messick 1982; Marston 1987). Indeed, special education students typically respond to the same instructional strategies that are successful with students who do not have disabilities, although these strategies may need to be applied more slowly and more systematically when used with special education students (Larrivee 1985; Scruggs and Mastropieri 1992). If individual adjustments are needed in these generally effective instructional strategies, adjustments cannot be made on the basis of diagnostic labels because individuals within diagnostic groups differ as much from each other as do students without disabilities (Snow 1984).

Another reason why diagnosis cannot be linked to treatment is that treatment utility requires a form of assessment that can be used to monitor student progress on a regular basis. Only with regular monitoring of progress can appropriate instructional modifications be introduced as needed. Current assessment practices in special education are designed to place students into rigid categories, and they lack the sensitivity to detect the small changes in students' behavior that so often guide instructional modifications (Marston 1989). In other words, with current assessment procedures, students "are not evaluated using individualized, treatment sensitive measures" (Reschly and Ysseldyke 1995, 21). Furthermore, most standardized tests cannot be administered frequently enough to make ongoing decisions about the instructional process.

Technical Adequacy

Many of the standard criticisms of special education assessment focus on the psychometric properties of the tests, surveys, behavioral checklists, and interviews that are typically used. Although the technical adequacy of these instruments varies widely, problems exist with even the best instruments. For example, intelligence tests such as the Wechsler Intelligence Scale for Children, both the revised (WISC-R) and third editions (WISC-III) are generally considered to have very strong psychometric properties (Wechsler 1991).[1] But as Sedlacek (1994) points out, minority populations are typically underrepresented in the normative samples for these tests. More than 90 percent of the normative sample for the WISC-III was composed of Whites and more than 90 percent of the group of Whites were without disabilities. These sampling biases are particularly relevant to special education assessment because special education serves students with disabilities and because minorities are overrepresented in special education.

Although biased sampling is often viewed as a purely technical problem, such thinking represents what Sedlacek (1994) calls the "Three Musketeers Problem" in assessment. This problem is an "all for one and one for all" attitude that an ideal standardized test can be developed for use with all people. Research, however, indicates that the same test can actually measure different things in different subpopulations. For example, Wechsler IQ scores have been found to reveal differences based on gender for students with Attention Deficit Hyperactivity Disorder (Slate, Little, Prince, and Blaske 1995) and for students with hearing impairments (Slate and Fawcett 1996). When scoring fails to account for such differences, as is the case with the WISC-III, scores are confounded with subgroup membership, and this confusion has an adverse effect on assessment results (Phelps and Ensor 1987). Similar confounding involving ethnicity has been reported. For example, Reynolds and Jensen (1983) and Taylor and Richards (1991) reported that the factor structure of WISC-R for African Americans differed from the factor structure reported for the predominantly White normative sample. More recently, Slate and Jones (1995) reported a similar difference in factor structure for African Americans on the WISC-III.

---

1. Although intelligence tests generally have well-established psychometric properties, the psychometric properties of achievement tests are highly variable. Indeed, the reliability and validity data that are provided for many achievement tests do not meet established guidelines (American Psychological Association 1985). The poor quality of many achievement tests raises important issues for special education assessment that we do not address because they are tangential to our thesis.

A second technical problem involves the comparability of test scores. This problem has two facets: comparability from one version of a test to the next and comparability of scores from different tests purporting to measure the same construct. With regard to comparability of test scores from one version of a test to another, Bracken (1988) has described how test scores tend to decline from one version of a test to the next, in part because of norming artifacts. For example, several recent studies have shown that children's scores on the WISC-III are significantly lower than the scores the same children would receive if tested with the WISC-R (Newby, Recht, Caldwell, and Schaefer 1993; Slate 1995; Slate, Jones, and Saarnio 1997; Wechsler 1991). Slate and colleagues (1997) argued that WISC-III scores were discrepant enough from WISC-R scores that many students who were originally diagnosed as having a learning disability based on WISC-R scores would be reclassified as slow learners if the WISC-III were used at the time of reevaluation. That is, the lower WISC-III score would bring the IQ-achievement discrepancy to below the cutoff needed for the learning disability diagnosis. Thus, these students would lose eligibility for special services on reevaluation, even though their actual functioning was unchanged. Just because the WISC-III is newer is not a reason to automatically assume that WISC-III scores are more accurate than WISC-R scores (Slate, Jones and Saarnio 1997).

The other facet of this problem is that two tests, purportedly measuring the same construct, often measure different constructs. Bracken (1988) provides a review of the reasons why this phenomenon can occur. His arguments are supported by data from a number of studies (e.g., Caskey 1985; Caskey, Hylton, Robinson, Taylor, and Washburn 1983; Slate and Saarnio 1996; Webster and Braswell 1991) in which statistically significant and conceptually important differences were found between people's scores on frequently used achievement tests, even though the scales involved supposedly measured the same construct. As a result, the outcome of assessment can be an artifact of test selection rather than an indicator of a student's functioning.

Categorical Diagnosis

As noted above, special education assessment is currently a search for pathology to justify placing students in diagnostic categories (Sarason and Doris 1979). Much of this search is conducted with standardized intelligence tests and standardized achievement tests. Because a large percentage of students who qualify for special education receive a diagnosis of either mental retardation or learning disability, intelligence tests have become the centerpiece of special education assessment, with the Wechsler Intelligence Scale for Children being the test most frequently administered to children and adolescents (Reschly and Wilson 1990). Achievement tests, though second in overall importance to intelligence tests, are still quite important to special education diagnosis because of the IQ-achievement discrepancy approach to diagnosing learning disabilities.

Unfortunately, the constructs of intelligence and achievement as assessed by standardized tests have little relevance to instruction and, therefore, have low treatment utility (Reschly and Wilson 1990). Indeed, Hilliard noted that "in no studies of successful teachers and successful schools is there ever any mention of reliance on IQ measures. In other words, IQ is irrelevant to successful instruction" (cited in Kamphaus 1993, 467). Although standardized achievement tests might seem to have more relevance to instruction, they are also fatally flawed (Marston 1989). These tests measure achievement as a generalized construct rather than assess students' progress in the curriculum being used to instruct them. They are also insensitive to small changes in students' achievements, and they cannot be given frequently enough to inform instructional decision making.

Finally, the use of a diagnostic classification system assumes that students can be placed into discontinuous categories of having or not having a disability. This assumption has been called scientifically questionable at best (e.g., Reynolds, Wang, and Walberg 1987), and scandalous at worst (e.g., Scriven 1983). Edgar and Hayden (1984/1985) noted that the current diagnostic system was not designed to identify students who need services but, rather, to withhold special services from all but a discrete, limited group of students. In short, special education assessment currently serves the political purpose to restrict the flow of tax dollars to a limited number of students rather than serves the educational purpose to identify needed changes in instruction.

The distortions created by politically motivated diagnoses are best illustrated by the category of learning disability. First, as defined in PL 94–142, a learning disability supposedly represents a disorder of basic psychological processes such as memory, perception, and language. The diagnosis of a learning disability, however, does not involve assessment of any of these processes. Instead, diagnosis is based on an IQ-achievement discrepancy.

Second, students with learning disabilities are an extremely heterogeneous group. The nature of a learning problem for any student in this group represents that student's individual characteristics more than the characteristics of any group of learners (Reynolds 1984/1985). In addition, depending on a student's age, these individual learner characteristics may manifest themselves differently. Thus, the only thing that students with learning disabilities share in common is low achievement (Edgar and Hayden 1984/1985). If low achievement alone were used as the criterion for diagnosing learning disabilities, however, 20 to 30 percent of school children would qualify for this diagnosis. Including IQ in the diagnostic criteria reduces the number of children who qualify and, consequently, places the many low-achieving students in the slow-learner category.[2]

Although slow learners do not qualify for legally mandated special services, research indicates that their instructional needs are no different from those of students who receive the learning disability diagnosis (Edgar and Hayden

2. The regression equations that are used to diagnosis learning disabilities on the basis of IQ and achievement scores create assessment problems that are beyond the scope of this chapter. See Slate, Hall, and Jones (1993) for a discussion of some of the more serious problems.

1984/1985). One of the ironies of the use of IQ as an exclusionary criterion is that, given two students with the same level of achievement, the student who is excluded from special services is the student with the lower IQ. As Reynolds (1984/1985) noted, PL 94–142 specifically intended to exclude slow learners on the assumption that teachers would receive special assistance to meet these children's needs even though these children did not qualify for special services. To us, this thinking appears to be Red Queen logic from Alice in Wonderland.

Of course, the ultimate criticism of the use of diagnostic categories is that it involves applying pejorative labels to students. Heward and Orlansky (1984) summarized the potential dangers of labeling, which include focusing attention on students' weaknesses rather than their strengths, causing self-fulfilling prophecies of low achievement, lowering students' self-esteem, causing peer rejection, and providing a rationale for removing students from regular classrooms. In addition, Heward and Orlansky noted that students from minority backgrounds are more likely to be labeled than are other students and that, once these labels are applied, they are difficult to remove. Given that categorical diagnosis has failed to demonstrate treatment utility, the potential damage of labeling cannot be justified.

PREDICTIONS FOR THE FUTURE

Reschly (1988) argued that assessments made for diagnosis alone will be replaced by assessments made to focus on treatment utility.[3] One can easily be pessimistic about the likelihood that Reschly's prediction will come true. School psychologists, for example, still spend roughly two-thirds of their time administering standardized tests for the sole purpose of classification (Reschly and Ysseldyke 1995). The current system may be too deeply entrenched to be dislodged. If one is optimistic, however, and believes that Reschly's prediction will come true, then what assessment practices will look like in the future is unclear. In the decade since the concept of treatment utility was introduced, little research has been conducted to determine the assessment practices that best contribute to this goal (Kratochwill and McGivern 1996). A few current practices do exist, however, that can serve as a basis for speculation.

Curriculum-based Measurement

Curriculum-based measurement (CBM) is "a procedure that directly assesses student performance within the course content for the purpose of determining that student's instructional needs" (Tucker 1985, 200). A sample is taken from the curriculum that is used to teach students, and students are given a fixed amount

---

3. Our emphasis on treatment utility differs from standard calls for noncategorical assessment. Rather than link assessment to intervention, typical noncategorical approaches simply create a large superordinate category for all students with mild disabilities.

of time in which to complete as much of the sample as possible. Scores reflect response rates such as number of words read correctly per minute or the number of arithmetic problems solved correctly per minute. Researchers have supported the reliability and validity of CBM measures (Marston 1989). In fact, Marston argued that CBM measures of arithmetic are less influenced by reading ability and other extraneous variables than are scores on traditional standardized tests. Recently, Baker and Good (1995) showed that CBM reading measures, unlike traditional norm-referenced measures, are as reliable and valid for bilingual Hispanic students as for students who speak only English.

With regard to treatment utility, CBM has a number of advantages over traditional assessment:

- CBM measures are closely tied to instruction because they employ material that is actually being used to instruct students.
- CBM measures require little time to administer and can be used frequently so that teachers can monitor students' progress on a regular basis without interfering with instruction.
- CBM measures are sensitive to small changes in students' performance, which allows teachers to adjust instruction quickly when students are not learning.
- Cultural biases do not affect CBM scores.
- The analysis of students' mistakes on CBM measures provides a direct indicator of student weaknesses.
- CBM measures assess response fluency, which is a better measure of achievement than is accuracy alone.
- The need for special instruction can be identified without labeling students with diagnostic categories (Shinn 1989).

CBM has been the subject of much debate, but most of the criticism has been based on myths (Schendel 1993). One of these myths is that CBM is a comprehensive assessment system. At present, it clearly is not, and its practitioners do not contend that it is. CBM has been highly successful at assessing student achievement in reading, spelling, writing, and mathematics, especially in the elementary grades (Shinn 1989). Its success in these areas shows clear promise for approaches that focus on treatment utility. CBM has yet, however, to demonstrate its effectiveness at higher grade levels, especially in relation to content area subjects such as history. Unless and until CBM can cross these barriers, other assessment approaches will be needed.

Precision Teaching

Precision teaching involves adjusting instruction for individual students based on regular, objective assessment of their academic performance (Lindsley 1991). The assessment system that is used to adjust instruction reflects an application of the response rate measures that are used in operant conditioning experiments about decision making. Each student's performance is assessed on a daily basis in terms of the number of responses per minute. Both the number of correct and the number of incorrect responses per minute are charted on a standardized graph called a "celeration chart." *Celeration* is a general term reflecting the fact that performance can show both accelerations (increasing response rates) and decelerations (decreasing response rates). A log scale is used so that equal changes in angle reflect a doubling of response rate. A goal line can be drawn on the celeration chart between the students' response rate at the beginning of instruction and the response rate that is desired by the last day of instruction. The decision whether or not instructional modifications are needed can be made by comparing a student's level of performance to his or her goal line. If student performance falls below the goal line for more than two days, modifications in instruction should be made (Binder 1996).

Because assessment in precision teaching is based on response rates, it shares all the advantages of CBM. Precision teaching, however, has a number of additional advantages:

1. Precision teaching establishes absolute standards for student performance by using the response rates of fully competent individuals to establish goals (Binder 1996). (CBM, however, often relies on local norms for making education decisions. Thus, low-functioning students in some schools may not receive special services because overall performance in the school is low.)

2. Precision teaching can directly assess progress toward fulfillment of the Individualized Education Program (IEP) when response rate goals are included in a student's IEP.

3. Response rates can be directly linked to instructional planning. For example, a student is not properly prepared to learn computational arithmetic unless he or she can read at least 100 random digits per minute (Haughton 1972; Starlin 1972). If a student fails to meet this criterion, a teacher knows that the student needs additional practice recognizing numbers before arithmetic instruction is begun.

4. Precision teaching has been used to assess student performance in a broader range of subjects than has CBM and has been used at all grade levels as well as in higher education (Pennypacker, Heckler, and Pennypacker 1977), including at least one graduate course in education (Lindsley 1996).

Precision teaching faces two major obstacles. First, the database for precision teaching in the professional literature is relatively scant for a system that has been in use for more than three decades, and much of what has been published has appeared only in the *Journal of Precision Teaching* (Binder 1996; Potts, Eshleman, and Cooper 1993). Clearly, the database must have more extensive publication so that it can be subjected to critical evaluation by other researchers.

Second, the assessment approach that is used in precision teaching grew out of the experimental analysis of behavior, an orientation poorly understood and often rejected by educators (Jones and Slate 1996).

Functional Analysis

Functional analysis, as the name implies, represents an assessment approach that is used to identify how a specific behavior functions to obtain reinforcement or avoid punishment. A complete functional analysis would describe the behavior of interest in observable terms, the situations under which behavior is likely or unlikely to occur, and the consequences that maintain or inhibit the behavior (O'Neill, Horner, Albin, Storey, and Sprague 1990).

Functional analysis involves a wide variety of procedures ranging from structured interviews to observation of naturally occurring behavior to experimental modification of a student's environment. Because space limitations prevent detailed description of functional assessment procedures here, readers are referred to a recent miniseries in the *Journal of Applied Behavior Analysis* (Neef and Iwata 1994). Although many of the methods used in functional analysis have long been used in conjunction with behavior modification, Iwata and colleagues (1982) reenergized interest in functional analysis by returning it to its operant roots. They systematically regulated environmental variables in a single-subject design to identify the causes of self-injurious behavior in nine individuals with developmental disabilities.

The overwhelming advantage of functional analysis over other approaches is that it has demonstrated treatment utility (Kratochwill and McGivern 1996). In fact, the National Institutes of Health (NIH) recommended that functional analysis precede treatment of destructive behavior by persons with developmental disabilities (NIH 1989). Functional analysis has proved to be superior to conventional behavior modification because functional analysis directly addresses the causes of problematic behavior instead of imposing artificial rewards or punishment (Mace 1994). Although much of the recent research on functional analysis has addressed problematic behavior by individuals with developmental disabilities, functional analysis has also been used to increase academic achievement (e.g., Cooper et al. 1992; McComas, Wacker, and Cooper 1996).

The disadvantages of functional assessment are related to the specific procedures that are employed (Kratochwill and McGivern 1996; Mace 1994). Although experimental procedures provide the most accurate results, they are expensive, time consuming, and require a knowledge of single-subject designs. If experimental procedures are used in an analog setting, they can fail to identify important factors that are operating in the student's natural setting. Observational procedures have ecological validity but cannot directly establish causality. They can also be expensive and time consuming. Interviews and rating scales are cost effective but may not provide valid data. Whatever procedures are used, functional assessment shares with precision teaching the problem of being associated with behavior analysis.

CONCLUSION

CBM, precision teaching, and functional analysis are not the only direct approaches to psychoeducational assessment. For example, a number of other approaches were addressed in a special issue of the *School Psychology Review* (Braden 1990). CBM, precision teaching, and functional analysis, however, currently offer what are, we believe, the most complete and best-documented alternative approaches to special education assessment. As such, they provide the best view of what an ideal future might look like. But we are skeptical about what the future actually holds for special education assessment. The current system may not meet the instructional needs of students but does meet administrative (Batsche and Knoff 1995) and political needs (Edgar and Hayden 1984/1985). Special interest groups that lobby for the needs of students with disabilities are more likely to argue for more of the current approach than to argue for substantive change. As Franklin commented, the "goal appears to be obtaining eligibility under IDEA or Section 504. These well-meaning 'advocates' continue to believe that students will obtain 'individual help' in small classes and will receive one-on-one attention if only they qualify for special services" (1996, 515). The belief that children are better served in school if only they can obtain the proper label is, unfortunately, mistaken.

REFERENCES

Algozzine, B., and L. Korinek. 1985. Where is special education for students with high prevalence handicaps going? *Exceptional Children* 51:388–94.

American Psychological Association. 1985. *Standards for educational and psychological tests.* Washington, D.C.: American Psychological Association.

Baker, S. K., and R. Good. 1995. Curriculum-based measurement of English reading with bilingual Hispanic students: A validating study with second grade students. *School Psychology Review* 24:561–78.

Batsche, G. M., and H. M. Knoff. 1995. Best practices in linking assessment to intervention. In *Best practices in school psychology III*, ed. A. Thomas and J. Grimes, 569–85. Washington, D.C.: National Association of School Psychologists.

Binder, C. 1996. Behavioral fluency: Evolution of a new paradigm. *The Behavior Analyst* 19:163–97.

Bracken, B. 1988. Ten psychometric reasons why similar tests produce dissimilar results. *Journal of School Psychology* 26:155–66.

Braden, J. P., ed. 1990. Mini-series on experimental methods for assessing intelligence. *School Psychology Review* 19.

Caskey, W. E., Jr. 1985. The use of the Peabody Individual Achievement Test and the Woodcock Reading Mastery Tests in the diagnosis of a learning disability in reading. *Diagnostique* 11:14–20.

Caskey, W. E., Jr., S. Hylton, J. B. Robinson, R. L. Taylor, and F. F. Washburn. 1983. Woodcock and PIAT reading scores: A lack of equivalency. *Diagnostique* 9:49–54.

Cooper, L. J., D. P. Wacker, D. Thursby, L. A. Plagmann, J. Harding, T. Millard, and M. Derby. 1992. Analysis of the effects of task preferences, task demands, and adult attention on child behavior in outpatient and classroom settings. *Journal of Applied Behavior Analysis* 25:823–40.

Deno, S. L. 1989. Curriculum-based measurement and special education services: A fundamental and direct relationship. In *Curriculum-based measurement: Assessing special children*, ed. M. R. Shinn, 1–17. New York: Guilford.

Edgar, E., and A. H. Hayden. 1984/1985. Who are the children special education should serve and how many children are there? *Journal of Special Education* 18:523–39.

Franklin, M. 1996. A practitioner's view of school reform: Does it really matter? *School Psychology Review* 25:512–16.

Haughton, E. C. 1972. Aims: Growing and sharing. In *Let's try doing something else kind of thing*, ed. J. B. Jordan and L. S. Robbins, 20–39. Reston, Va.: Council for Exceptional Children.

Hayes, S. C., R. O. Nelson, and R. B. Jarrett. 1987. The treatment utility of assessment: A functional approach to evaluating assessment quality. *American Psychologist* 42:963–74.

Haywood, H. C., A. L. Brown, and S. Wingenfeld. 1990. Dynamic approaches to psychoeducational assessment. *School Psychology Review* 19:411–22.

Heller, K., W. Holtzman, and S. Messick, eds. 1982. *Placing children in special education: A strategy for equity*. Washington, D.C.: National Academy Press.

Heward, W., and M. Orlansky. 1984. *Exceptional children*. 3d ed. Columbus, Ohio: Merrill.

Hilgard, E. R. 1987. *Psychology in America: A historical survey*. San Diego: Harcourt Brace Jovanovich.

Howell, K. W. 1986. Direct assessment of academic performance. *School Psychology Review* 15:324–35.

Iwata, B. A., M. F. Dorsey, K. J. Slifer, K. A. Bauman, and G. S. Richman. 1982. Toward a functional analysis of self-injury. *Analysis and Intervention in Developmental Disabilities* 2:3–20.

Jones, C. H., and J. R. Slate. 1996. Educators' attitudes toward educational practices based in behavior analysis. *Journal of Research and Development in Education* 30:31–41.

Kamphaus, R. W. 1993. *Clinical assessment of children's intelligence*. Boston: Allyn and Bacon.

Kratochwill, T. R., and J. E. McGivern. 1996. Clinical diagnosis, behavioral assessment, and functional analysis: Examining the connection between assessment and intervention. *School Psychology Review* 25:342–55.

Larrivee, B. 1985. *Effective teaching for effective mainstreaming*. New York: Routledge.

Lindsley, O. R. 1991. Precision teaching's unique legacy from B. F. Skinner. *Journal of Behavioral Education* 1:253–66.

———. 1996. The four free-operant freedoms. *The Behavior Analyst* 19:199–210.

Mace, F. C. 1994. The significance and future of functional analysis methodologies. *Journal of Applied Behavior Analysis* 27:385–92.

Marston, D. B. 1987. Does categorical teacher certification benefit the mildly handi-capped child? *Exceptional Children* 53:423–31.

———. 1989. A curriculum-based approach to assessing academic performance: What it is and why do it. In *Curriculum-based measurement: Assessing special children,* ed. M. R. Shinn, 18–78. New York: Guilford.

McComas, J. J., D. P. Wacker, and L. J. Cooper. 1996. Experimental analysis of academic performance in a classroom setting. *Journal of Behavioral Education* 6:191–201.

National Institutes of Health. 1989. *NIH consensus development conference on the treat-ment of destructive behaviors in persons with developmental disabilities.* Bethesda, Md.: National Institutes of Health.

Neef, N. A., and B. A. Iwata. 1994. Current research on functional analysis methodologies: An introduction. *Journal of Applied Behavior Analysis* 27:211–14.

Newby, R., D. Recht, J. Caldwell, and J. Schaefer. 1993. Comparison of WISC-III and WISC-R IQ changes over a 2-year time span in a sample of children with dyslexia [Monograph]. *Journal of Psychoeducational Assessment: Advances in Psychoeduca-tional Assessment, Wechsler Intelligence Scale for Children: Third Edition* 11:87–93.

O'Neill, R. E., R. H. Horner, R. Albin, K. Storey, and J. R. Sprague. 1990. *Functional analy-sis of problem behavior: A practical assessment guide.* Sycamore, Ill.: Sycamore.

Pennypacker, H. S., J. B. Heckler, and S. F. Pennypacker. 1977. The personalized learning center: A university-wide system of personalized instruction. In *Handbook of applied behavioral research,* ed. T. A. Brigham and A. C. Catania, 591–617. New York: Irving-ton Press.

Phelps, L., and A. Ensor. 1987. The comparison of performance by sex of deaf children on the WISC-R. *Psychology in the Schools* 24:210–14.

Potts, L., J. W. Eshleman, and J. O. Cooper. 1993. Ogden R. Lindsley and the historical de-velopment of precision teaching. *The Behavior Analyst* 16:177–89.

Reschly, D. J. 1988. Special education reform: School psychology paradigm shift. *School Psychology Review* 17:459–75.

Reschly, D. J., and M. S. Wilson. 1990. Cognitive processing versus traditional intelligence: Diagnostic utility, intervention implications, and treatment validity. *School Psychol-ogy Review* 19:443–58.

Reschly, D. J., and J. E. Ysseldyke. 1995. School psychology paradigm shift. In *Best prac-tices in school psychology III,* ed. A. Thomas and J. Grimes, 17–31. Washington, D.C.: National Association of School Psychologists.

Reynolds, C. R. 1984/1985. Critical measurement issues in learning disabilities. *Journal of Special Education* 18:451–76.

Reynolds, C. R., and A. Jensen. 1983. WISC-R subscale patterns of abilities of Blacks and Whites matched on Full Scale IQ. *Journal of Educational Psychology* 75:207–14.

Reynolds, M. C. 1979. Categorical versus noncategorical teacher training. *Teacher Educa-tion and Special Education* 2:5–8.

Reynolds, M. C., and K. C. Lakin. 1987. Noncategorical special education for mildly hand-icapped students. A system for the future. In *The handbook of special education: Re-search and practice,* vol. 1, ed. M. C. Wang, M. C. Reynolds, and H. J. Walberg, 331–56. Oxford: Pergamon.

Reynolds, M. C., M. C. Wang, and H. J. Walberg. 1987. The necessary restructuring of special and regular education. *Exceptional Children* 53:391–98.

Sarason, S., and J. Doris. 1979. *Educational handicap, public policy, and social history.* New York: Free Press.

Schendel, J. 1993. The top ten myths and curriculum-based measurement (CBM). *NASP [National Association of School Psychologists] Communique* 21 (March):3–4.

Scriven, M. 1983. Comments on Gene Glass. *Policy Studies Review* 2:79–84.

Scruggs, T., and M. Mastropieri. 1992. Effective mainstreaming strategies for mildly handicapped students. *Elementary School Journal* 92:389–409.

Sedlacek, W. E. 1994. Issues in advancing diversity through assessment. *Journal of Counseling and Development* 72:549–53.

Shinn, M. R., ed. 1989. *Curriculum-based measurement: Assessing special children.* New York: Guilford.

Slate, J. R. 1995. Two investigations of the validity of the WISC-III. *Psychological Reports* 76:299–306.

Slate, J. R., and J. Fawcett. 1996. Gender differences in Wechsler performance scores. *American Annals of the Deaf* 141:19–23.

Slate, J. R., J. D. Hall, and C. H. Jones. 1993. Using regression in determining eligibility for specific learning disabilities: More complex but not necessarily more valid. *Arkansas School Psychology Association Newsletter* (November):3–6.

Slate, J. R., and C. H. Jones. 1995. Preliminary evidence of the validity of the WISC-III for African American students undergoing special education evaluation. *Educational and Psychological Measurement* 55:1039–46.

Slate, J. R., C. H. Jones, and D. A. Saarnio. 1997. WISC- III diagnosis and special education diagnosis. *Journal of Psychology* 131:119–20.

Slate, J. R., V. Little, M. Prince, and D. Blaske. 1995. Subgroups, sex differences, and factorial structure of WISC-R and WRAT-R performance for students with Attention Deficit Hyperactivity Disorder. *Assessment in Rehabilitation and Exceptionality* 2:197–206.

Slate, J. R., and D. A. Saarnio. 1996. Differences in reading and math achievement of scores for students with mental retardation. *British Columbia Journal of Special Education* 20:34–45.

Snow, R. 1984. Placing children in special education: Some comments. *Educational Researcher* 13:12–14.

Starlin, A. 1972. Sharing a message about curriculum with my friends. In *Let's try doing something else kind of thing,* ed. J. B. Jordan and L. S. Robbins, 13–19. Reston, Va.: Council for Exceptional Children.

Taylor, R. L., and S. B. Richards, 1991. Patterns of intellectual differences of Black, Hispanic, and White children. *Psychology in the Schools* 28:5–9.

Tucker, J. A. 1985. Curriculum-based assessment: An introduction. *Exceptional Children* 52:199–204.

U.S. Department of Health, Education, and Welfare. 1977. Education of handicapped children: Implementation of Part B of the Education of the Handicapped Act. *Federal Register* 42:42474–518.

Webster, R. E., and L. A. Braswell. 1991. Curriculum bias and reading achievement test performance. *Psychology in the Schools* 28:193–99.

Wechsler, D. 1991. *Wechsler Intelligence Scale for Children-III.* San Antonio: The Psychological Corporation.

Ysseldyke, J. E., and S. L. Christenson. 1988. Linking assessment to intervention. In *Alternative educational delivery systems: Enhancing instructional options for all students,* ed. J. L. Graden, J. E. Zins, and M. J. Curtis, 91–109. Washington, D.C.: National Association of School Psychologists.

5

Technology and Special Education

Cleborne D. Maddux

One of the more notable trends of the second half of the twentieth century has been the rapid pace of technological change. This phenomenon has been particularly dramatic during the last two or three decades. For example, Sawyer and Zantal-Wiener point out that as recently as 1972 we had "no MRIs or CAT scans, space stations, Walkmans, camcorders, VCRs, CDs, personal computers, Fax machines, cordless telephones, cellular phones, bar codes, genetic fingerprinting, laser surgery, and automatic teller machines" (1993, 70).

Of these innovations, the development and popularization of personal computers is possibly the most significant and, certainly, the most amazing. Today, computers are ubiquitous, and we have come to take them so much for granted that we can easily forget they have been available since only 1974 when they were introduced in kit form. Incredibly, by the late 1980s, "small computers had found their way into nearly every walk of life, millions of people considered them indispensable, and there were more small computers in the United States than there were people!" (Maddux and Cummings in press).

Small computers first proved themselves in the business world where electronic spreadsheet and word processing software revolutionized accounting and composing tasks. Soon, educators began bringing them into schools as aids to both teaching and learning. At first, the machines were expensive but crude; educational software was scarce and of poor quality. There was substantial resistance to the educational computer movement. For these and other reasons, schools were slow to acquire computers. In fact, in 1983, the ratio of students to computers in U.S. schools was about 125 to 1, and many schools had no computers (Okolo, Bahr, and Rieth 1993). Advocates continued to press for more and better computers, and the latest surveys show that 98 percent of schools have computers, 28 percent of those schools have more than fifty computers, and the ratio of students to computers is approximately 10 to 1 (McDaniels 1996; Quality Education Data 1995).

Although computers are not generally being used to their best advantage in schools, many experts believe that computers have the potential to be the most revolutionary teaching and learning tools ever developed. Although other electronic innovations in education have failed to bring about significant improvements in schooling, computers differ in a highly significant way: They can be highly interactive (Maddux, Johnson, and Willis 1997). Sixteen-millimeter film projectors, slide projectors, overhead projectors, televisions, and the other electronic teaching aids of the past lend themselves most readily to relatively passive use by learners. Computers, in contrast, can be programmed to respond differently to input by individual learners. This crucial difference in learner engagement is what gives computing its exciting and unique educational promise.

RESISTANCE TO COMPUTERS IN SCHOOLS

The road to the acceptance of computing in schools was not entirely smooth. There was and continues to be resistance to the idea that computers have an important place in education. This resistance has multiple causes, which are elaborated as follows.

Cultural Lag

We have long known that certain elements of culture tend to change faster than other elements. Anthropologists call this tendency "cultural lag" (Kneller 1965). In the United States, changes in the culture at large tend to occur long before changes in education. The primary reason for this tendency is that the most conservative members of a culture are typically chosen as education policymakers. School board members, for example, are almost always "disproportionately white, male, middle-aged, high in education, occupation, and income, and well established in their local communities" (Boocock 1980, 250). Such affluent individuals, many of whom have distinguished themselves in business and are models of a conventional lifestyle, have a vested interest in maintaining the status quo and in resisting change. After all, for these individuals, the existing culture has led to wealth and recognition. They are suspicious of change and support changes in education only after they have been adopted and proven advantageous in other cultural arenas. This suspicion helps explain why computers were highly successful and well accepted in business environments before education policymakers across the country began to make funds available to purchase computers for schools.

Overly Optimistic Claims of Educational Computing Advocates

Ironically, one of the most damaging trends was brought about by well-meaning early advocates who sought to convince school administrators and other policymakers that funds should be provided for computer hardware and software for schools. These advocates, who often approached educational computing with the kind of frantic enthusiasm that is usually demonstrated only by religious zealots, frequently portrayed computers and various computer applications as education panaceas and established unreasonably optimistic expectations in the minds of education policymakers and the public at large. Maddux, Johnson, and Willis describe this phenomenon as follows:

> We cannot imagine any educational innovation that could possibly live up to such inflated claims. Such promises set up unrealistic expectations that have a way of coming back to haunt the incautious innovator. This happens when those who control resources eventually (and inevitably) begin to demand evidence that expenditures have been worthwhile. When they realize that most promises have gone unfulfilled, they may quickly change from advocates to opponents of the innovation. The danger, of course, is that the resulting backlash may be so severe that the innovation is abandoned. (1997, 8)

The Poor Quality of Early Educational Software

Another contributing factor to the resistance to using computers in schools was the poor quality of much of the early educational software. Educational software of any kind was scarce because most early software developers concentrated on business applications. By comparison, the education market was tiny, and because computers were scarce in school, software houses were reluctant to commit resources to such a specialized and limited potential market in which computer implementation was considered controversial.

The educational software that was available was often technically and pedagogically flawed. Some of it was rushed to market before it was properly tested and contained so many programming errors that it would not run at all or would "crash" when students keyed in certain responses. Some other available software would run as planned, but it contained many spelling, punctuation, and grammar errors—even factual or conceptual errors in the subject matter content. Much of the software that was technically and mechanically adequate had been developed by programmers and others who had little knowledge concerning schools, scope and sequence of curricula, human development, or educational psychology. Consequently, much of the software was pedagogically flawed or simply boring. Very little of the software was based on learning theory, and when learning theory was used, it tended to be oversimplified, mechanical reinforcement theory in the tradition of programmed instruction. This was an unfortunate circumstance, because programmed instruction had proven to be an educational failure decades before when it was used on the ill-fated and only briefly popular "teaching machines" of the 1960s.

THE BACKLASH AGAINST INFORMATION TECHNOLOGY IN EDUCATION

For these and other reasons, the late eighties and early nineties were characterized by a backlash against the idea of using information technology in general education or in special education. Scores of articles opposing the use of computers in schools appeared in academic journals, popular magazines, newspapers, and other publications.

The opposition to computing in schools became so intense that the entire movement was in danger of the same kind of disillusionment and abandonment that had accompanied all previous attempts to bring electronic innovations into education. From teaching machines to educational television, the historical precedent for failure was all too obvious. Although some electronic devices such as overhead projectors are still found in today's schools, none lived up to the initial optimism that accompanied their introduction, because none revolutionized teaching or learning.

Although the threat to computing in schools was real, it no longer has the potential to destroy the modern movement to bring information technology into the teaching and learning process. Even though educational software has improved somewhat, the danger of disillusionment and abandonment of computing in schools was ended by trends in the culture at large, not by events in education. Computers will not be abandoned in schools simply because they are so ubiquitous in the culture at large. The need for small computers is taken for granted in business, government, the military, the mass media, and the home. Indeed, because computers pervade every walk of modern life and are so well accepted by so many people, it would probably not be possible now for educators to prevent the continued proliferation of computers in schools. In short, computing has gained so much cultural momentum that the presence of computers in schools of the future seems secure. What remains in question, however, is whether computers will be used well or poorly and, consequently, whether their proliferation in schools will qualitatively improve education or merely provide minor, laborsaving conveniences for teachers and students.

Poor Use of Computers in Education

Although computing is unlikely to be abandoned in present or future schools, there are serious concerns about the poor way computers are sometimes used and whether such use can help significantly improve the educational environment. Although many examples are available of exemplary and imaginative computer use in schools, such laudatory examples are not typical. Many experts have called attention to this fact since computers first began to be brought into the education enterprise. Simonson and Thompson, in considering the role that technology is playing in the current school reform movement, conclude:

> Although technology, tied to the goals of the restructuring movement, can change the roles of students and teachers, it is not being used to its full potential. Research findings suggest, in fact, that computers are generally still used to accomplish traditional tasks in schools, rather than to support new directions for teachers and students.... Whatever the reasons, it is clear that technology has not yet come close to its potential. (1997, 12)

Additionally, the President's Committee of Advisors on Science and Technology recently submitted its findings, *Report to the President on the Use of Technology to Strengthen K–12 Education in the United States*. The group addresses the role of technology in school reform:

> At the elementary school level, computers are often employed for teaching isolated basic skills and for playing educational games. Word processing is used to a significant extent at all levels, but in most cases as part of an effort to teach computer skills, and not as a tool for writing in connection with English, social studies, or other academic classes. The situation would appear to be similar in the case of spreadsheet use, which is generally treated as an aspect of computer literacy, and less commonly integrated into, for example, the math or science curriculum. It should be noted that some schools have, in fact, integrated computers extensively and effectively within many aspects of the learning process, in many cases relying on information technology as an essential element of educational reform. Such schools, however, would thus far appear to represent a very small fraction of our nation's k–12 institutions. (1997, 21)

Leuhrmann (1994) suggests that computers and information technology have had profound effects on every walk of life except education. Ely (1993) agrees and provides the following assessment of computing's effect on education in the United States: "On a national scale, one would have to conclude that computer-based instruction in U.S. schools and universities has had minimal impact. By any measure of learning achievement, of significant changes in styles of teaching and learning, or of curriculum reform, the conclusion is 'little or no effect'" (1993, 55).

Why Are Computers Often Used Poorly in Schools?

There are many reasons for the poor use of computing in schools. One reason is that excellent educational software is still in short supply. The President's Committee of Advisors on Science and Technology identifies a lack of excellent educational software as a continuing problem: "There is widespread agreement that one of the principal factors now limiting the extensive and effective use of technology within American schools is the relative dearth of high-quality computer software and digital content designed specifically for that purpose" (1997, 21).

The panel then lists five reasons for the scarcity of good educational software, which are elaborated below.

Inadequate software acquisition budgets. The panel points out that schools spend a yearly average of between ten dollars and sixteen dollars per pupil on computer software, and suggests that this figure must be increased "substantially." Otherwise, the panel suggests that software houses will continue to be unwilling to spend the money for necessary research and development activities prior to producing excellent software.

Market fragmentation. The educational market is fragmented not only by diverse subject areas and grade levels but also by many varying specifications imposed by different states, school districts, and schools.

Lack of modern hardware in schools. Antiquated hardware in schools leads to a scarcity of software, which contributes further to antiquated hardware. This insidious circularity occurs because educational software developers fear that schools will not be able to use their products on antiquated hardware and are thus reluctant to commit the resources needed to develop up-to-date software. School policymakers, however, are reluctant to provide funds to buy state-of-the-art hardware because they know there is very little educational software available that can take advantage of such hardware.

Procurement related problems. These problems are related, in general, to cumbersome state, district, and local bureaucratic regulations and, specifically, to procurement procedures that were developed originally to acquire traditional print media and other media that did not need frequent revisions. The committee points out that these problems are particularly acute in the twenty-two "adoption states," where state approval of materials is required prior to consideration for approval by district or local school authorities. Such states often provide such approvals, granted by large committees, only every five years, thus inadvertently discouraging more frequent updating of materials. Although five-year cycles may be realistic for revision of print materials, such a long period of time guarantees that hopelessly outdated software will be used by schools toward the end of the cycle. Even then, states often charge software developers thousands of dollars in application fees when materials are submitted for committee consideration of approval, and many states also require large numbers of computers to be made available free of charge to committee members during the adoption proceedings.

Unintended economic consequences related to innovation. The committee emphasizes the lack of initiatives by the private sector to develop products that will facilitate school reform:

> The commercial availability of software and information resources designed to support student-centered, constructivist approaches to education is ... limited, and there is little evidence to date of large-scale, well-funded efforts by either traditional educational software vendors, multimedia developers, or

textbook publishers to develop such content. Moreover, in spite of a general appreciation of the potential for long-term growth in the market for educational software, there has thus far been only limited activity within the venture capital community aimed at launching startup companies focused on the provision of software designed for such pedagogic approaches, and targeted specifically at the nation's elementary and secondary schools. (President's Committee of Advisors on Science and Technology 1997, 22)

The panel concludes that the federal government must make funds available to subsidize the development of such resources.

TAKING CONTROL OF THE EVEREST SYNDROME

In the past, I have contended that the future success of information technology in education depends primarily on whether or not we think critically about technology and its proper role in education and then make good decisions about how it will be used in schools. All too often, advocates of information technology in education have fallen prey to what I have termed "the Everest Syndrome." That is, they have acted as though they believe that computers should be brought into schools simply "because they are there" (Maddux, Johnson, and Willis 1997). Such thinking leads to the unspoken assumption that computers are valuable for their own sake and that they should be used in schools to do whatever they can be made to do. This view is unfortunate for many reasons, not least of which is the fact that it is entirely possible to apply computers to problems for which they are entirely unsuited and inappropriate.

Then too, the success of information technology in education requires us to apply technological solutions to important rather than trivial problems (Maddux and Cummings 1986; Maddux, Johnson, and Willis 1997). After all, using information technology in education is expensive, both in economic terms and, perhaps more significantly, in human terms. The human cost of information technology in education occurs because both educators and students have a finite amount of time, energy, and enthusiasm to devote to learning to use new tools such as computers. If these precious resources are squandered on technology that does not help solve important education problems, then teachers, students, policymakers, and the general public cannot be expected to continue to favorably view or highly value the use of technology in the schools.

A simple, dichotomous categorization system for educational applications of information technology can help in thinking about appropriate goals for technology, whether in general or special education. I have called the categories "Type I" and "Type II" applications.

Type I and Type II Applications of Information Technology

Type I applications are those that make teaching in traditional ways easier, faster, or otherwise more efficient. Type II applications, in contrast, make available new and better ways of teaching—ways that would not be accessible without technology.

The use of Type I applications in schools is not at all inappropriate. In fact, teachers should take advantage of such applications, especially if their use releases teachers from routine teaching tasks so that they can devote their time and attention to more creative and important teaching. However, the success of information technology in general education and in special education will be judged by the degree to which computers are successful in providing Type II applications.

Information technology is costly in both monetary and human terms. If the technology's only contribution is to make teaching the same things in the same ways we have always taught them more convenient, then taxpayers and policymakers will not willingly continue to invest heavily in computers, peripherals, and software, and teachers will not be willing to devote the considerable time and effort needed to learn to use the technology. Although relatively trivial goals must be pursued and achieved in schools, information technology is too expensive to devote solely to such goals. Instead, for it to be considered successful by education critics, the media, school board members, legislators, taxpayers, and parents, information technology must also be applied productively to the most important education problems and goals. Therefore, although teachers should make use of Type I applications, a successful and productive information technology program in general education and in special education should be balanced and should include both Type I and Type II applications.

Unfortunately, Type I applications of information technology in education are much more common than are Type II applications, probably because Type I applications, such as drill-and-practice software, can be developed by those with little or no expertise in theories of education, curricula, or learning and are much easier, quicker, and cheaper to develop.

Characteristics of Type I Applications

As explained earlier, Type I applications support traditional teaching content and methods. Most Type I applications also share the following five characteristics:

- *The intellectual involvement of the user is relatively passive.* Almost all software requires interaction between the user and the computer. However, Type I applications generally involve lower-level rather than higher-order, or complex, cognition. Rote responses and memorization, for example, are typical activities of software in this category. A common example of such an application is drill-and-practice software that is designed to help children learn number facts such as the multiplication tables.

- *Most of what happens on the screen has been predetermined by the software developer.* The user may type in brief number responses or respond to multiple choice items, but most of what happens is predetermined by whoever planned and developed the software.

- *User input is restricted to a limited repertoire of acceptable responses.* Most Type I software permits only a single number, letter, or word to be entered by the user. The spacebar, the arrow keys, or the ENTER key may also be acceptable, but complex responses such as entire mathematical formulas or complete sentences are usually not options.

- *The goal is the acquisition of facts by rote memory.* Again, there is nothing wrong with such a goal. Many things must be memorized, and computers can help students do so. Rote memory applications are problems only when they constitute the only type of applications being used.

- *Everything the software is capable of doing can be observed in a short period of time, usually ten minutes or less.* Even if the software can be customized with regard to speed, level of difficulty, and type of reinforcement, almost everything can be sampled in only a few minutes.

Characteristics of Type II Applications

Type II applications make teaching and learning accessible in new and better ways. "If use of the computer improves teaching or learning and if it would be impossible (or extremely difficult) to teach or learn in this manner without the use of the computer, then the application in question is most likely a Type II application" (Maddux, Johnson, and Willis 1997, 22). Most Type II applications have characteristics that are almost opposites of Type I application characteristics:

- *The user is intellectually involved in a relatively active way.* Because Type II uses do not generally deal primarily with rote learning or memorization, they tend to stimulate much more cognitively complex user involvement than do Type I uses. Contrast the cognitive activity level, for example, of a student using a desktop publishing program to produce a classroom newspaper with that of a student responding to software that provides drill and practice with the multiplication facts.

- *Most of what happens on the screen is determined by the user.* In fact, a great many Type II applications such as word processing, electronic spreadsheets, or desktop publishing programs provide the user with a blank computer screen and a powerful way for the user to determine what will appear there.

- *The user has a great deal of the control over the type of interaction with the computer, and there is an extensive selection of acceptable user input.* The user makes most of the decisions about when to invoke various tools such as spelling and grammar checkers or programs to resize, recolor, or otherwise edit images. The list of appropriate or acceptable user input is nearly unlimited.

- *Most Type II software is designed to accomplish much more complex and creative tasks than the tasks that are characteristic of Type I software.* Managing simulations of city management or cell metabolism or constructing "what if" budget scenarios are obviously more complex and creative than responding to electronic multiplication flashcards.

- *It usually takes hours, days, weeks, or months before a user experiences everything a Type II program is capable of doing.* Sophisticated educational simulations, desktop publishing programs, or modern word processing programs, to name a few examples, are so complex and varied that many, if not most, users never experience every nuance or possibility.

Examples of Type I Applications

Five general categories of Type I software are most typically found in schools: drill-and practice, tutorial, assessment, administrative, and computer-managed instruction.

Drill-and-practice software. Drill-and-practice software does not attempt to teach the user anything. Instead, it provides drill and practice to memorize facts or to establish a rote skill that was originally taught some other way. Common examples are programs that provide drills on number facts, sight vocabulary, parts of speech, names of the fifty states, and so on (Maddux, Johnson, and Willis 1997). Research has shown that drill-and-practice software is the most common software in schools and is even more common in special education.

Tutorial software. Unlike drill-and-practice software, which is aimed at providing practice at something that was originally taught some other way, tutorial software is aimed at teaching the skill in the first place. Most tutorial software is Type I software, although it is possible to develop Type II tutorial software. Most tutorial software falls into the Type I category because most such programs make use of only traditional teaching methods such as lecture or demonstration. Programs that are designed to prepare users to take the Graduate Record Exam or to use Windows 95 or some specific word processing, spreadsheet, or database management software are examples of tutorial software.

Assessment software. A growing body of software is being designed to support the assessment process in schools. Much of this software is aimed at special education. Assessment software is designed to perform one or more of the following functions: administer, score, report, or interpret tests or test results. Many technical and philosophical problems are related with such software. Although writing a software program to administer some tests is relatively easy to do, most experts agree that doing so makes it necessary to restandardize the test because norms developed through human administration will not necessarily apply if the test is machine administered.

Scoring a machine-administered test can also be a problem because the scoring of many individual psychological and education tests that are used in special education require a great deal of expert judgment. Although computers and computer programs are excellent at performing straightforward and repetitive tasks as well as mathematical calculations, they are completely inadequate at performing any tasks that require human affective qualities such as empathy or compassion. In addition, their use as problem solvers is limited to structured problems in which logical, "if-then" problem-solving strategies are sufficient (Dreyfus 1992). The interpretation of test results is an example of a very unstructured problem for which computers are not well suited. However, as long as the computer is used only for performing the kind of rote, tedious calculations of scores or the secretarial tasks that are involved in report writing, this type of application can be useful.

Administrative applications. A wide variety of software is designed to assist in the secretarial or routine tasks that are connected with running a school. A few examples in this category include software that is intended to automate the registration process, record and compile attendance data, produce graphics for presentations or reports, prepare mailing labels, and balance budgets. In special education, a growing body of software is intended to partially or fully automate the process of writing Individualized Education Programs (IEPs). Some of this software is intended only to relieve the IEP committee of the tedious paperwork involved in filling out forms. However, other programs effectively usurp the mandated decision-making role of the committee by accepting test scores and other data, then providing a diagnosis. Some such software even generates the long-term goals and short-term objectives required by the law. This software is clearly against the spirit and, arguably, against the letter of the Individuals with Disabilities Education Act (IDEA). Lawmakers intended the IEP meeting to be a problem-solving meeting of parents and diverse professionals who would engage in discussion and debate concerning each student. It was believed that out of this process would come the best possible thinking and decision making. Those who develop or implement software that automates this process clearly do not understand the limitations of computers and are misusing them.

Computer-managed instruction (CMI). Software in this category performs a variety of tasks including "organizing student data, monitoring student progress, testing student mastery and prescribing further instruction or remediation, recording student progress, and selecting the order of instructional modules to be completed" (Maddux, Johnson, and Willis 1997, 27).

Examples of Type II Applications

Seven general categories of Type II software are often used in education: word processing, spreadsheets and databases, simulations, programming languages, problem-solving software, prosthetic aids, and the Internet.

Word processing. It should be obvious by now that the particular educational use a piece of software is put to can determine whether it is a Type I or Type II application. For example, a word processing program that is used by a teacher simply to compose and then print out a traditional test would be a Type I application. However, use of the same word processing program with students to permit new and better ways of teaching creative writing would be an example of a Type II application.

When the first research on word processing and its effect on writing began to appear, word processing did not seem as helpful as many advocates had hoped. At first, one of the few advantages of writing with a word processor was that it stimulated a greater quantity of writing, even though overall quality was not improved. Nevertheless, many advocates made the point that because word processing takes the drudgery out of writing and revising, it should be considered worthwhile even if it were equal only to writing with paper, pen, or typewriter.

The earliest research on creative writing and word processing was crude, and today, the results of more recent research are much more optimistic. Researchers have identified advantages that fall into the following categories: ease of production and revision, cognitive advantages, social advantages, and attitudinal advantages (Maddux, Johnson, and Willis 1997). Roblyer, Edwards, and Havriluk do an excellent job of summarizing the research on word processing and writing:

> Generally, studies seem to conclude that students who use word processing software in the context of writing instruction programs tend to write more, revise more (at least on a surface level), make fewer errors, and have better attitudes toward their writing than students who do not use word processing software. Teachers who use word processing software with their students should not expect writing quality to improve automatically. Improvements of that kind depend largely on other factors such as the type of writing instruction. But the potential value of word processing has been established, making it one of the most validated uses of technology in education. (1997, 131)

Electronic spreadsheets and databases. Spreadsheets were originally developed for use as electronic accounting ledgers for business. They were an instant success because accountants could easily investigate various "what if" scenarios. Accounting ledgers are tedious to use in such a fashion because changing the value in one row and column may mean that hundreds or even thousands of other affected values must be recalculated. But electronic spreadsheets automatically recalculate any affected values when one value is changed.

Spreadsheets as Type I applications are often used by school administrators to do the accounting on budgets and by teachers to maintain electronic grade books. As Type II applications,

> Spreadsheets can be used to teach mathematical concepts, science, and problem solving. There are also other uses: Students can use the spreadsheet to investigate a variety of social issue questions. One such question might be, When will city X reach a critical water shortage? The students would then conduct library research to obtain the statistics called for in the spreadsheet template or be provided with invented data for a fictitious city. Once the statistics were entered, population growth could be projected and correlated with available water supply, and a report could be written suggesting the year when the

available water resources would not be adequate to meet the city's needs. (Maddux, Johnson, and Willis 1997, 290)

Electronic databases, also originally developed for use in business, can be used additionally as a Type II teaching tool. Hoelscher describes how this adaptation can be accomplished: "The process of using the computer as a data workhorse creates more openings for students to peer into the information they have and to play out their strategies for creating and sharing new information. It may now make more sense to look at things in a number of very different ways before deciding upon 'the answer.' And, once decided upon, the answer may be more fully understood" (1986, 25). Databases provide unique opportunities for students to search out information, learn how to locate desired information, and put that information into a report. Students can design and fill a database of their own, which provides a unique opportunity for them to think about organizational processes and structure.

Simulations. Educational simulations make experiences available to students that are too expensive, too dangerous, too distant, too difficult to observe, or are otherwise unavailable in schools. Simulations are available for many diverse activities—from traveling the Oregon Trail as a pioneer to managing a farm.

Programming languages. The use of programming languages in schools has been controversial, and although languages like BASIC were often taught in the beginning of the educational computing movement, this practice is seldom advocated today.

The early advocates argued that programming would be a useful vocational skill in all professions, a claim that has not been substantiated by needs in the modern job market. However, another argument was that learning to program could teach certain important cognitive skills. That is, programming was viewed as a cognitive amplifier.

The leading advocate of this latter view was Seymour Papert (1980), a mathematician and computer scientist at the Massachusetts Institute of Technology. Papert studied with Jean Piaget and created a programming language especially for children called "Logo." Papert suggested that certain school reforms, when combined with the teaching of Logo to children, could result in children developing formal operational thinking (adult thinking) skills at far younger ages than most psychologists had ever suspected.

Although Logo is a full, general-purpose programming language, it is best known for its ability to draw graphics using the Logo turtle, a screen object that Papert conceived as analogous to the Euclidean "point in space." Children can move the turtle about the screen in immediate mode, leaving a visible line of any color in its wake. Papert asserts that Logo can be used to make abstractions, such as the point in space, concrete enough to be understood and mastered by young children.

Although Papert's contentions about Logo as a cognitive amplifier have not been fully verified through research, Maddux and Cummings (in press) list other reasons for using Logo with children, particularly with children in special education:

- *Logo is highly accessible to children.* Unlike other computer languages, interesting and enjoyable tasks can be accomplished after only a short orientation to the language, yet it is sophisticated enough to challenge computer programmers. Although Logo will not do anything that cannot be done in other computer languages such as BASIC, the low threshold of Logo is what makes it unique and ideal for use with children with disabilities, many of whom have developed the habit of giving up on basic skills of all kinds before learning enough to progress to more interesting levels. Because the basics of Logo can be learned in a single sitting, such children are often motivated to persevere in learning this language. Such children would be unlikely to stick to the task of learning a language such as BASIC, which requires many hours of learning and practice before anything very interesting can be accomplished.

- *Logo can provide a success experience for children with disabilities.* Many of these children have come to regard school as an environment for failure. Thus, Logo may provide a means to break the cycle of expectancy of failure that is followed by poor performance by providing the child with an opportunity to achieve successful control of a highly prestigious machine in an academic setting.

- *Logo is self-correcting and nonjudgmental.* Programming is a trial-and-error process that eliminates the need for adult criticism and correction. If a Logo command is incorrect, then the screen does not look as the child wished and another command must be tried. This feature is highly beneficial for many children with disabilities who have difficulty monitoring their own performance but who are oversensitive to criticism or correction by adults.

- *Logo graphics provide practice in spatial relations, including right-left orientation and directionality.* Because many children with disabilities are deficient in these concepts and skills, Logo can provide motivating and beneficial practice.

- *Logo does not require long periods of sustained attention and effort.* Therefore, children who are distracted can resume work where they left off without beginning over. Because many children with disabilities are easily distracted, they are often frustrated by tasks such as traditional arithmetic algorithms that require many variables to be held in the mind. Children whose attention wanders must begin over when they resume their efforts. The Logo turtle can be moved into immediate mode, and a child who temporarily stops work can resume where he or she left off.

- *Logo programming tasks can be used to promote social interaction and peer acceptance.* Programming assignments or activities are often carried out in groups of two or three students. Thus, they are ideal tasks for cooperative learning activities and peer tutoring (Okolo, Bahr, and Rieth 1993). Teachers can use programming in Logo to help disabled children learn social skills and gain peer acceptance. Disabled children who are good Logo programmers can be used as peer tutors and thus acquire improved self-concepts.

- *Logo provides a highly motivating reason for using mathematics and mathematical concepts.* Because many children with disabilities have not had success in school mathematics, Logo can provide a way to help eliminate some of the negative emotional associations that they have toward numbers.

Problem-solving software. Two different types of software fit into the problem-solving category. One type is based on the assumption that there are general problem-solving skills that can be taught in any knowledge domain and will then transfer to other domains. For example, one piece of software in this tradition uses a chemistry simulation that is designed to teach children to use the process of elimination. The research on generalizable problem-solving skills is not encouraging. It appears that problem-solving skills are relatively domain-specific and are not highly generalizable from one domain to another.

The other type of software in this category is intended to be used as a tool in solving problems in a specific domain. For example, some software packages present visual representations of mathematical functions. The research on problem-solving tool software is more encouraging than the research on software that is based on the generalizable skills hypothesis.

Computers as prosthetic aids. This application is not highly controversial and is intended as a compensatory aid for children with disabilities. Many such applications exist, including text-to-speech synthesizers that accept keyboard input and convert it to speech. A much more advanced application that is often used with deaf children or with children who have speech disabilities converts nonstandard speech to synthetic speech or print.

Other applications involve special input or output devices that permit individuals with restricted motor abilities to use a computer. Many special input switch devices have been developed, some permitting the use of the head, the chin, a straw-like device, the tongue, or even eyebrow movement. Large-print word processors and word processors that translate keyboard input to braille have been developed for individuals with visual disabilities.

Telecommunications and the Internet. Telecommunications applications involve one computer communicating with another. Until recently, telecommunications usually required a subscription to a private information utility, and these subscriptions were simply too expensive for schools in general. Recently, however, the development of the Internet and a specialized part of it called the World Wide Web has made telecommunications a useful educational tool. The Web holds particular promise and is growing at a phenomenal rate. In fact, a recent survey shows that as much total time is spent each month using the Web in the United

States and Canada as the total monthly playback time of all rented videotapes in those two countries (Maddux and Johnson 1997; Masotto 1995).

The educational potential of the Web is almost unlimited. However, a number of difficult problems must still be solved before it can be expected to live up to its potential. Maddux and Cummings (in press) have outlined many of these problems:

- Making sure that educators focus on how best to use the Internet in teaching, rather than on simply providing access to the Internet and assuming that educational advantage will automatically follow

- Attempting to make good educational use of the Internet with a limited supply of diverse and often antiquated hardware and software

- Ensuring that access to the Internet remains free to schools and to students

- Providing the preservice and in-service training necessary for teachers to learn how to use the Internet as a useful teaching and learning tool

- Making sure that school districts can provide ongoing support and excellent documentation, both technical and curricular in nature

- Ensuring that groups that object to the content of the Internet do not persuade school authorities to attempt to censor it or block its access to children

- Providing ways for teachers and students to judge the quality and accuracy of information found on the Internet

CURRENT RESEARCH ON INFORMATION TECHNOLOGY IN SPECIAL EDUCATION

A growing body of literature supports the use of information technology in special education. Some of this literature is in the form of case studies and anecdotes, such as the following assessment by Lewis:

> In classrooms throughout the nation, from preschool to graduate school, technology makes learning easier for persons with disabilities. Telecommunications and multimedia technologies such as interactive video bring the world into the classroom. Electronic communication devices allow students to speak and add their voices to those of their classmates. And adapted computers provide access to instruction in myriad subject areas, from learning to count to calculus. In a few short years, technology has changed the way people with disabilities live, work, and learn. (1993, 3)

Research is also supportive. Hannaford (1993) reviewed the research literature on the efficacy of using information technology in both regular and special education and came to the following conclusions:

- Computers help both regular and exceptional students to learn material faster.

- Computers lead to better attention, motivation, and time-on-task behaviors for both groups.

- Both groups have a positive attitude toward computer instruction.

- Drill-and-practice software is the most common, is effective for all students, and is most effective for the lowest-ability students in a group.

- For computer instruction to be most effective in either group, it must be integrated with the entire curriculum.

- When used with small and large groups rather than with individuals, computers improve peer interaction in both regular and special education.

- Computers do not automatically depress creativity in either group or result in dehumanized schools or curricula.

- Computer instruction is neither better nor worse than traditional instruction. Whether disabled or nondisabled students benefit depends on the way teachers implement computer instruction.

- Teachers of disabled and nondisabled students have positive attitudes about computers but use them in isolated ways. They seldom integrate computers into the instructional mainstream.

A great deal of research shows that drill-and-practice software is the most commonly used software in special education. Thormann and colleagues (1987) reviewed all the available research in which teachers listed complaints about educational software. The most common complaint about drill-and-practice software was that very little of it could be modified to meet the diverse needs of students. Specifically, teachers complained that most software did not allow teachers to vary either presentation rate or response rate. They also criticized the lack of provision for teachers to submit their own content, such as spelling or vocabulary words. Furthermore, teachers felt that the predetermined software content did not fit the school curriculum. Even more seriously, they complained that most software violated basic principles of good instructional design or teaching methodologies, particularly in regard to reinforcement and corrective feedback techniques.

Vockell and Schwartz (1992) provide useful recommendations aimed at preventing the misuse of drill-and-practice software:

- Because productive drill should result in students providing the correct answer at least 90 to 95 percent of the time, use drill-and-practice software only during the practice and never during the learning stage.

- The teacher should ensure that students thoroughly understand the material before using drill-and-practice software.

- Use drill-and-practice software sparingly. Restrict such use to no more than fifteen-minute sessions at the elementary level and no more than thirty-minute sessions at the secondary level.

- Regard drill-and-practice software as a way only to reinforce material that was successfully taught some other way.

- Stop drill-and-practice sessions the moment that students appear frustrated or bored. If drill and practice is not stopped at this point, students will conclude that the topic or concept itself is difficult or boring or that understanding of the material is irrelevant.

Howell (1990) reviews research on the use of word processing with disabled children and concludes that such children are frequently hampered by their lack of familiarity with the computer keyboard and lack of mastery in the use of the specific word processing software. He suggests that students with disabilities first master keyboarding and the use of specific word processors before teachers begin actual writing instruction, and he cautions that simply providing word processing without such instruction is unlikely to result in improved writing ability for any group of students.

Male investigated word processing in special education and makes the following recommendations for use with children with disabilities:

- Read what the student has written and react to it on a personal level ("After reading that paragraph, I feel like I can almost taste that horrible meal you describe.")

- Help the child clarify or expand his or her writing by asking questions that directly relate to what the child has written. ("What is it about the room that makes it feel cheery?")

- Suggest strategies for expanding or clarifying what the child has written. ("Think back to when you went through the doors into the emergency room. Write about what was going through your mind.")

- Type what the child is saying. The teacher is most likely to type for a student when ideas are flowing and the student is unable to type fast enough to get his or her ideas down or when the student is stuck. Teachers can type short phrases on the computer, based on what the child says aloud, which the student can then expand into complete sentences.

- When the child encounters difficulties with the word processor, help him or her focus on the writing itself by assisting with particularly difficult commands or steps.

- Build the child's self-image as a writer by commenting on the strengths he or she has in common with real authors and by assuring the child that authors share some of his or her same frustrations. (1994, 95)

Lewis (1993) reviews word processors that include features for special learners and devices that can be used with word processors to adapt them for use in special education. For example, she describes a device that modifies input. The device, called "Ke:nx" operates in several different modes:

- Normal keyboard mode, so that students who do not require adapted input can use the same computer as those who do
- Scanning mode, for students who respond by pressing a switch
- On Screen mode, for students who can use the mouse or TouchWindow to make selections from an on-screen keyboard containing letters, words, and/or icons (graphics)
- Alternate keyboard mode, for students who use devices such as the Unicorn Expanded Keyboard, Unicorn Model 510, TASH Mini-keyboard, TASH King Keyboard, or the Key Largo Keyboard
- Morse code input, for students who use one, two, or three switches to send Morse code signals to the computer
- Assisted keyboard mode, for students who can use the standard keyboard with some adaptations
- ASCII mode, to allow students to access the Macintosh through an electronic communication device (1993, 288)

Lewis (1993) also reviews specific word processing programs including programs for beginning writers; with large text displays; that orally read letters, words, or sentences; that run on Macintosh programs; and that predict the next word and offer suggestions. She reviews programs that provide writing aids such as outliners; suggested writing activities and assignments; frozen text (a feature that allows teachers to insert text that cannot be changed by the student); spelling checkers; thesauruses; and grammar and style checkers.

Lazzaro (1993) reviews assistive technology applications that fall into three categories. These are adaptive technologies for people who are blind or visually impaired, for people who are deaf or hard of hearing, and for people with motor or speech impairments.

Applications for people who are blind or visually impaired include word processors that enlarge type or that convert type to synthesized speech; traditional braille; embossed braille; or (by using a tactile display device employing retractable pins) refreshable, paperless braille. Braille notetakers are also available. These can be carried to a class and later connected to a regular or braille printer. Other devices will convert illustrations to raised line drawings so they can be sensed by touch.

Lewis (1993) also reviews programs for use by individuals who are deaf or hard of hearing. She recommends programs that can change the "beeps" that some programs sound as warnings to visual cues. In addition, she suggests that interactive videodiscs have the potential to provide many supplementary aids, such as sign language and various levels of captioning, for deaf individuals.

Microswitches are adaptations of great value for many individuals with motor impairments. These switches can be set to operate under the control of almost any muscle in the body, and they can be set to operate lights, appliances, or a computer. Through the use of microswitches, individuals with motor impairments can gain partial or full control over their physical environments. Such control may help them avoid the development of learned helplessness, a common problem among such individuals.

Many different types of microswitches are on the market, including push switches, pull switches, grasp switches, wobble switches (activated by bending in any direction), pneumatic switches (activated by sucking or puffing on a straw), and sensor switches (activated by extremely small movements). York, Nietupski, and Hamre-Nietupski (1985) provide a useful, six-step decision process to be followed in choosing microswitches.

Another application involves augmentative or alternative communication aids. These applications are for individuals who cannot use normal speech. Augmentative devices are for those who have some speech. Glennen (1992) classifies specific examples of augmentative or alternative communications as either low-technology aids or high-technology aids. Low-technology aids may involve pointing to pictures or letters or may involve gesturing and do not involve computers, printed output, or speech output. According to Glennen, "High technology communication aids have speech output, printed output, or sometimes both output modes. On some systems, the size, location, and type of symbols displayed on the communication aid overlay can be completely customized for the user" (1992, 94).

High technology aids sometimes include the use of prerecorded messages or message prediction strategies. The stored messages are those that are very frequently used, such as greetings or farewells, and users can select them by striking a predetermined key. Message prediction systems scan text as it is input, then use language probabilities to anticipate the next letter or word. The anticipated next letter or word is typed in for the user, who can elect to accept or reject it. This feature greatly simplifies composition by eliminating the need for a great many keystrokes.

High technology aids may employ direct selection or scanning (Glennen 1992). With direct selection, the user points at a specific symbol, often on a special touch screen. If necessary, the pointing can be augmented through the use of headsticks, handsplints, mouthsticks, lightbeams, joysticks, or eyegaze monitors that react to the eye movements of the user. With scanning, the system quickly presents the entire sequence of possibilities, and the user indicates his or her choice. For example, a word processor for individuals with limited fine-motor ability might present a grid of all the letters and other characters at the upper corner of the screen. Each character might be highlighted briefly, and the user strikes the spacebar or uses any of the input aids discussed above when the desired character is highlighted.

PREDICTIONS FOR THE FUTURE

Making predictions about technology is hazardous. The so-called "futurists" have not done a good job with regard to technology. For example, ten years ago, no one predicted the evolution of the World Wide Web, yet today, the Web includes more than 100 million Web pages, and one of the more popular search engines (AltaVista) is used by more than 18 million different users each month to perform more than 20 million searches of the Web each day (Digital Equipment Corporation 1997). In fact, with regard to technology, the predictions of futurists have almost always been far less startling than what actually takes place. Nevertheless, some predictions most likely can be made safely with regard to technology and special education. These predictions stem from observing some of today's problems in the field:

- *Better solutions will be found to some of the financing problems for technology in special education.* Although excellent technological solutions to some special education problems have been developed, many of these are very expensive. Because demand is low, they cannot be mass produced. It is unclear who, if anyone, is responsible for paying for such technology, and many individuals who could benefit from it do not currently have access to sufficient resources.

- *Technological aids that are currently available will become much easier to use and will require much less maintenance.* Many people with disabilities have tried specialized technology such as the Optacon (a device for translating print into tactile impulses for individuals who are blind) and have abandoned them for lower technology such as braille. Some of these individuals express disillusionment with technological solutions because they are so difficult to learn to use and because they seem to break down at the exact times when they are most needed.

- *Preservice and in-service technology education for educators will improve greatly.* Many studies have shown that such training is inadequate and is a major stumbling block to effective implementation in both general and special education.

- *More and better research will be done to investigate the use of technology in special education.*

- *The Internet and World Wide Web will continue to improve and will continue to grow in importance.* More and more classrooms will gain access to them.

The above predictions seem highly likely to take place based on current trends. Another even more likely and more general prediction is that technology will continue to become more important in both general and special education. Undoubtedly, other developments will happen that are, at the moment, completely unpredictable. If the last ten years are any indication, many of these new developments will be both startling and exciting. We certainly have cause for cautious optimism about the future. If educators and policymakers avoid the error of assuming that technology should be brought into schools simply "because it is there" and if efforts are made to balance Type I and Type II applications, then computers and information technology have the potential to become the most important innovation in the history of special education.

REFERENCES

Boocock, S. S. 1980. *Sociology of education: An introduction.* 2d ed. Boston: Houghton Mifflin.

Digital Equipment Corporation. 1997. *Digital's AltaVista search site unveils largest and freshest web index.* Available: http://www.altavista.digital.com/av/content/pr101497.htm.

Dreyfus, H. L. 1992. *What computers still can't do.* Cambridge, Mass.: MIT Press.

Ely, D. P. 1993. Computers in schools and universities in the United States of America. *Educational Technology* 33:53–57.

Glennen, S. 1992. Augmentative and alternative communication. In *The handbook of assistive technology,* ed. G. Church and S. Glennen, 93–122. San Diego: Singular Publishing Group.

Hannaford, A. E. 1993. Computers and exceptional individuals. In *Computers and exceptional individuals,* 2d ed., ed. J. Lindsey, 3–26. Austin: Pro-Ed.

Hoelscher, K. 1986. Computing and information: Steering student learning. *Computers in the Schools* 3:23–34.

Howell, R. 1990. Technology and change in special education: An interactional perspective. *Theory into Practice* 29:276–82.

Kneller, G. F. 1965. *Educational anthropology: An introduction.* New York: Wiley.

Lazzaro, J. J. 1993. *Adaptive technologies for learning and word environments.* Chicago: American Library Association.

Leuhrmann, A. 1994. Computers: More than latest in ed-tech: Why technology has so little impact in schools. In *Computers in education,* 6th ed., ed. J. J. Hirschbuhl, 6–8. Guilford, Conn.: Dushkin.

Lewis, R. B. 1993. *Special education technology: Classroom applications.* Pacific Grove, Calif.: Brooks/Cole.

Maddux, C. D., and R. E. Cummings. 1986. Educational computing at the crossroads: Type I or Type II uses to predominate? *Educational Technology* 26 (7):34–38.

———. In press. *An introduction to special education.* Columbus, Ohio: Merrill.

Maddux, C. D., and D. L. Johnson. 1997. The World Wide Web: History, cultural context, and a manual for developers of educational information-based Web sites. *Educational Technology* 37:5–12.

Maddux, C. D., D. L. Johnson, and J. W. Willis. 1997. *Educational computing: Learning with tomorrow's technologies.* 2d ed. Boston: Allyn and Bacon.

Male, M. 1994. *Technology for inclusion.* 2d ed. Boston: Allyn and Bacon.

Masotto, T. 1995. *Commerce Net/Nielsen Internet demographics survey executive summary.* Available: <http://www.commerce.net/work/pilot/nielsen_96/exec_95.html> (accessed on Jan. 6, 1999). Cupertino, Calif.: Commerce Net.

McDaniels, G. 1996. *How many computers do schools really need?* Available: <http://www.skellsbank.com/garry3.html>. Novato, Calif.: The Learning Company.

Okolo, C. M., C. M. Bahr, and H. J. Rieth. 1993. A retrospective view of computer-based instruction. *Journal of Special Education Technology* 12:1–27.

Papert, S. 1980. *Mindstorms: Children, computers, and powerful ideas.* New York: Basic Books.

President's Committee of Advisors on Science and Technology. 1997. *Report to the president on the use of technology to strengthen k–12 education in the United States.* Washington, D.C.: President's Committee of Advisors on Science and Technology.

Quality Education Data. 1995. *Technology in public schools.* 14th ed. Denver: Quality Education Data.

Roblyer, M. D., J. Edwards, and M. A. Havriluk. 1997. *Integrating educational technology into teaching.* Columbus, Ohio: Merrill.

Sawyer, R. J., and K. Zantal-Wiener. 1993. Emerging trends in technology for students with disabilities. *Teaching Exceptional Children* 26:70–77.

Simonson, M. R., and A. Thompson. 1997. *Educational computing foundations.* Columbus, Ohio: Merrill.

Thormann, J., R. Gersten, L. Moore, and M. Morvant. 1987. Microcomputers in special education classrooms: Themes from research and implications for practice. *Computers in the Schools* 3 (3/4):97–109.

Vockell, E. L., and E. M. Schwartz. 1992. *The computer in the classroom.* 2d ed. New York: Mitchell McGraw-Hill.

York, J., J. Nietupski, and S. Hamre-Nietupski. 1985. A decision-making process for using microswitches. *Journal of the Association for the Severely Handicapped* 10:214–23.

6

Teacher Education: Reform and Restructuring

Thomas W. Sileo   *Mary Anne Prater*

Numerous issues and policies—social, political, and economic—influence education reform and restructuring at all levels. This chapter explores considerations related to litigation and legislation, approaches to educational assessment and service delivery, and technological applications to education. The focus of the discussions concerns children and youth with disabilities and others who may be at risk of educational failure. The discussions also have a direct relationship to postsecondary education and the field of teacher preparation, particularly as we consider the need to prepare special educators to work with diverse student populations.

This chapter considers reform and restructuring in teacher education and focuses primarily on the importance of preparing special educators with competencies in multicultural education. Within the discussion, we address the ever changing demographics in public school settings and the misrepresentation of children and youth from diverse racial, ethnic, and cultural backgrounds who receive special education services. Next, we discuss teacher supply and demand as well as the concomitant need to recruit college and university students with diverse backgrounds into special education teacher preparation programs and retain them. Finally, we consider curricular and pedagogical changes that must occur in teacher education to adequately prepare all teachers for a changing school population.

CHANGING DEMOGRAPHICS

We live in an ever changing society that is characterized by diversity in all aspects of our daily lives, especially our educational systems. Projections indicate that the elementary and secondary public school populations in the United States are expected to increase approximately 12 percent and 28 percent, respectively, by the year 2005, at which time an estimated 55.9 million students will be enrolled in America's schools (National Center for Educational Statistics 1995). Growth is particularly acute in the southern and western geographic regions of the country as a result of increased births and migration.

Significant changes in school demographics also result from increasing numbers of immigrants who enter the United States. A recent report from the U.S. Census offers new evidence of the expanding diversity in the country (cited in "Ethnic diversity ..." 1999; "One American ..." 1999). The report, which considers the population changes between 1990 and 1998, indicates that 9.3 percent of the nation's population is foreign born, with new arrivals emigrating primarily from countries to the south and east of the United States. The report also indicates that the African American population increased almost 13 percent, due in large part to an influx of 7 million immigrants. African Americans remain the largest underrepresented minority population and comprise approximately 34.4 million people or 12.7 percent of the approximate 270 million people living in the United States.

Hispanics comprise one of the largest foreign-born groups immigrating to the U.S., however. The number of Hispanics, already one of the largest underrepresented groups, swelled more than 35 percent between 1990 and 1998. Hispanics now make up 30.3 million people or 11 percent of the overall population and are expected to overtake the non-Hispanic Black population by the year 2004. The Hispanic population is the most varied group and consists of Cubans, Puerto Ricans, Mexicans, and Latin Americans, among others; approximately 10.7 million Hispanics are foreign born.

Asians and Pacific Islanders, however, evidenced the most growth and increased more than 40 percent; they now comprise roughly 10.5 million people or 4 percent of the total population. A similar phenomenon occurred during 1980–1990, when the growth among the Asian and Pacific Islander population exceeded that of African Americans and Hispanics, collectively, primarily because of the growing numbers of immigrants and refugees from East and Southeast Asia (Harry 1992). Approximately 6.4 million Asian and Pacific Islanders are recent immigrants whereas only 4.1 million Asian Pacific Islanders are born in the United States. Projections indicate that within the next ten years, the U.S. population will be composed primarily of African Americans, Hispanics, Asian Pacific Islanders, and Native Americans as well as other non-White, non-Hispanic groups from South Asia and the former communist bloc countries (Hodgkinson 1992).

In addition to recent immigrants, diversity among school-aged students includes an ever increasing number of children and youth who are of mixed racial backgrounds and are members of indigenous groups such as Native Alaskans, Eskimos, Hawaiians, and Native Americans. School demographics also reflect a composite of students who differ regarding the length of time they have been in the country, individual and ethnic identities, and changing family constellations. Many of these youngsters typically live in less affluent neighborhoods, and their backgrounds may include factors such as low socioeconomic levels and poverty, single-parent families, low parent education levels, inner-city housing, and limited English proficiency, all of which are associated traditionally with high risk for poor student outcomes (McWhirter et al. 1998; Rodriguez 1998).

The majority of public school teachers, in contrast, are from middle-class socioeconomic levels and live in the suburbs; they normally reside in communities other than those in which they teach. Consequently, they are removed from the cultures of their school communities and may have few shared experiences with—and may lack understanding about—the children and parents with whom they interact (Koerner and Hulsebosch 1996). These teachers are often unable to provide equal access to meaningful educational opportunities for the youngsters in their classes whose cultures differ from their own cultural background and values (Bradfield-Krieder 1999; Wald 1996).

Sociocultural diversity is greater within the general population than among teachers. Only 58 percent of the nation's public schools have any teachers who are members of diverse racial, ethnic, and cultural groups (Henke et al. 1996). The differences between the teaching force and the school population create a potential lack of cultural compatibility in school settings, which may result in inadequate or inappropriate services to students (Shimabukuro 1998; Wald 1996). Approximately 32 percent of all public school students in the nation represent non-White racial, ethnic, and cultural populations whereas only 14 percent of their teachers are from similar heritages (Choy et al. 1993; Henke et al. 1996). A similar situation may be found in special education where the student population is increasing in diversity while the teaching force remains predominantly White, middle-class, and female (Cook and Boe 1995).

In addition to the discrepancy between the racial, ethnic, and cultural backgrounds of teachers and students, the number of teachers from traditionally underrepresented populations continues to decline despite an increase in enrollment trends among these groups in teacher preparation programs (Wald 1996). The projections in the early 1990s—which indicated that fewer than 5 percent of public school teachers would represent racially, ethnically, and culturally diverse populations at the beginning of the millennium (American Association of State Colleges and Universities 1991)—have become a reality. In 1994, the American Association of Colleges for Teacher Education (AACTE) estimated that 88 percent of all undergraduate students who were enrolled in teacher preparation programs nationwide were White. Twelve percent comprised African Americans, Hispanics, Asian Americans, and Native Americans (AACTE 1994). Finally, the attrition rate among teachers from underrepresented populations is significantly higher than among their White colleagues (Henke et al. 1996; Wald 1996).

SPECIAL EDUCATION REPRESENTATION OF DIVERSE STUDENTS WITH DISABILITIES

Disproportionate numbers of students from diverse backgrounds are often inappropriately identified with disabilities and misrepresented in special education programs (Adger et al. 1993; Artiles and Trent 1994; Chinn and Hughes 1987; Fleishner and Van Acker 1990; Grossman 1995; Harry 1992; Ramirez 1990). The phenomenon, of over- and underrepresentation of students from linguistically and culturally diverse heritages, which has persisted throughout the years, continues today. For example, African American, Native American, and Pacific Islander students tend to be overrepresented in classes for students with emotional and behavior disorders, learning disabilities, and mental retardation. Hispanic students tend to be overrepresented in programs for students with learning disabilities. Students from each of these population groups are more likely to be underrepresented in programs for those identified as gifted and talented (Grossman 1995; Harry 1992; Hawaii State Department of Education 1994). Asian American students, in contrast, tend to be underrepresented in the areas of learning disabilities as well as emotional and behavior disorders, and they tend to be overrepresented in programs for students with speech disorders (Grossman 1995; Hawaii State Department of Education 1994).

Data substantiate the overrepresentation of many indigenous children and youth who receive special education services. The data also indicate that students in this same group are represented in disproportionately large numbers in many social and physical demographic statistics that indicate special educational needs: high levels of poverty, low levels of maternal education, excessive incidences of child abuse and neglect, remarkably high use of drugs and alcohol, retention in grade level, inordinate absences in secondary school, and increased dropout rates (Children's Defense Fund 1999; Oswald et al. 1999).

CONTRIBUTING VARIABLES

A number of variables contribute to the increasing numbers of students from diverse backgrounds who are at risk of educational failure and for the identification of a disability. These factors may include a lack of balance between teachers and students who share linguistic and cultural backgrounds, as noted above; school district size and concentration of diverse students; inadequate teacher preparation; and attitudinal considerations (Harry 1992; Oswald et al. 1999; Rice 1998).

Quite often, teachers are not prepared adequately to address the sociocultural needs of students from diverse backgrounds; they may find the students' presence in the classroom unsettling and even disruptive at times. Students may not present a "goodness of fit" with teachers' perceptions of a standardized educational delivery system and Eurocentric instructional practices (Carey, Boscardin, and Fontes 1994; Garcia and Malkin 1993; Grossman 1995). Students from diverse backgrounds experience difficulty in classroom settings despite the efforts that have been made to prepare teachers to be culturally sensitive and responsive to their academic and social learning needs (Welch 1996).

Teachers' attitudes and reactions to diverse student populations are extremely important because they influence classroom climate as well as students' self-concept, sense of belonging, and expectations for achievement and behavior. Teachers' beliefs determine whether they acknowledge and assume responsibility to address students' academic and social learning needs in a culturally responsive manner or whether they shift the responsibility to others (Talbert-Johnson and Cochran 1999). Language and color barriers often separate students from the educational institutions they attend and place them at greater risk for educational and behavioral difficulties, as well as for discrimination and cultural bias related to referrals and assessments for special education and related services (Adger, Wolfram, and Detwyler 1993; Grossman 1995; Lambie and Daniels-Mohring 1993).

Educators acknowledge the disparities in the educational outcomes for many students from diverse backgrounds. Students may not receive an appropriate, responsive education that enables them to experience academic success. For example, their educational programs may have little or no relevance to their family and community cultures, languages, and values. In addition, they may be threatened by ostensibly unrealistic expectations for academic and behavioral performance and, therefore, become easily distracted and seemingly unmotivated in school settings. Quite often, they become alienated from family members, peers, and teachers. Students' feelings of isolation may lead them to drop out of school, become gang members, and engage in criminal behavior.

It is incumbent on schools and teachers, therefore, to make appropriate accommodations and to create educational environments that address the academic and social learning needs of all students. In essence, by continuing to ignore the changing demographics among school populations, we deny equal access to educational opportunities to America's diverse populations, we sustain negative attitudes that disenfranchise students and perpetuate their concomitant academic failure, and we reinforce social class and racial stratification (Sileo, Sileo, and Prater 1996).

TEACHER SUPPLY AND DEMAND

The United States is currently experiencing a nationwide teacher shortage. It is estimated that more than 2 million new teachers will be needed within the next ten years (National Commission on Teaching and America's Future 1996). These estimates are based on the projected increases and changing demographics in school-aged populations, as noted above, and on the current supply of teachers and identified shortages in content-area disciplines and geographic regions. High-poverty communities face the greatest challenge in recruiting, supporting, and retaining new teachers. Current attrition rates suggest that schools in lower-socioeconomic and high-poverty areas will need an excess of 700,000 teachers over the next decade. Approximately one-half of those additional teachers will be first-time teachers (Henke et al. 1996).

The available supply of teachers is dwindling, as evidenced by the approximate annual attrition and retirement rates of 7 percent and 30 percent, respectively. In addition, the "graying" of America's teachers is a major factor with which we must contend within the next decade as the teachers who were born during the baby-boom years approach retirement age. The projected wave of retirements portends severe teacher shortages for disadvantaged urban and rural schools as well as in the fields of special education, bilingual education, mathematics, and science (Henke et al. 1996).

The current pool of teaching students nationwide may not fill the demand for new teachers, considering the minimal number who enter teacher preparation programs and the concomitant low number of program completers who actually apply for teaching positions. Many individuals with high qualifications, especially women and members of populations traditionally underrepresented in education, are often drawn to more lucrative and prestigious professions. Circumstances that contribute to their decisions to choose other professions include readily available financial aid packages that offset college tuition and living costs, equal employment opportunities and affirmative action standards, a perceived lack of societal respect for teachers, the notion that "those who can—do, and those who can't—teach," low salary levels in comparison to other professions, poor working conditions, and national conditions of employment (Sileo and Edelen-Smith 1993). In addition, the length and more stringent entry and exit requirements of teacher education programs—especially exit requirements that necessitate passing national or state examinations in basic skills, content areas, and pedagogy—are often cited as reasons for not enrolling in teacher preparation programs (Wald 1996).

Teachers' initial classroom experiences may be both personally and professionally difficult, and without support, approximately 22 percent of new teachers leave the field within their first three years of employment. Attrition rates in urban districts can reach 50 percent during the first five years of employment. Reasons that are attributed to the high attrition rates include new teachers' perceived lack of support for and investment in their personal and professional well-being by the public schools (Recruiting New Teachers 1997). Another variable may include the continually changing roles and responsibilities of classroom teachers in which they are required to develop and carry out an ever expanding curriculum that addresses family values, social skills education, and prevention education programs in the areas of domestic and school violence, drug and alcohol abuse, and HIV/AIDS, among others. Specific factors that contribute to the high attrition rate among special education teachers concern conditions of employment that often include ill-equipped classrooms, limited supplies, an overwhelming amount of paperwork, and students who have widely differing abilities. In addition, special education teachers often teach in isolation from their peers, under the direction of multiple supervisors, and as consultants and advocates in a system that experiences a constant state of flux and opposition from employers and peers (Sileo and Edelen-Smith 1993; Wald 1997, 1998). A high attrition rate among special education teachers undermines the quality of education not only because it affects the number of vacant positions in a school but also because it affects the number of positions that must be filled by unqualified teachers (Wald 1998).

The demand for teachers is not uniform. In general, surpluses may be found in elementary education, English, and social studies education; yet these surpluses may decrease depending on the projected teacher retirements as noted above. Currently, the shortages are primarily in special education, bilingual and multicultural education, and the secondary academic content fields of mathematics and science (Henke et al. 1996). In addition, teachers who are hired in these fields may not possess the appropriate teaching qualifications. For example, a remarkable number of public school teachers whose primary assignments are in foreign language (13 percent), English (25 percent), mathematics (34 percent), science (40 percent), and social studies (59 percent) lack suitable subject-area majors or minors in their respective teaching fields. The problem of underprepared teachers is exacerbated in high-poverty schools where more than 50 percent of the teachers may not have a college major or minor in their primary teaching field (Henke et al. 1996). Estimates indicate a range of 10 percent to 30 percent of teachers who lack the appropriate credentials in the field of special education (Cook and Boe 1995; National Commission on Teaching and America's Future 1996).

Teacher shortages in special education have existed for more than a decade as evidenced by the overall 35 percent national decline in the number of special education teacher training program graduates. For example, in 1991, the National Center for Education Statistics reported that the 15,543 graduates in special education teacher preparation met only 55 percent of the demand for special education teachers. This shortage, coupled with the increasing numbers of students identified with disabilities, has resulted in a critical need for qualified special education teachers, especially those who are prepared to work in the area of emotional and behavior disorders. The shortage of qualified special education teachers necessitates that school districts and universities support programs that promote professional success and satisfaction in the early years of teaching, thereby increasing the likelihood of retaining qualified teachers in the profession (Cheney, Krajewski, and Combs 1992).

Recruitment and Retention

The recruitment of qualified special education teachers to work in urban, rural, and geographically remote school districts with a high proportion of students from lower socioeconomic levels and diverse backgrounds remains a challenge. Some states and school districts, therefore, are making concerted efforts to address current and future teacher shortages and to balance the racial, ethnic, and cultural representation among teachers and students. These efforts include enticements such as (1) increased salaries, cash bonuses, and reimbursements for the cost of education; (2) incentive funding programs, such as tuition waivers, for public, four-year institutions to recruit students in high-demand areas; (3) alternative routes to special education teacher credentials that target military personnel, former teachers, professionals making midcareer changes, and those who were prepared as teachers but never entered the profession; and (4) teacher induction programs designed to increase novice teachers' competencies in content and pedagogy as well as classroom organization and management skills to ensure their retention in the profession (Rodriguez 1998).

The disproportionate ratios among students and special education teachers from similar backgrounds and the increasing numbers of linguistically and culturally diverse school-age students necessitate that colleges and universities recruit and retain individuals from like student populations to the teaching profession. Diverse cultural representation among the teaching force helps to prepare all children and youth for citizenship in pluralistic societies. It provides students with an enriched and diverse educational experience, ensures equitable opportunities, and provides role models for all students (Craft 1996). Diversity also promotes awareness of cross-cultural understanding, tolerance, and collaboration among school personnel as well as heightened cultural decision making. Although no clear evidence supports the idea that students of color learn better when taught by teachers of color (Ladson-Billings 1994), research does indicate that teachers from underrepresented populations often engage in culturally responsive instruction, using communication styles that are similar to students' home and community settings (Au and Mason 1981; Foster 1994). Other studies suggest that teachers who share students' cultural backgrounds may be more effective in maintaining classroom discipline, establishing ongoing communication with family members, and reducing the numbers of students who are referred for special education services (Ewing 1995; Garcia and Malkin 1993; Meier, Stewart, and England 1989).

The recruitment of university students from underrepresented populations cannot be separated from efforts to retain them once they enter teacher preparation programs. A number of guiding principles may enhance student recruitment and retention endeavors to ensure that minority students complete their programs and graduate at a rate similar to other students. First, teacher educators must acknowledge the diversity within and among underrepresented student populations. Inter- and intragroup differences may include variables of class, subcultures, family affiliations and loyalties, gender definitions, and role perceptions, among others. We therefore must devise and implement numerous ways to attract and support students.

Second, we should recognize that all students need assistance in setting and attaining goals. Students from underrepresented populations are often the first generation of family members to attend college; they may need institutional support, such as career counseling, and opportunities to reflect on career directions. It is also critical to provide students with various support networks during their initial semesters of enrollment in a special education teacher preparation program. These support networks include a range of campus-based services such as tutoring; instruction in study skills, note taking, and test preparation; and assistance with developmental reading, writing, and mathematics skills. In addition, we should create communities of learners with a common goal or focus, who can help each other as tutors, academic advisors, mentors, editors, consultants, and sources of encouragement (Lewis 1997). One means of creating learning communities is to rely on a cohorted approach to teacher preparation.

Third, intangibles such as campus climate and classroom environment are important to facilitating students' subject matter mastery. University students often become disenchanted and disengaged if they cannot relate to instructional materials and teaching approaches or if they are unable to derive personal meaning and satisfaction from their learning. We must ensure, therefore, that curriculum, instruction, and assessment practices are set within appropriate contexts, are culturally sensitive, and are responsive to students' backgrounds, values, and learning styles.

Fourth, institutional leadership and commitment that supports underrepresented students and responds to special education teacher shortage areas must be highly visible. Task forces, committees, and department commissions of universities, colleges, and states must provide students with educational and moral support as well as financial resources to help them reach their career goals. Institutional commitment to diversity is also demonstrated by actively recruiting faculty members with diverse heritages and others who have varied experiences with racial, ethnic, and cultural groups; by forming partnership agreements with schools and school districts that have large numbers of underrepresented students; and by systematically providing professional development for teacher education faculty regarding the various aspects of educating teachers for diversity (Zeichner 1996). Faculty development programs may consider the following ways to improve teacher education for diversity and to enhance the teaching and learning climate in higher education: infuse multicultural content throughout the teacher education curriculum; create an enabling learning environment; prepare teachers for language-related issues, including culturally sensitive instructional strategies and assessment of student learning; and ensure that teacher preparation textbooks and instructional materials reflect diverse populations.

Finally, a recruitment and retention plan is likely to be more effective if progress is evaluated with systematic and thorough data collection, analysis, and synthesis processes. Ongoing monitoring of program efforts and outcomes should be a collaborative undertaking among university faculty members and student support services personnel.

Teacher education plays a pivotal role in cultivating a teaching force that skillfully enhances individual opportunities and identities, in expanding the talent pool, in contributing to the economy, and in strengthening social cohesion (Craft 1996). The recruitment and retention of preservice teachers who represent culturally diverse populations, therefore, is an important function of special education teacher preparation. The efforts that colleges and universities make to support diverse students help to identify culturally responsive assessment and instructional practices that form a foundation for improving the learning behaviors and academic achievement of racially, ethnically, and culturally diverse university students as well as for informing teacher preparation programs of needed changes.

Special Education Teacher Preparation Programs

Special education teacher preparation programs can be catalysts. These programs can provide preservice teachers with training that promotes cultural diversity by ensuring that, as program graduates, they are well prepared to teach children and youth from diverse racial, ethnic, and cultural backgrounds. Future teachers must be taught appropriate instructional strategies that will ensure the success of diverse student populations and that will empower and engender confidence in parents and other family members to become partners in their children's education (Sileo and Prater 1998). This is critically important given the recent reform related to restructuring teacher education and infusing multicultural competencies into the curriculum (Cochran-Smith 1991; National Commission on Teaching and America's Future 1996; Zeichner and Hoeft 1996).

The charge to special education teacher educators, therefore, is to transform university courses to ensure that they address multicultural curricular and pedagogical considerations and that they promote tolerance of and appreciation for all diverse cultures, ideas, and perspectives. Teacher education faculty are responsible for preparing all teachers to hold all students to the same high academic standards (Zeichner 1996). In essence, these faculty are models as they integrate the principles of multicultural education, provide field-centered experiences, and use appropriate instructional strategies (Bell and Munn 1997/1998). They are responsible for ensuring that education—at both the k–12 and college levels—offers a global view of human affairs that concerns the evolution and interconnectedness of human cultures (Craft 1996).

CURRICULAR CONSIDERATIONS

Special educators who are preparing to teach in today's schools must increase their multicultural competencies, develop a clear understanding of the multicultural worlds in which they and their students reside, and learn how to celebrate and share these cultures with others. Preparation programs, therefore, must promote the value and strength of diversity within society by ensuring that future teachers gain the necessary knowledge to interact with students and family members from varying cultural backgrounds, nurture pride in students' cultural heritage, foster human rights and alternative life choices, and develop positive understandings of and attitudes toward diverse cultures (Sileo and Prater 1998; Sileo, Sileo, and Prater 1996).

Banks (1994, 1996) identified five practices that must be considered when developing culturally responsive instruction. They include (1) curricular integration of concepts, principles, and theories across diverse groups; (2) knowledge construction whereby students understand the interactions and contributions of diverse populations to culture and civilization; (3) prejudice reduction and the promotion of positive regard toward all populations; (4) pedagogical equity and use of instructional strategies that complement students' cultures, learning, and behavior styles; and (5) the empowerment of school cultures and social structures to advance social justice and to ensure that all students experience educational equity.

As an overriding theme, special education preparation programs should enhance teachers' awareness of and sensitivity to their own cultural values and ethics as bases for ensuring that their interactions with diverse students facilitate equitable educational opportunities. In essence, teachers must veer from traditional ways of looking at and thinking about their worlds and, if necessary, confront the values that shape their exchanges with students. In addition, preparation programs should provide teachers with knowledge of and foster sensitivity to students' language and cultural characteristics and should develop their cognizance of diversity within and among cultural groups, while at the same time avoiding homogeneity and stereotypical beliefs.

Some commonality exists within and among various racial, ethnic, and cultural groups. However, we must also acknowledge the diversity within their languages, religions, and perceptions of life. It may be helpful to remember the saying "each individual is like all other people, like some other people, and like no other person" as we consider the variance within and across diverse populations. For example, when considering American Indians and Native Alaskans, educators should acknowledge the heterogeneity that exists across the various Indian tribes, Aleuts, and Eskimos, among others. Although a certain cultural heritage and worldview are shared by many Native Americans, "tribal differences are very real and tribal affiliations are quite important to Indian people.... There is no such thing as a single 'Indian' culture. Navajos are as different culturally from the Sioux as Canadians are from Mexicans" (Little Soldier 1990, 66, 68). Similar situations exist within African American, Hispanic, Asian American, and Pacific Islander populations. It is imperative that educators understand the many cultures that students bring into the classroom.

Language, as a communication and interaction tool, is the foundation for students' success in school. Special education teachers, therefore, must develop sensitivity to the dynamics of linguistic diversity, including nonstandard language dialects and the pragmatics of language—such as when to speak and what to discuss. For example, language characteristics of Asian and Pacific Americans that contribute to their being overidentified for special education services may include phonology difficulties, traditional reliance on oral communication, and use of dialects such as Hawaii Creole English (Sileo and Prater 1998; Trueba, Cheng, and Ima 1993).

Nonverbal communication styles also vary across cultures (Sileo and Prater 1998; Sileo, Sileo, and Prater 1996). Touching a child's head, for example, may be considered threatening or offensive in several cultures, yet other touching is a sign of friendship or affection. Lack of eye contact may indicate, among other things, deference to and respect for adults. When interacting with students of Hispanic, Native American, or Asian backgrounds, lack of eye contact is often misinterpreted by teachers, however, as an indication of disrespect or disinterest in the conversation. For example, Luis is expected to look the teacher in the eye when he is talking to her, yet at home, such eye contact would be considered defiance of parental authority.

Special education teachers also need to be aware of students' working styles. Some Asian Americans are concerned with task orientation, personal achievement, and independence. Pacific Islander students, in contrast, generally maintain a group focus through cooperative work and dependency on others. Variations in working styles affect structures within the traditional American educational system that have often relied on independent assignments and fostered competition among students.

In addition, special educators must consider the effect of cultural background on students' behavioral styles, especially when interpreting behavior, defining defiance, and designing appropriate management systems that are intended to foster achievement and behavioral change. For example, students may react differently to personal praise. Many Asian Americans are modest and humble about their achievements and do not seek public recognition. They may indicate less than they know and not volunteer knowledge. Similarly, Hawaiian students are often embarrassed by excessive praise (Sileo and Prater 1998).

Special education teachers should also identify as role models individuals who represent a wide variety of cultural backgrounds and who promote positive images of diverse cultural groups. In addition, instructional approaches must be appropriate and sensitive to students' cultural identity. For example, the focus on time in classrooms may be very different for students from a variety of cultural backgrounds. European cultures place a great emphasis on using time wisely. Native Americans and Pacific Islanders, however, may be less time-conscious and may focus more on the task; for them, time is flexible. Sileo and colleagues (1998) indicated that when they were not very well-grounded in Native-American cultural values and working as novice teachers on the Navajo Indian Reservation, they were often intrigued with the notion of Navajo time in which an event began when people arrived—perhaps fifteen or more minutes later than the scheduled time.

Cultures also differ in the degree to which they value individualization, cooperation, and competitiveness. This information should affect the special education teacher's design for instruction. Students from cultural groups that endorse collaborative processes, for example, will respond well to cooperative learning and peer tutoring opportunities. In addition, many cultures reinforce the principles that rely on teacher-directed instruction. In some Polynesian cultures, for example, children are expected to watch and memorize to learn how to do something. Modeling, repetition, and practice, therefore, may promote effective learning in students from the Hawaiian cultural background (Sileo and Prater 1998).

Special education teachers who are sensitive to the diverse communication, curricular, and pedagogical needs of the students in their classes, then, rely on instructional strategies that recognize learning as a process whereby students create and construct new meanings within the context of their current knowledge. These teachers provide instructional opportunities that enable students to integrate information across modalities and to interact physically with the learning environment. New experiences are related to learners' developmental levels, interests, and problems.

Culture-specific strategies that are designed to increase preservice teachers' awareness of their personal cultures and inherent values as well as their sensitivity to linguistic differences and cultural values may be found in Prater, Sileo, and Sileo (1997), Sileo and Prater (1998), Sileo, Sileo, and Prater (1996), Thorp (1997), and Voltz (1994, 1995). The authors also consider teachers' interactions with and their advocacy roles on behalf of children and youth with disabilities, their parents, and other family members as a foundation for developing realistic parental involvement programs.

Pedagogical Considerations

Special education teacher preparation programs are becoming increasingly more diverse than in past years, as demonstrated by the growing percentage of students from diverse cultural heritages and language backgrounds, nontraditional career-change students, and students with disabilities who are enrolled in preparation programs. Therefore, when transforming university courses to ensure that special education teachers are culturally sensitive and responsive to the diverse student populations with whom they work in public school settings, faculty must go beyond merely infusing multicultural content knowledge into the courses. Multicultural course transformations in higher education require that faculty in special education teacher preparation programs adhere to the same practices as those addressed above regarding curricular considerations. In addition, they should design and deliver programs that model cultural inclusiveness and that use culturally sensitive curricular materials as well as instructional and assessment strategies that are appropriate to the diverse university students who are enrolled in teacher preparation programs.

The application of culturally sensitive and responsive instructional considerations in special education teacher preparation programs has a dual benefit. First, it models effective pedagogical approaches that may be replicated by university students in their own classrooms. Second, it illustrates faculty's sensitivity to the academic and social learning needs of university students from diverse backgrounds.

Curricular Materials

Textbooks and instructional materials that use politically correct language, portray positive images of diverse cultural groups, and acknowledge those groups' contributions to society help faculty to integrate content about diversity issues into university courses. These materials also help develop students' awareness of diversity and reduce prejudice (Banks 1994). Educators of special education teachers, therefore, must be aware how textbooks and other curricular materials treat diversity. They should ensure that the texts and materials represent a wide range of diversity, particularly as it concerns the students in their university classes and the cultural groups with whom their students will interact as future teachers (Prater, Sileo, and Sileo 1997).

The textbooks and instructional materials should also be free of biases that may debase specific populations. These biases may include (1) *invisibility*, whereby specific racial, ethnic, and cultural populations as well as women, individuals with disabilities, and the aged are either neglected or underrepresented; (2) *stereotypes*, in which traditional and rigid roles are ascribed to certain populations; (3) *selectivity and imbalance*, where authors fail to discuss the roles of various groups; and (4) *linguistic bias*, where authors rely solely on masculine pronouns or Anglo names (Hunt and Marshall 1994). Textbooks, for example, may show Cuban Americans engaged in unskilled, semi-skilled, and skilled labor activities such as dishwashing, housekeeping, gardening, and entertaining as long as they are also represented in professional roles such as physicians, teachers, and lawyers.

Textbooks and other curricular materials vary considerably regarding the inclusion of cultural diversity issues and the representation of diverse groups. The coverage should be inclusive and contain both textual and pictorial examples to help ensure that preservice educators are knowledgeable about subject matter and populations. Teacher educators may need to supplement textbooks and curricular materials to enhance both students' sensitivity and the application of their new learning to practical situations (Prater, Sileo, and Sileo 1997; Sileo and Prater 1998).

Field-Centered Special Education Teacher Preparation

Increasing preservice teachers' cultural responsiveness requires a change in special education teacher preparation programs. The programs should model inclusiveness and afford future teachers with opportunities to experience culturally responsive interactions with diverse students, parents, and other family members in contrast to just studying about diversity (Morris et al. 1997; Zeichner and Hoeft 1996). According to Lynch, "honoring differences by providing access to others ... from diverse cultural, language, gender, and racial groups invigorates the curriculum and creates a climate that supports diversity" (1997, 65). Opportunities may be provided through field-centered programs for groups of students that ground special education teacher preparation in practices where preservice teachers complete field-based activities and student teaching experiences in settings that embody the basic tenets of multicultural education. The experiences and accompanying seminars should provide mediated cultural immersions for university students in which they encounter in-depth interactions with children, parents, and colleagues from minority backgrounds as a foundation for developing critical constructs of teaching related to social justice and educational equity (Bradfield-Krieder 1999; Talbert-Johnson and Cochran 1999).

Field-centered special education teacher preparation occurs most often in partnership schools that reflect simultaneous commitment, shared responsibility, and collaboration among university and public school personnel to improve not only the curriculum and instruction for all children and youth but also the quality of special education teacher preparation. Field-centered programs allow preservice special education teachers to become fully acquainted with the complexities of teaching and to learn actively and simultaneously about pedagogical and academic content, diverse students, and the contexts in which teaching and learning occur. For example, candidates may be required to design and implement a culturally responsive and developmentally appropriate curriculum and concomitant instructional activities that address their students' diverse cultural and linguistic needs. As a way to learn about the cultural community, they may also be asked to interview parents and other family members from diverse backgrounds, identifying culturally based perceptions of disability or determining parents' attitudes about the educational system. In essence, students are required to think and act as teachers in situated circumstances where they apply and analyze their newly acquired skills and competencies, identify potential discrepancies with their existing knowledge base, and suggest alternative ways to use and test their new understandings in real-world situations (Goodlad 1990; Holmes Group 1990, 1995; National Commission on Teaching and America's Future 1996).

Instructional Strategies

In many cultures, learning is perceived as worthwhile only when it is relevant to real-world issues and solutions to real-world problems, such as those related to social equity. In addition, learning is worthwhile when it provides opportunities for social interaction. University-level instructional and assessment strategies, therefore, should model cultural inclusiveness and should provide appropriate contextual settings to help university students learn successfully, particularly those from diverse backgrounds. The ensuing discussion considers selected instructional and assessment strategies that seem especially suitable for working with diverse student populations in higher education settings (Lewis 1997; Lynch 1997; Sileo et al. 1998).

Learning Journals

Journal writing is a powerful, reflective practice that promotes adult learning and context-embedded critical thinking (Cooper 1994, 1995). Educators of special education teachers, therefore, may wish to use journals as one means to validate the contributions that preservice teachers make to their own learning and provide accounts of personal observations, impressions, and insights regarding university course content. Journal keeping heightens preservice teachers' awareness of diversity issues, enhances understanding of events in their lives, provides a description of personal and professional growth and problem-solving processes, functions as a means to explore solutions to life's problems, and enables writers to examine and clarify their knowledge and values as the foundation for decision making (Black, Sileo, and Prater 2000; Cooper and Heck 1995).

One way to structure learning journal entries is to rely on the following categories for entries: diary, notebook, dialogue, integrative, and evaluative (Black, Sileo, and Prater 2000; Sileo et al. 1998). The categories afford preservice special education teachers with opportunities to think about student teaching activities, practicum, and course content; to examine the values and assumptions on which their experiences are based; and to construct personal knowledge. Students' journal entries and dialogue with the instructor provide a way for instructors to personalize instruction and get to know students in ways that are seldom possible in class (Lynch 1997). Journals and subsequent dialogues also allow students the privacy to examine difficult issues and the permission to share their thoughts in a safe, nonjudgmental atmosphere. All communication between the instructor and students is confidential; students' reflections allow instructors to provide personalized feedback. The journal is a focusing tool for themes and concepts that are related to diversity issues, where writers refine their learning to higher levels of understanding as they harmonize course content with individual experiences. Students' written products provide a window into their learning and form a basis for university instructors to refine instructional strategies. In addition, they enable instructors to observe students' attempts to make sense of their lives and to construct meaning. One particularly poignant journal entry provides insight into a student's struggle to understand personal issues around diversity. He wrote:

> For the first time, I am really starting to take a look at how race and ethnicity affect my life as a Filipino who was raised in Hawaii. There is a lot going on within the minority populations—primarily cultural issues—and, lot of [sic] energy is going into making connections to our culture, language, rights, and place in society. With this in mind, I wonder if nonminority teachers can make an difference [sic] in children's' [sic] lives. Would a curriculum not have to be integrated or even start with their contributions first and then address other issues? A strong background in students' culture and knowledge of their language would seem necessary because without these, one could not be an effective teacher.

Journals may also serve a specific purpose. For example, in a university course in which we discuss the development of cross-cultural competence, preservice teachers are asked to submit journal entries that focus on ethnic self-awareness. The journal format, adapted from Sorrell (1997), asks students to address the following: (1) ancestors' origins; (2) family description in terms of assimilation, accommodation, segregation, and amalgamation; (3) cultural characteristics and values related to verbal and nonverbal communication, spatial and temporal orientation modes, social and behavioral patterns, and preferred ways of learning; and (4) current functioning levels regarding ethnic identity. The latter aspect of the journal entry asks students to describe themselves in terms of ethnic self-rejection, superiority and ethnocentrism, identity clarification, biethnicity, multi-ethnicity, and global competencies (Banks 1991).

Reflective teachers think about their behaviors and experiences in the context of classroom environments and then make informed and intelligent decisions regarding multicultural curricular and instructional issues as well as their interactions with students. Reflection is critical to effective teaching practices, yet it is often a difficult process because teachers are unable to look objectively at their experiences and because they lack time and structured opportunities for reflection. Preservice special education teachers need a structure, such as journaling, that enables them to grow in reflective teaching practices and in their interactions with students and parents from diverse heritages (Pultorak 1993, 1996).

Videotapes with Peer-assisted Reflection

Peer-assisted reflection is another way to increase students' awareness and understanding of their educational experiences with linguistically and culturally diverse children and youth or their parents. When using videotapes and peer-assisted reflection, special education teacher preparation students videotape themselves while they are engaged in a predetermined learning or assessment activity. The videotaped activity may be viewed in a small peer-group setting in which the preservice teacher requests constructive feedback about particular culturally responsive teaching behaviors. The videotapes, when combined with peer-assisted reflection, encourage preservice students to take an objective critical look at their teaching behaviors and potential roles as teachers. Their ability to reflect about content, process, and the premises on which their instructional decisions are based are central to their future successes with students and parents.

Videotapes give added value to reflection because they provide preservice special educators with the structure and expression of past experiences in field-centered settings. They afford opportunities to think thoroughly and systematically about teaching practices and interactions, alter those behaviors, and become thoughtful practitioners. Using videotapes with peer-assisted reflection is a nonthreatening way to encourage constructive discussion and review of others' teaching behaviors and to reflect on additional learning techniques and activities.

Service Learning

Service learning emphasizes giving to or caring for others as a way to create change in preservice teachers' understanding of the social contexts in which others live, particularly the children and youth in their classes who may reside in impoverished communities (Kahne and Westheimer 1996). In essence, university students volunteer, or "give something back" to schools or communities. They also decenter, or "walk in another's shoes," to develop a foundation for caring relationships and responsiveness to others' needs. Caring involves fostering social reconstruction, acquiring skills to advocate on behalf of students with disabilities, and forming social bonds with parents and other community leaders. University students enjoy using the community as a classroom because it enables them to act as responsible citizens and to engage in complex social endeavors. The community classroom teaches problem solving skills, provides additional means to attain educational objectives, and enhances student teachers' performance on traditional learning measures (Bringle and Hatcher 1996; Kahne and Westheimer 1996).

Service learning practices are an appropriate extension of experiential learning opportunities such as field experiences, practica, student teaching, and internships, all of which are designed to develop preservice special education teachers' professional skills. Experiential learning activities promote powerful outside-of-class learning experiences that help to transform preservice teachers' understanding of course content and social issues, and they are a direct link to preparing special educators to work with diverse students and others at risk for educational failure. Service learning activities provide opportunities for meaningful reflection: University students analyze issues of social concern as a basis for stepping outside of their current understandings to find solutions to problems that may conflict with their own predisposition and self-interests. In essence, students move their newly acquired learning to higher levels of understanding.

Service learning activities provide preservice special education teachers with enriched learning experiences in appropriate contexts that address challenging social issues and that renew communities. They also provide opportunities for interdisciplinary study that connect theory with practice, develop higher-order thinking skills, and promote self-esteem (Bringle and Hatcher 1996; Kahne and Westheimer 1996). They afford university students with "know-how" information that is acquired through active learning—in contrast to "know-about" information that may be acquired passively in a classroom setting (Checkoway 1996).

Role Playing

Role playing is an additional way to provide university students with effective learning experiences in realistic contexts that enable them to handle the everyday roles, responsibilities, and challenging situations that confront teachers (Espiner, Hartnett, and Lyons 1991; Hartnett, O'Brien, and Espiner 1992; Murray and Steadman 1992). It allows preservice special educators to identify and conceptualize roles in flexible and imaginative ways that allow them to define the cultural and linguistic characteristics and values that guide their behaviors.

Role playing may be used to involve preservice special educators actively in the teaching–learning process, allow exploration of reactions or responses to various situations, provide opportunities to practice newly acquired knowledge and skills, and permit students to make mistakes in a supportive environment. Role playing is also useful in helping preservice teachers to (1) focus on decision-making alternatives and anticipate the consequences of those decisions, (2) recognize and develop an appreciation for others' viewpoints, and (3) manage and appreciate personal frustrations and other feelings. A role-playing situation that is applicable to preservice special educators may entail a collaborative team effort to design a student's Individualized Education Program (IEP) with professionals as well as the parents and student who are from a minority racial, ethnic, and cultural background. Another situation may involve demonstrating effective listening and confrontation skills when dealing with a difficult professional situation.

Role playing activities may also be appropriate for working parents of Hispanic, Native-American, Asian, and Pacific Islander backgrounds, among others. Quite often, the overt communication styles that are prevalent in the schools and the parents' uncertainty about their legal rights and responsibilities may cause parents to defer to teachers in determining their children's educational programs. "Role play and simulations may assist parents to acquire new behaviors needed to participate as equal team members in their interactions with school personnel" (Sileo, Sileo, and Prater 1996, 148).

Action Methods

Action methods involve university students in structured learning experiences to clarify concepts, gain new information, and change their perceptions. Selected action methods that we find particularly appropriate include icebreaker and continuum activities, opinion maps, story boarding, concept mapping, and cooperative learning groups.

Icebreaker activities. These activities allow university students to become better acquainted with each other and facilitate spontaneity in their class interactions. Icebreakers also build trust, energize group members, and illustrate the instructor's style as one of facilitation rather than dissemination of information through lectures. Icebreakers may be related to specific subject matter that will be discussed throughout the course. For example, we have used icebreaker activities in which students locate someone in the class who has similar racial, ethnic, and cultural characteristics and then identify what they like best (and least) about their heritage. In other instances, students describe their initial encounters with individuals with disabilities or those at risk of educational failure, their success or failure with an academic task, or their rejection by peers or teachers because of membership in an underrepresented group.

Continuum activities. In a continuum activity, preservice special educators place themselves on an imaginary line that represents a continuum of stances on a particular issue (Espiner, Hartnett, and Lyons 1991; Hartnett, O'Brien, and Espiner

1992; Murray and Steadman 1992). The activities usually require students to initially indicate their positions on relatively black-and-white issues and then progress to indicating their positions along continuums for complex gray-area issues that require situational responses.

Students must state their reasons for choosing a particular point along the continuum. They can be paired with group members who are at opposite ends of the continuum or with others who are closest to themselves as a basis for discussion regarding an issue; they may change locations after communicating with others about the issue. Issues that may be used in this activity include the use of nonstandard forms of English (such as Ebonics or Hawaii Creole English) in classroom settings or the inclusion of students with disabilities in general education classrooms. A variation of the activity asks students to place themselves along the continuum according to perceptions of where their parents would stand regarding an issue such as interracial marriage. Subsequent discussion often highlights intergenerational differences in people's viewpoints. Continuums can also be used to create cooperative learning groups, particularly when a mix of opinions or experiences is important to the group's composition. For example, mixing students based on knowledge and experiences may be worthwhile if a cooperative learning group is designing a curriculum or a lesson in multicultural education.

Opinion maps. Opinion maps are similar to continuum activities (Espiner, Hartnett, and Lyons 1991; Hartnett, O'Brien, and Espiner 1992; Murray and Steadman 1992). Group members make an individual statement about an issue and simultaneously place themselves on a position in the room. Other students place themselves farther from or nearer to the person according to the stated opinion. Opinion maps encourage preservice teachers to take a stand on an issue and to clarify their positions on controversial topics such as the viability of bilingual education and the role of public schools in advocating cultural assimilation or cultural pluralism.

Story boarding. Story boarding is a brainstorming strategy designed to engage a total group of students in team learning about a particular subject and to develop a sense of ownership for a learning product. It is particularly useful when the major outcome of the activity is to maximize students' input and to tell a powerful and compelling story with multiple dimensions. During the story boarding process, participants generate and write ideas on adhesive notes of various colors and sizes. Each idea is posted prominently in front of the room under one of a predetermined set of categories that helps a story to unfold. The group reflects on the ideas that have been generated during the brainstorming process and arranges them into a sequence that links the themes under consideration. The final aspect of story boarding involves a group summary. The ensuing dialogue, which concerns how the ideas address the themes, reinforces the collective power of group learning.

An example of story boarding that we use considers the effect of homelessness on students from diverse cultural heritages. The activity is particularly relevant in Hawaii, where many Native Hawaiians choose to live on the beach as part of the sovereignty movement. Preservice teachers brainstorm ideas regarding the positive and negative influences of homelessness on students' personal beliefs and aspirations, health, family relationships, and perceptions toward society and the world order. The ideas are organized to create a comprehensive narrative about homelessness and its effects on the lives of school-age children, youth, and their family members. The story boarding activity serves as a springboard to generate strategies for working with children and their families in educational settings.

Concept mapping. Concept mapping techniques are visual representations and expressions of preservice teachers' understanding about a topic. They facilitate meaningful learning and may be used with individuals or small groups of students. The value of concept mapping lies in its development, where university students consciously and explicitly link new knowledge to previously acquired concepts. Concept mapping encourages the construction of holistic, associative patterns in which the user relates concepts to understand a topic. Concept mapping techniques can be used to summarize a textbook chapter, a class unit, or course content.

The concept mapping technique has a number of variations. One approach that we like allows students to place the principal idea in the center of the map. Major subtopics radiate from the main idea, although the angle, direction, and order of the branches are not logically sequenced. A random arrangement is permissible because a sequence is not essential (Sileo et al. 1998). Adhesive notes, each bearing a concept, can be rearranged to facilitate the mapmakers' understanding of the concept. We often use concept mapping to initiate class discussion about Asian and Pacific Islanders, who are commonly aggregated as a single ethnic group even though they have diverse geographic, historic, religious, and linguistic origins. In addition, these groups differ in their approaches to cultural values and beliefs, social structure, child-rearing practices, language and communication styles as well as their perceptions about health, illness, and disabilities. With a little imagination, preservice teacher educators can apply concept mapping techniques in a variety of ways to ascertain students' knowledge and understandings about specific topics.

Cooperative learning activities. These activities consist of structured, systematic instructional strategies where small heterogeneous groups of preservice special education teachers work together to attain a shared learning outcome. The activities afford opportunities for students to develop broader understandings than those they would develop if they each were to explore a topic individually. Cooperative learning activities are powerful teaching strategies that promote students' acquisition of knowledge and development of valuable life skills such as critical thinking, effective communication, and respect for others' diverse academic abilities, disabilities, languages, and cultural backgrounds. Cooperative learning enables instructors to structure the learning environment in a way that addresses course content in a meaningful and relevant manner and ensures that each class member contributes to the group's goal.

The elements of cooperative learning include positive interdependence among group members for project completion; face-to-face interaction in which students assist, encourage, and support each other's efforts; individual accountability where each participant is responsible for the total content; appropriate use of social skills; and the identification of group processes that facilitate or hinder effective and efficient teamwork (Johnson, Johnson, and Holubec 1990). Evaluating group dynamics and providing feedback are critical to successfully carrying out cooperative learning activities and to preparing preservice educators to teach these skills in their own classrooms.

Cooperative learning is receiving increased attention in higher-education settings where, in a group effort, students may study together for an examination; respond to teacher-generated questions or check the accuracy of an assignment as an in-class activity; and complete a research project, class presentation, or study guide. Three types of cooperative learning groups are applicable to college and university classes: formal groups, informal groups, and base groups (Johnson, Johnson, and Smith 1991).

Formal groups may be used to teach specific content by having them cooperatively complete an assigned task that follows formal instruction. The jigsaw approach is one that may be used with formal groups. In this approach, each student is assigned a particular essential aspect of a selected topic. Each group member contributes an individualized response that is integrated with the other participants' work to yield a group product. Projects that seem relevant for formal cooperative learning activities include identifying the basic provisions of U.S. federal legislation on behalf of students with disabilities; organizing litigation on behalf of students with disabilities based on the right to treatment, education, and nondiscriminatory education; and developing school-based action plans that help to involve parents from diverse cultural backgrounds in their children's education (Sileo et al. 1998).

Informal cooperative learning groups help focus students' attention on the subject matter; set expectations and a mood conducive to learning; ensure students' active participation; and provide closure to an instructional session (Johnson, Johnson, and Smith 1991). A good example of an informal group activity is a review strategy that allows students to discuss content from the previous class meeting for three to five minutes before they continue with the topic under consideration. Another informal cooperative learning group activity, think-pair-share (Kagan 1992), allows groups of four students to brainstorm solutions to a problem individually (think), discuss the individual responses with a group partner (pair), and, finally, exchange the answers between the two pairs (share).

Cooperative base groups provide students with support, encouragement, and assistance to progress academically. The base groups are permanent and assemble every time the class meets; they help to improve students' attendance, personalize their university experience, and improve the quality of their learning (Johnson, Johnson, and Smith 1991).

Cooperative learning strategies require university students to process course content actively, reflect on the content, and communicate their thoughts and discoveries to others. The activities seem to be particularly appropriate in higher-education settings with students from underrepresented populations who may need a supportive classroom environment that nurtures their learning and success. Cooperative learning activities also create an atmosphere that reduces competition among students and, therefore, may be suitable for students who prefer a group orientation and an atmosphere of sharing as the basis for goal attainment. The application of cooperative learning strategies in university classes depends on students' needs and characteristics, their previous cooperative learning experiences, and the content of the assignments. It has unlimited uses depending on the focus of the course and the instructor's imagination.

Assessment Strategies

Culturally sensitive and responsive instructional strategies involve framing students' learning within appropriate contexts so they perceive its relevance and are eager to solve real-world problems. These strategies accommodate the need to provide students with opportunities for social interaction. These variables should be taken into account when contemplating the assessment process and how students demonstrate mastery of course content and pedagogical competency. Lewis (1997) suggests that students be provided with alternative response modes, which may include but are not limited to (1) reading logs, (2) a series of abstracts that are annotated with students' personal reactions, (3) concept mapping exercises, and (4) performance-based assessment. Students' pedagogical competence may be assessed through artistic expression, music, or other performance venues such as role play, video- and audiotaped presentations, and real-life interactions in field-centered and student teaching settings.

Portfolio assessment seems to be a particularly appropriate vehicle for students from underrepresented groups to demonstrate their knowledge and pedagogical competence as well as interpersonal skills. Portfolio assessment incorporates a wide range of response modes and provides a representative selection of evidence that demonstrates the unfolding of teaching and learning over time. In addition, portfolio assessment allows students the chance to affirm their cultural heritage and to promote the tenets of multicultural education. It also provides evidence of students' performance beyond factual knowledge and offers the opportunity to identify a broader and more in-depth portrayal of their abilities. Finally, the process of portfolio assessment allows preservice teachers to reflect on and to assess their learning and to determine the work samples that best demonstrate their abilities.

The opportunity to make choices about work products acknowledges preservice students' competence and the value of their preferences. Choice making empowers them to assume responsibility for setting goals as well as for directing and participating in the evaluation of their learning. In essence, portfolio assessment is the basis for reflecting on the lifelong nature of learning. It enables students to (1) examine their past and current behaviors, (2) reflect on their significance, and (3) generate knowledge that informs future decisions. Thoughtful reflection helps teachers to identify the ethical, social, political, and legal forces that drive their decision making and that shape their personal and professional behaviors as they strive to address the ever changing learning and behavioral needs of the school population.

SUMMARY

This chapter focused on the need to prepare special educators with competencies in multicultural education that enable them to work more effectively with youth from diverse racial, ethnic, and cultural backgrounds. Discussion considered the changing demographics in public school settings and the misrepresentation in special education settings of youth from diverse racial, ethnic, and cultural backgrounds. The chapter also discussed teacher supply and demand as well as the concomitant need for special education teacher preparation programs to recruit and retain college and university students with diverse backgrounds. Finally, we addressed curricular and pedagogical changes that must occur in teacher preparation programs to ensure that future special education teachers are prepared adequately for a changing school population. This discussion attempted to link the changes in special education teacher preparation programs that need to be made to support multicultural education in public school settings with the improved instruction in higher education classrooms that complements the learning needs of university students with diverse cultural heritages.

REFERENCES

Adger, C. T., W. Wolfram, and J. Detwyler. 1993. Language differences: A new approach for special educators. *Teaching Exceptional Children* 26:44–47.

Adger, C., W. Wolfram, J. Detwyler, and B. Harry. 1993. Confronting dialect minority issues in special education: Reactive and proactive perspectives. Paper presented at the National Research Symposium on Limited English Proficient Students, July 15–16, 1999, Washington, D.C. (ERIC Document Reproduction Service No. ED 356 673).

American Association of Colleges for Teacher Education. 1994. Teacher education pipeline III: Schools, colleges, and departments of education enrollments by race, ethnicity, and gender. Washington, D.C.: American Association of Colleges for Teacher Education.

American Association of State Colleges and Universities. 1991. Short takes. *AASCU Memo to the President* 32 (22):1.

Artiles, A. J., and S. C. Trent. 1994. Overrepresentation of minority students in special education: A continuing debate. *Journal of Special Education* 27:410–37.

Au, K. H., and J. M. Mason. 1981. Social organizational factors in learning to read: The balance of rights hypotheses. *Reading Research Quarterly* 17:115–52.

Banks, J. A. 1991. *Teaching strategies for ethnic studies.* 3d ed. Boston: Allyn and Bacon.

————. 1994. Transforming the mainstream curriculum. *Educational Leadership* 51:4–11.

————. 1996. Transformative knowledge, curriculum reform, and action. In *Multicultural education, transformative knowledge, and action: Historical and contemporary perspectives,* ed. J. A. Banks, 335–48. New York: Teachers College Press.

Bell, E. D., and C. G. Munn. 1997/1998. Can we create dreamkeepers for diverse classrooms? *National Forum of Teacher Education Journal* 7:14–21.

Black, R. S., T. W. Sileo, and M. A. Prater. 2000. Learning journals, self-reflection, and university students' changing perceptions. *Action in Teacher Education* 21 (4):71–89.

Bradfield-Krieder, P. 1999. Mediated cultural immersion and antiracism: An opportunity for monocultural preservice teachers to begin the dialogue. *Multicultural Perspectives* 1:29–32.

Bringle, R. G., and J. A. Hatcher. 1996. Implementing service learning in higher education. *Journal of Higher Education* 67:221–39.

Carey, J. C., M. L. Boscardin, and L. Fontes. 1994. Improving the multicultural effectiveness of your school. In *Multicultural counseling in schools: A practical handbook,* ed. P. Pedersen and J. C. Carey, 239–49. Boston: Allyn and Bacon.

Checkoway, B. 1996. Combining service and learning on campus and in the community. *Phi Delta Kappan* 77:600–606.

Cheney, C. O., J. Krajewski, and M. Combs. 1992. Understanding the first year teacher: Implications for induction programs. *Teacher Education and Special Education* 15:18–24.

Children's Defense Fund. 1999. *The state of America's children yearbook.* Washington, D.C.: Children's Defense Fund.

Chinn, P. C., and S. Hughes. 1987. Representation of minority students in special education classes. *Remedial and Special Education* 8:41–46.

Choy, S. P., R. R. Henke, M. N. Alt, E. A. Medrich, and S. A. Bobbitt. 1993. *Schools and staffing in the United States: A statistical profile.* Washington, D.C.: U.S. Department of Education, National Center for Education Statistics.

Cochran-Smith, M. 1991. Learning to teach against the grain. *Harvard Educational Review* 61:279–310.

Cook, L., and E. Boe. 1995. Who is teaching students with disabilities? *Teaching Exceptional Children* 28:70–72.

Cooper, J. E. 1994. Digging, daring, and discovering: Sifting the soil of professional life through journal writing. In *Ethical and social issues in professional education,* ed. C. Brody and J. Wallace, 103–16. New York: State University of New York Press.

————. 1995. The role of narrative and dialogue in constructivist leadership. In *The constructivist leader,* ed. L. Lambert, D. Walker, D. Zimmerman, J. E. Cooper, M. D. Lambert, M. E. Gardner, and P. J. Ford-Slack, 121–33. New York: Teachers College Press.

Cooper, J. E., and R. H. Heck. 1995. Using narrative in the study of school administration. *Qualitative Studies in Education* 8:195–210.

Craft, M. 1996. Cultural diversity and teacher education. In *Teacher education in plural societies: An international review,* ed. M. Craft, 1–15. London: Falmer Press.

Espiner, D., F. Hartnett, and D. Lyons. 1991. Action methods in teaching. Unpublished manuscript, University of Auckland.

Ethnic diversity increases in the U.S. 1999. *The Honolulu Advertiser* (September 15):A3.

Ewing, N. 1995. Restructured teacher education for inclusiveness: A dream deferred for African American children. In *Effective education of African American exceptional learners,* ed. B. A. Ford, F. E. Obiakor, and J. Patton, 189–208. Austin: Pro-Ed.

Fleishner, J. E., and R. Van Acker. 1990. Changes in the urban school population: Challenges in meeting the need for special education leadership and teacher preparation personnel. In *Monograph on critical issues in special education: Implications for personnel preparation,* ed. L. M. Bullock and R. L. Simpson, 73–91. Denton: University of North Texas.

Foster, M. 1994. Effective Black teachers: A literature review. *In Teaching diverse populations: Formulating a knowledge base,* ed. E. R. Hollins, J. E. King, and W. C. Hayman, 225–41. Albany: State University of New York Press.

Garcia, S. B., and D. H. Malkin. 1993. Toward defining programs and services for culturally and linguistically diverse learners in special education. *Teaching Exceptional Children* 26:52–58.

Goodlad, J. I. 1990. *Teachers for our nation's schools.* San Francisco: Jossey-Bass.

Grossman, H. 1995. *Special education in a diverse society.* Boston: Allyn and Bacon.

Harry, B. 1992. *Cultural diversity, families, and the special education system.* New York: Teachers College Press.

Hartnett, F., P. O'Brien, and D. Espiner. 1992. Use of facilitation within a system of training for direct service personnel. Paper presented at the Ninth World Congress of the International Association for the Scientific Study of Mental Retardation, August 5–9, Gold Coast, Australia.

Hawaii State Department of Education. 1994. *Ethnicity by handicap for state.* Honolulu: Office of Instructional Services, Special Education Section.

Henke, R. R., S. P. Choy, S. Gies, and S. P. Broughman. 1996. *Schools and staffing in the United States: A statistical profile, 1993–94.* Washington, D.C.: U.S. Department of Education, National Center for Education Statistics.

Hodgkinson, H. L. 1992. *A demographic look at tomorrow.* Washington, D.C.: Institute for Educational Leadership. (ERIC Document Reproduction Service No. ED 359 087).

Holmes Group. 1990. *Tomorrow's schools: Principles for the design of professional development schools.* East Lansing, Mich.: The Holmes Group.

———. 1995. *Tomorrow's schools of education.* East Lansing, Mich.: The Holmes Group.

Hunt, N., and K. Marshall. 1994. *Exceptional children and youth: An introduction to special education.* Boston: Houghton Mifflin.

Johnson, D. W., R. T. Johnson, and E. J. Holubec. 1990. *Circles of learning: Cooperation in the classroom.* 3d ed. Edina, Minn.: Interaction.

Johnson, D. W., R. T. Johnson, and K. A. Smith. 1991. *Active learning: Cooperation in the college classroom.* Edina, Minn.: Interaction.

Kagan, S. 1992. *Cooperative learning.* San Juan Capistrano, Calif.: Resources for Teachers.

Kahne, J., and J. Westheimer. 1996. In the service of what? The politics of service learning. *Phi Delta Kappan* 77:592–99.

Koerner, M. E., and P. Hulsebosch. 1996. Preparing teachers to work with children of gay and lesbian parents. *Journal of Teacher Education* 47:347–54.

Ladson-Billings, G. 1994. What we can learn from multicultural education research. *Educational Leadership* 51:22–26.

Lambie, R., and D. Daniels-Mohring. 1993. *Family systems within educational contexts: Understanding students with special needs.* Denver: Love Publishing Co.

Lewis, R. B. 1997. Assessment of student learning. In *Multicultural course transformation in higher education,* ed. A. I. Morey and M. K. Kitano, 71–88. Boston: Allyn and Bacon.

Little Soldier, L. 1990. The education of Native American students: Where makes a difference. *Equity and Excellence* 24:66–69.

Lynch, E. W. 1997. Instructional strategies. In *Multicultural course transformation in higher education,* ed. A. I. Morey and M. K. Kitano, 56–70. Boston: Allyn and Bacon.

McWhirter, J. J., B. T. McWhirter, A. M. McWhirter, and E. H. McWhirter. 1998. *At-risk youth: A comprehensive approach.* Pacific Grove, Calif.: Brooks/Cole.

Meier, K., J. Stewart, and R. England. 1989. *Race, class, and education.* Madison: University of Wisconsin Press.

Morris, V. G., S. I. Taylor, J. Knight, and R. Wasson. 1997. Preparing teachers to reach out to parents. *ATE [Association of Teacher Educators] Newsletter* 30:5.

Murray, R., and C. Steadman. 1992. Group skills and interpersonal relations. Unpublished manuscript, University of Auckland.

National Center for Educational Statistics. 1995. *Projections of education statistics to 2005.* Washington, D.C.: National Center for Educational Statistics.

National Commission on Teaching and America's Future. 1996. *What matters most: Teaching for America's future.* New York: National Commission on Teaching and America's Future.

One American in 10 born elsewhere. 1999. *Kauai Times* (September 19):A4.

Oswald, D. P., M. J. Coutinho, A. M. Best, and N. N. Singh. 1999. Ethnic representation in special education: The influence of school-related economic and demographic variables. *Journal of Special Education* 32:194–206.

Prater, M. A., T. W. Sileo, and N. M. Sileo. 1997. Introduction to the field of exceptionalities: Do textbooks reflect cultural diversity? *Teacher Education and Special Education* 20:11–21.

Pultorak, E. G. 1993. Facilitating reflective thought in novice teachers. *Journal of Teacher Education* 44:288–95.

———. 1996. Following the developmental process of reflection in novice teachers: Three years of investigations. *Journal of Teacher Education* 47:283–91.

Ramirez, B. 1990. Preparing special education and related services personnel to serve culturally and linguistically diverse children with handicaps: Needs and future directions. In *Monograph on critical issues in special education: Implications for personnel preparation,* ed. L. M. Bullock and R. L. Simpson, 92–95. Denton: University of North Texas.

Recruiting New Teachers, Inc. 1997. *National study of urban teacher induction programs: Preliminary findings.* Belmont, Mass.: Recruiting New Teachers, Inc.

Rice, L. M. 1998. Research report. *DDEL [Division for Culturally and Linguistically Diverse Exceptional Learners] News* 8:1–3.

Rodriguez, E. M. 1998. *Preparing quality teachers: Issues and trends in the states.* Denver: State Higher Education Executive Officers.

Shimabukuro, S. M. 1998. Adolescents with disabilities from diverse cultures and human service providers: Cultural mismatch. Paper presented at the Council for Exceptional Children Symposium on Culturally and Linguistically Diverse Exceptional Learners, November 5–6, Washington, D.C.

Sileo, T. W., and P. Edelen-Smith. 1993. Alternative certification programs in special education teacher preparation. *Pacific Proceedings* 2:9–23.

Sileo, T. W., and M. A. Prater. 1998. Creating classroom environments that address the linguistic and cultural backgrounds of students with disabilities: An Asian Pacific American perspective. *Remedial and Special Education* 19:323–37.

Sileo, T. W., M. A. Prater, J. L. Luckner, B. Rhine, and H. A. Rude. 1998. Strategies to facilitate preservice teachers' active involvement in learning. *Teacher Education and Special Education* 21:187–204.

Sileo, T. W., A. P. Sileo, and M. A. Prater. 1996. Parent and professional partnerships in special education: Multicultural considerations. *Intervention in School and Clinic* 31:145–53.

Sorrell, A. L. 1997. Ethnic self-awareness is the key to multicultural teaching. Paper presented at the Council for Exceptional Children Symposium on Culturally and Linguistically Diverse Exceptional Learners, January 8–10, New Orleans, Louisiana.

Talbert-Johnson, C., and L. L. Cochran. 1999. Prominent issues in teacher preparation: Managing diverse, disabled, and disadvantaged students. Paper presented at the Seventh Annual Comprehensive System of Personnel Development Conference on Leadership and Change, May 2–5, Arlington, Virginia.

Thorp, E. K. 1997. Increasing opportunities for partnership with culturally and linguistically diverse families. *Intervention in School and Clinic* 32:261–69.

Trueba, H. T., L. R. L. Cheng, and K. Ima. 1993. *Myth or reality: Adaptive strategies of Asian Americans in California.* Washington, D.C.: Falmer Press.

Voltz, D. L. 1994. Developing collaborative parent-teacher relationships with culturally diverse parents. *Intervention in School and Clinic* 29:288–91.

———. 1995. Learning and cultural diversities in general and special education classes: Frameworks for success. *Multiple Voices for Ethnically Diverse Learners* 1:1–11.

Wald, J. L. 1996. *Culturally and linguistically diverse professionals in special education: A demographic analysis.* Reston, Va.: The Council for Exceptional Children.

———. 1997. OSEP funded projects recommend strategies for retention of special education personnel. *NCPSE [National Clearinghouse for Professions in Special Education] News,* 1, 1, 5.

———. 1998. *Retention of special education professionals: A practical guide of strategies and activities for educators and administrators.* Reston, Va.: Council for Exceptional Children.

Welch, M. 1996. Teacher education and the neglected diversity: Preparing educators to teach students with disabilities. *Journal of Teacher Education* 47:355–66.

Zeichner, K. M. 1996. Educating teachers for cultural diversity in the United States. In *Teacher education in plural societies: An international review*, ed. M. Craft, 141–58. Washington, D.C.: Falmer Press

Zeichner, K. M., and K. Hoeft. 1996. Teacher socialization for cultural diversity. In *Handbook on research on teacher education*, 2d ed., ed. J. Sukula, T. J. Buttery, and E. Guyton, 525–47. New York: Simon and Schuster.

PART 3

Including Special Populations

Introduction

As educators grapple with the issue of equitable treatment for all students, the question of how the integration of students with disabilities is to be accomplished remains a hotly debated issue. Discussions on the merits of inclusion as a philosophy are not as prominent as apprehension about putting inclusion into practice. Few dispute the contention that every child, regardless of his or her type and severity of disability, has the right to a free and appropriate education in a setting that is as normal as possible. Nevertheless, our philosophical commitment far outstrips our practice: The barriers to successful and universal inclusion remain complex, diverse, and numerous.

The question of how the integration of students with exceptional conditions is to be accomplished is the focus of this section. Authors examine inclusive practices and other germane issues for specific groups of students with exceptionalities.

How to effectively program education services for gifted students is an ongoing issue in special education. Although there is a general consensus that too many gifted students are inadequately served in our schools (Lupart 1998), the field is divided on the issue of placement. Some promote general classroom placement with enrichment activities that are provided by the classroom teacher. Others question whether this practice is enough and promote models such as acceleration, ability grouping, and mentorships.

McFadden and Ellis open this section with a critical assessment of the education of gifted students within inclusive settings, focusing on the Canadian situation. They begin with an historic overview of the education of students with gifts and talents; present the arguments about inclusion, pro and con; indicate ways to accommodate these students; and make predictions about the future of education for gifted and talented students within inclusive schools.

Continuing the discussion of inclusion, the education of students with behavioral disorders is, as a practical matter, one of the most vital issues for classroom teachers. However, the great disparity between teachers' perceptions and expectations and their experiences with difficult-to-teach students paints a murky picture of inclusion for such children. Some contend that, with support, all students with behavioral disorders can function in general classrooms. Others do not see the general classroom as a safe haven for child or teacher; they argue that it is deleterious to the child with a behavioral disorder, the teacher, and other students to retain in general classes those who cannot conform to the basic expectations of that classroom. They question the premise that regular classroom teachers will increasingly welcome more difficult-to-teach children as they become proficient in the use of effective instructional skills. They contend that such welcoming will not occur unless the gain of effective skills is accompanied by a change of attitudes (Kauffman, Gerber, and Semmel 1988). Still others argue that expecting general education teachers to welcome, tolerate, and successfully teach and manage the most disruptive students is extremely naive and illogical, both from the viewpoint of common sense and from the perspective of available research (Fuchs et al. 1991). In addition, the outlay of energy and resources needed for a student with behavioral disorders to succeed in the regular classroom may not be commensurate with the questionable gains that are achieved (see MacMillan, Gresham, and Forness 1996).

Students with behavioral disorders are not included in a vacuum; they are in real classrooms in which the characteristics of teachers, children, and programs differ markedly. With this idea in mind, Landrum and Tankersley examine inclusive practices with this most difficult group of students. They look critically and comprehensively at reform efforts and question both where and how students with behavioral disorders should be educated. In essence, they discuss the overarching questions of whether fundamental changes to accommodate children with exceptionalities are possible in the majority of today's public schools and whether all teachers can or should be expected to accommodate all children with special needs.

The inclusion of children with severe and profound disabilities is another area of concern for general educators. Although much that is positive is emerging in the literature about children's progress, peer tolerance, and teacher acceptance, many teachers still remain unconvinced.

In a far-reaching chapter on the inclusion of students with severe and profound disabilities, Deborah Peters Goessling outlines the history of the field and the positive developments that have occurred, but also the major barriers that remain to full and universal inclusion for students with significant disabilities. She details recent litigation and presents ideas for successful inclusion as well as predictions for the future.

In 1986, PL 99–457 extended the population to be served to infants and preschool children with exceptional conditions. The growth in services for young children with disabilities stimulated widespread interest in the special knowledge and skills that are needed to provide effective and supportive educational services to infants, preschoolers, and their families within infant programs and preschool settings.

Parents who discover that a child has a disability share a common set of tasks. They must learn about the disability, become aware of their child's educational and therapeutic needs, identify the range of services that potentially can assist the child, and gain access to these services (Bailey et al. 1999). Hence, many argue that early intervention has a broader purpose than child development. The expanded purpose acknowledges that early intervention also should support families of children with disabilities (Bailey et al. 1998). In a comprehensive survey of early childhood special education, Wall addresses these issues. She explores the dimensions of PL 99–457 in terms of the new directions and the mandates it presents to educators and to schools. She discusses inclusion from the view of early childhood education and, in particular, the way in which teacher education may meld early childhood and special education. The core of the paper centers on the challenges to teachers and the means and methods by which young children with exceptionalities may be included.

The discussion of inclusion shifts to consider the search in America for the most effective way to educate students who are deaf, a search that has a history of conflict among advocates of different approaches (Drasgow 1998). In fact, determining which communication mode is most appropriate in the education of students who are deaf has formed one of the longest running controversies in the entire field of education.

Today, the debate concerns bicultural/bilingual education, simultaneous communication approaches, and oral/aural approaches. Specific methods are driven by the philosophy to which a person subscribes—a clinical model or a cultural model. Clinical models, which regard deafness as a deficit, stress overcoming or compensating for hearing loss. Other models regard deafness as a culture and view the condition as a difference, not a disability.

Because they hold that American Sign Language (ASL) is the natural language of the deaf community throughout anglophone United States, many deaf adults favor bilingualism for all deaf children. They argue that young deaf children who are taught a conventional sign system develop language in sign that is comparable in both content and form to the language that young hearing children develop in speech (Goldin-Meadow and Morford 1985). Because a strong language base in one language facilitates learning another language, young deaf children who sign arrive in school with a firm linguistic base. Further, say these deaf adults, the deaf child is a member of a unique linguistic and cultural group and "forcing deaf children to be part of the hearing world denies them the right to themselves" (Elliott 1993, 11).

Bilingual education for deaf students uses ASL and English. Children use ASL as the major medium of instruction in preschool through the primary grades, with a major focus on sign production and comprehension. Development of English literacy begins in third grade, and from then on, ASL and English are used fairly equally for instructional purposes (McAnally, Rose, and Quigley 1987).

Miller and Moores speak to the values of bilingual/bicultural education for students who are deaf. They address the enduring controversy surrounding oral vs. manual methods and contend that a bilingual/bicultural philosophy frees individuals from the restraints of such a dichotomy. It allows people who are deaf to use a language that defines them as a recognizable minority group and that acknowledges the unique culture and language of individuals.

As we see throughout this text, many schools are experiencing major educational challenges and reform efforts. In the final chapter, Winzer and Mazurek begin on a similar note: One of the most pressing problems within special education is improving the quality and opportunity of education for students with special needs who come from diverse cultural backgrounds and who may also be limited in English proficiency. They then discuss the means by which teachers can create opportunities to bridge ethnic and cultural boundaries. The authors acknowledge that the diversity among school-aged students requires that teachers add new pedagogical skills to their repertoires (Voltz, Dooley, and Jeffries 1999). They also recognize that considerations of curriculum, pedagogy, and the environment become complex as teachers attempt to address cultural diversity and limited English proficiency as well as the developmental consequences of a condition.

This final chapter on multicultural special education moves from theory to implementation. It shows that effective program design for students with disabilities from culturally and linguistically diverse backgrounds is based on the same principles and purposes as multicultural education. However, some of the teacher competencies and teaching strategies that are needed to achieve the goals of multicultural special education—especially those that create supportive learning environments in general education—may be different. The educator's task is to provide age-relevant and developmentally appropriate instructional programs that take advantage of cultural congruence while promoting the value of diversity and fostering achievement. To accomplish this task, teachers need knowledge about various exceptional conditions, their developmental consequences, the way those conditions affect the teaching and learning processes, and the legal perspectives related to educating children with exceptionalities so they can build meaningful pedagogical bridges across different cultural systems. Teachers need to know about and be sensitive to the structures, values, attitudes, communication, and ways of interacting of different cultures (see Winzer and Mazurek 1998).

REFERENCES

Bailey, D. B., R. A. McWilliam, L. A. Darkes, K. Hebbeler, R. J. Simeonsson, D. Spiker, and M. Wagner. 1998. Family outcomes in early intervention: A framework for program evaluation and efficacy research. *Exceptional Children* 64:313–28.

Bailey, D. B., D. Skinner, P. Rodriguez, D. Gut, and V. Correa. 1999. Awareness, use, and satisfaction with services for Latino parents of young children with disabilities. *Exceptional Children* 65:367–81.

Drasgow, E. 1998. American Sign Language as a pathway to linguistic competence. *Exceptional Children* 64:329–42.

Elliott, L. 1993. Mainstreaming opposed by deaf community. *ATA [Alberta Teachers' Association] News* (May 18):11.

Fuchs, D., L. S. Fuchs, P. Fernstrom, and M. Hohn. 1991. Toward a responsible reintegration of behaviorally disordered students. *Behavioral Disorders* 16:133–47.

Goldin-Meadow, S., and M. Morford. 1985. Gestures in early child language: Studies of deaf and hearing children. *Merrill-Palmer Quarterly* 31:145–76.

Kauffman, J. M., M. M. Gerber, and M. I. Semmel. 1988. Arguable assumptions underlying the Regular Education Initiative. *Journal of Learning Disabilities* 21:6–11.

Lupart, J. 1998. Setting right the delusion of inclusion: Implications for Canadian schools. *Canadian Journal of Education* 23:251–64.

MacMillan, D. L., F. M. Gresham, and S. R. Forness. 1996. Full inclusion: An empirical perspective. *Behavioral Disorders* 21:145–59.

McAnally, P., S. Rose, and S. Quigley. 1987. *Language learning practices with deaf children.* Boston: College Hill Press.

Voltz, D. L., E. Dooley, and P. Jeffries. 1999. Preparing special educators for cultural diversity: How far have we come? *Teacher Education and Special Education* 22:66–77.

Winzer, M. A., and K. Mazurek. 1998. *Special education in multicultural contexts.* Columbus, Ohio: Merrill.

7

What Happens to Gifted Education within Inclusive Schooling?

Margaret McFadden   *Julia Ellis*

S tudents who are gifted and talented are increasingly likely to receive all or most of their schooling in the regular education system. In many school districts, separate specialized programs are being curtailed or phased out. The expectation that students who are gifted and talented will have their needs met within the regular school and classroom environment is congruent with the inclusive schooling movement in special education (Willis 1995). As a result of current restructuring efforts, school-level administrators assume more responsibility for the operational and decision-making functions of special education. These functions include planning, coordinating, and evaluating services for students who are gifted and talented (Harris and Evans 1994; Myers and Sobehart 1994/1995). This trend is seen as resulting from a general philosophy that favors mixed-ability grouping and from the absence of priority funding for gifted-education programs (Evans 1995/1996; Jones 1991; Renzulli and Reis 1991a, 1991b; Rogers 1991a, 1991b, 1991c). This paper is intended to invite consideration about the future of education within the inclusive schooling movement for students who are gifted and talented.

ADVOCATING INCLUSIVE SCHOOLING

Inclusive schooling entails and invites a revisualization of education on a grand scale. Sapon-Shevin has described the societal movement toward inclusive schooling as "much bigger than special education, much bigger than individual classrooms; it's even bigger than the school. Inclusion really calls for a fundamental restructuring of the school districts and the schools. It means changes in the curriculum, changes of pedagogy, in staff allocation, teacher education, and so on" (in O'Neil 1994/1995, 9). The mission of inclusive schools is to restructure schools so they are responsive communities that meet the needs of the students within them. To achieve this mission, schools must be rich in resources and support for both teachers and students. Teacher preparation time, dedicated leadership, a vision statement, commitment, restructuring, and staff development are all required for inclusive schooling to thrive (Sapon-Shevin 1994/1995).

Like all students, students who are gifted and talented need to be in classrooms where their gifts are identified, their talents are nurtured, and their struggles are supported (Clark 1992a; Silverman 1996). VanTassel-Baska (1991) has suggested that students who are gifted and talented can receive the necessary support in inclusive classrooms through differentiated curricula, individualized instruction, and appropriate adjunct programs and services.

Stainback and Stainback (1990) have emphasized the difference between inclusive schooling for students who are gifted and talented and the movement to integrate or mainstream students with disabilities into their regular neighborhood schools. Inclusive schools do not focus on how to assist any particular category of students into the mainstream of education. Instead, they focus on how to develop, organize, implement, maintain, manage, and evaluate supportive classrooms and schools that include and meet the needs of all students.

Those who see inclusive classrooms as promising educational sites for students who are gifted and talented have large, complex visions. As one example, Sapon-Shevin (1994/1995) advocates for inclusive classrooms that establish and maintain warm, accepting, and challenging classroom communities. Such classrooms would embrace diversity; identify and honor gifts; develop and nurture talents; implement a multilevel, multimodal curriculum; incorporate flexible grouping and pacing for instruction; have teachers who are prepared and supported to teach interactively; have teachers who receive ongoing support; and actively involve parents and pertinent stakeholders in the planning, implementation, and evaluation process. In such ideal images of inclusive schooling, it should be possible to imagine appropriate educational experiences being made available to students who are gifted and talented as part of the regular school program.

CONCERNS ABOUT INCLUSIVE SCHOOLING

Among advocates for students who are gifted and talented are those who express concern that inclusive schooling will fail to support high-ability students (Belcastro 1987; Renzulli and Reis 1991b; Silverman 1996; Tomlinson 1993). Many such advocates insist that inclusive schooling is likely to accommodate the needs of only the mildly gifted students who are talented in specific domains (Clark 1992a; Gallagher 1991b; Rosenstein and Dettmer 1991; Ross 1991).

At the same time, a large number of advocates for gifted education have identified strategies for raising the level of challenge for students who are gifted and talented in regular classrooms (Harvey 1996; Maker 1993; Parke 1989, 1990; Renzulli 1994a, 1994b, 1994/1995; Renzulli and Reis 1991b; Sapon-Shevin 1992, 1994/1995; Sullivan 1991; Thorkildsen 1994). These strategies have included instructional options such as differentiating and personalizing curriculum as well as placement alternatives such as community-based mentor programs, independent study in specialized resource classrooms, accelerated classes, and specialized classes outside the students' age-grades. Instruction can be differentiated or personalized by providing opportunities for flexible groupings, tiered assignments, learning centers, learning contracts, research projects, curriculum compacting, curriculum enrichment, interest-based assignments, and small-group clusters of gifted and talented students within the regular classroom (Maker 1993; Parke 1989).

Some advocates for students who are gifted and talented have also acknowledged that the needs of such students may be met in regular classrooms when the curriculum is high powered. Also, when excellent teachers in regular classrooms are willing to use flexible grouping, students who are gifted and talented can work alone, with one another, and with the whole group, which provides a variety of challenges. Finally, if teachers use diagnostic and prescriptive techniques, they ensure that students who are gifted and talented are being appropriately challenged (Clark 1992a; Willis 1995).

Actually, the visions of inclusive schooling advocates and the practice recommendations that are proposed by advocates of gifted and talented students are fairly compatible. In any case, inclusive schooling has become recognized as an educational imperative. With this imperative in view, Treffinger (1995) has expanded on the notion of inclusive schooling by proposing the concept of significant schools. He suggests that inclusive schooling, which incorporates contemporary emphases on talent identification and development, holds substantial promise for contributions to gifted education.

AN EMPHASIS ON EDUCATIONAL EXCELLENCE FOR ALL

Some advocates see inclusive schooling as an opportunity for comprehensive school reform that involves imagining schools that are not stratified by ability or constrained by curriculum, having schools staffed by innovative teachers who are themselves supported, and having a goal of excellence for all students (Tomlinson, 1994/1995).

Although advocates of gifted education have traditionally recommended alternative settings for students who are gifted and talented, they see the importance of strengthening the quality of education that these students receive throughout the entire school day when specialized instruction is either not in progress or not available at all (Evans and King 1993; Parke 1990; Renzulli 1994/1995). Many advocates recognize that improving educational opportunities for students who are gifted and talented in the regular classroom is not unrelated to improving these opportunities for all students (Feldhusen 1995; Renzulli and Reis 1991a, 1991b; Ross 1991). The goals that are held for gifted and talented students are the goals held for all students (Treffinger 1991b), and the learning environments that support students with gifts and talents are also those that support all students (Clark 1992a). A simple example of this benefit for all is the de-emphasizing of both structured, teacher-centered curriculum and excessive group instruction (Johnston 1991).

Parke (1990) has suggested a number of ways that educational programs can meet the needs of students who are gifted and talented in inclusive school and classroom settings. These include (1) assessing individual differences; (2) encouraging students to take responsibility for their own learning; (3) developing Individualized Education Programs (IEPs); (4) using curriculum materials, resources, and activities appropriate for the individual needs of the students; (5) implementing flexible grouping and instructional pacing; (6) providing opportunities for in-depth explorations; (7) incorporating student interests into the curriculum; and (8) respecting, rather than exploiting, student strengths and talents. Thus, with an emphasis on excellence for all, the principles and practices of programming for students who are gifted and talented could conceivably become integral to inclusive schooling that seeks to address the needs of all students (Gallagher 1991a; Renzulli and Reis 1991a, 1991b; Treffinger 1991a, 1991b).

MILESTONES IN THE HISTORY OF TALENT DEVELOPMENT

One can better appreciate and consider current concerns about gifted education in the context of inclusive school initiatives by examining a brief outline of the history of talent development.

Early History of Talent Development

As early as 350 B.C., Plato urged that highly able students be identified and placed in gifted education programs with curricular emphases on philosophy, science, and metaphysics. He insisted that the very survival of Greek democracy depended on educating highly able students for leadership positions. Educators in the Roman Empire held similar views and made special provision for gifted students in the areas of their military training. In the 1500s, during the reign of Suleiman the Magnificent in the Turkish Empire, educators sought students who were talented in leadership and provided them with special programs to study philosophy, art, science, religion, and war (McCluskey and Walker 1986).

In the 1700s, Thomas Jefferson promoted a concept of a free public school system that was intended to strengthen the general education of all citizens and to identify gifted students and nurture their talents. He believed that leaders in a democracy must be the most gifted individuals and that these people could be found in all socioeconomic levels. While in office, Jefferson established full scholarships to encourage academically capable students to attend college (Clark 1992a; McDaniel 1993).

During the 1800s, Sir Francis Galton investigated the hereditability of human intelligence. Working from the premise that intelligence was fixed at birth, he emphasized individual differences in intelligence and developed the first prototype of the unitary, linear scale of intelligence (Bacto et al. 1991; Keating 1990). In the early 1900s, Alfred Binet developed the first standardized test of human intelligence, which was later revised by Lewis Terman of Stanford University. These tests became known as the Stanford-Binet Intelligence Scales, and later revisions of them continue to be used today. Standardized ability and achievement tests made way for a new educational emphasis on screening, identification, and provision of specialized education programs for students with gifts and talents. During the 1930s and 1940s, psychological testing became popular and made ability grouping a viable means of educating students who were gifted and talented (Borland 1986; Lupart 1992; McDaniel 1993).

Contemporary History of Gifted Education

Terman (1925) conducted extensive longitudinal work with more than 1,500 students with an average age of eleven years and IQs exceeding 140. His findings emphasized the contribution of intelligence test scores to the early identification of child precocity and clearly revealed a relationship between early promise and later fulfillment of potential. This research provided educators with a strong impetus for establishing special education programs for students who were gifted and talented (Bacto et al. 1991; Clark 1992a; Tannenbaum 1993; Vialle 1993).

In the 1930s, Leta Hollingworth established a laboratory school for exceptional students, including those who were gifted and talented. She developed curricula emerging from student interests and conducted research on curriculum enrichment for students who were gifted and talented (Silverman 1989; Tannenbaum 1993).

During the Sputnik era, policymakers became very concerned with academically talented students, and educators intensified their efforts to prepare scientists, leaders, and thinkers (McDaniel 1993). The Great Talent Hunt of the 1960s stimulated radical curriculum revision in the subject areas of mathematics, science, and social studies. At the same time, Harry Passow's research endeavor, known as the Talented Youth Project, assisted school administrators and their staff members in developing, carrying out, and evaluating programs for students who were gifted and talented (Tannenbaum 1993).

Legislation concerning students who are gifted and talented first took the form of the Gifted and Talented Children's Education Assistance Act of 1969 with revisions in 1974 and 1978 (Zirkel and Stevens 1987). In 1972, Sidney Marland, then Commissioner of Education, modified that definition in a report to Congress known as the Marland report (Marland 1972). A noteworthy milestone, the Marland report advanced a new definition of gifted and talented. It recognized many kinds of talents or giftedness: high performance in general intellectual ability, specific aptitude, creative or productive thinking, leadership ability, visual and performing arts, and psychomotor abilities. The Marland report stimulated policy development that led to the 1988 Javits Gifted and Talented Education Act that allocated funds for identifying and developing programs for disadvantaged students who were gifted and talented (Passow 1993; Passow and Rudnitski 1994). Legislation that affirmed the importance of specialized programs for students who were gifted and talented compelled educators to place education for these students within the context of education for all students, "making the identification and nurturing of talent potential an integral and central responsibility of the entire school system and process of schooling" (Passow and Rudnitski 1994, 272).

History of Gifted Education in Canada

Since 1969, all of the provinces and territories in Canada have enacted legislation guaranteeing education to all children, including exceptional children (Goguen 1993). The Canadian Charter of Rights and Freedoms, introduced by Parliament in 1982, had a dramatic effect on provincial legislation regarding the education of students who were gifted and talented because several of its sections were found to have implications for policy and practice in education programs for these students.

Three provinces—Alberta, Saskatchewan, and Ontario—have enacted legislation, developed departmental regulations, and issued corresponding policy statements on the education of students who are gifted and talented. These entail extensive guidelines for identification, categorical designation, and special education of students who are gifted and talented. The absence of educational resources and special education programs for students who are gifted and talented in the eastern provinces of Newfoundland, Nova Scotia, New Brunswick, and Quebec reflects the mainstream movement in Canada during the 1980s. Manitoba and British Columbia adapted a noncategorical approach to the provision of programs and services for students who are gifted and talented, endeavoring to meet the needs of all students within a regular education framework (Goguen 1993). British Columbia has also put into effect an inclusive schooling approach that avoids categorization and identifies every student as unique, while still providing sufficient environmental stimulation for the maximal development of potential (Nikiforuk 1993).

Although Alberta, Saskatchewan, and Ontario each have included programs and services for students who are gifted and talented as special education provisions for exceptional students, the opportunities to acquire related funding are different in each province. Only Alberta provides a funding formula that specifically includes programs to meet the needs of students who are gifted and talented (Alberta Education 1995b; Goguen 1993). Alberta Education (1991) has outlined a vision of schooling that emphasizes challenging students who are gifted and talented in specialized school settings so they meet and exceed the academic standards of the best postsecondary institutions in the world and receive recognition for excellence in a broad range of endeavors. In Saskatchewan, an Educational Development Fund designed to finance educational innovations may provide funding for approved gifted education programs (Saskatchewan Education 1989).

This historical outline of developments related to gifted and talented education has three important themes. One is the expectation that this society and those in the future will benefit if the most able people are given the best education that can be developed for them. Another theme relates to the value of identifying high potential at early ages and the implications of identifying ability groupings for special instruction. Third, throughout this history, the policy, legislation, and funding related to programs for students who are gifted and talented have been recognized as having significant effect.

PROGRAM DEVELOPMENT FOR STUDENTS WHO ARE GIFTED AND TALENTED

A review of some of the work that has been done to develop education programs for gifted and talented students will be useful as we consider the implications of incorporating such programs into inclusive schooling. This section will provide an overview of the ways that instruction has been organized in programs for students who are gifted and talented; how Individualized Education Programs (IEPs) for students who are gifted and talented have been conceptualized and carried out; and how schoolwide program development has been conceptualized.

Organizational Configurations in Programs for Gifted and Talented Students

A broad range of organizational configurations have been used in programs for gifted and talented students to support many diverse goals. These configurations include ability grouping, cooperative learning, acceleration, and enrichment, as well as adjunct programs and provisions such as independent study, computer technology, mentoring, counseling, and leadership education. Placement settings for these provisions have included regular classrooms, resource classrooms, classrooms for gifted students, charter schools, and community-based programs.

1. *Flexible ability grouping.* Clark (1992b) has recommended that flexible ability grouping be done based on considerations of academic abilities, interests, needs, and optimal learning pace. Grouping can be set up using within-class grouping, special classes or schools, magnet programs, special group meetings prior to or after school, or pullout programs during school hours or summer programs. Ability-grouping arrangements have been shown to result in significant academic advancement when programs provide in-depth study and acceleration, focus on developing a positive self-concept and a sense of well-being, increase

opportunities for individual expression, encourage high achievers, reduce cliquishness and friction among students, and increase attention to subject area content.

2. *Cooperative learning.* Within the research on grouping configuration, the knowledge base on cooperative learning is growing. Cooperative learning involves small heterogeneous groups of high-, medium-, and low-achieving students who work together to achieve a common academic goal while employing a multitude of strategies to promote peer interaction (Conroy 1993; Nelson, Gallagher, and Coleman 1993). Typically, cooperative learning groups assume and encourage heterogeneity, peer tutoring, partner teaching, and collaboration in groups larger than two (Nelson, Gallagher, and Coleman 1993; Robinson 1991).

3. *Acceleration.* Provisions for elementary students who are gifted and talented typically are designed to differentiate and individualize students' programs by accelerating and enriching curricular experiences. Acceleration can take many different forms: early entrance to kindergarten or first grade; grade skipping; continuous progress; self-paced instruction; subject matter acceleration; combined classes; curriculum compacting; telescoped curricula; mentorships; extracurricular programs; concurrent or dual enrollment; early graduation; compacted courses; advanced-level courses; advanced placement; credit by examination; correspondence courses; acceleration to university; and early entrance to junior high school, high school, or university. The various methods of acceleration entail progress through an educational program at rates that are faster or at ages that are younger than is considered the norm. Acceleration has been recognized as a valuable and necessary program option for ensuring the educational achievement of students who are gifted and talented (Daniel and Cox 1989; Schiever and Maker 1991).

4. *Enrichment.* Rather than increase the pace of progression through the regular education curriculum, enriched curricular experiences focus on adjusting the breadth and depth of the curriculum, the tempo or pace at which the curriculum is introduced, and the kind and content of material that is presented. Whether acceleration or enrichment is more appropriate depends on the needs of the students. Prominent acceleration programs are characterized by rapid advancement through the regular curriculum whereas enrichment programs typically incorporate advanced themes and subject areas, emphasize enhancing cognitive processes such as problem solving and creative productivity, and, at the same time, intensify the pace of instruction. To be appropriately carried out, acceleration must be enriching, and enrichment must, in the long run at least, be accelerative (Southern, Jones, and Stanley 1993).

5. *Independent study.* Independent study is intended to allow students who are gifted and talented to select and study topics in a personalized environment (Burns 1993). Independent study opportunities can individualize and extend classroom learning in ways that incorporate multidisciplinary basic skills and higher-level thinking skills into the curriculum. Such opportunities can enable

students who are gifted and talented to go beyond the confines of the classroom, explore the world of work, use school and community resources, participate in inquiry- and discovery-based activities that foster in-depth learning of a self-selected topic, and develop individual learning products that are both creative and worthwhile (Betts 1985; Friedman and Gallagher 1993). Benefits of successful independent study programs include more opportunities for discovery, increased motivation for learning, independence, and a life-long love for learning (Reis and Schack 1993).

6. *Using computer technology.* Jones (1990) has suggested that computers are "idea engines" for students who are gifted in that they allow students to ask and attempt to answer advanced questions, provide for individual learning styles and rates of learning, and enable students to meet others who are gifted and talented via Internet surfing. Hickey (1995) has underscored that computer technology can support independent, small-group, and whole-class instructional opportunities. Used independently, computer-assisted instruction can be direct, individualized, flexibly paced, and interactive.

7. *Guidance and counseling.* The unique personality characteristics of students who are gifted and talented place them at risk for certain kinds of endogenous and exogenous emotional difficulties (Clark 1992a; Douthitt 1992; Freeman 1985; Mendaglio 1995; Silverman 1993; Sowa et al. 1994; Webb 1993; Yewchuk and Jobagy 1991, 1992). For gifted students, crucial risks to achieving social and academic excellence appear to emanate from contextual factors, hence the need to distinguish between endogenous and exogenous problems. Guidance and counseling services to students who are gifted and talented span coordination, assessment, consultative and preventive guidance, counseling and psychotherapy, and advocacy (Andreani and Pagnin 1993; Brown 1993; Clark 1992a; Silverman 1993; Sisk 1987; Webb 1993; Yewchuk and Jobagy 1992).

8. *Mentoring.* Mentorship provisions have been identified as one of the most effective organizational configurations for helping students who are gifted and talented to realize their full potential (Batton and Rodgers 1993; Brown and Harper 1987; Zorman 1993). Three common types of mentorship programs include (1) career exploration, guidance, and development; (2) content-based programs that focus on enrichment in a particular area of interest to individual students; and (3) personal growth programs emphasizing self-awareness that leads to higher educational aspirations (Nash et al. 1993). Mentoring programs for students who are gifted and talented may involve parents, teachers, adults and retirees in the school community, and older students who are gifted and talented (Brown and Harper 1987; Nash et al. 1993; Zorman 1993).

9. *Leadership education.* Leadership education is considered appropriate for students who are gifted and talented given their advanced capacities for critical and creative thinking, problem solving, futuristics, planning, analysis, synthesis, and evaluation. Leadership programs emphasize an awareness of self as a potential leader and focus on creative leadership by developing leadership skills,

knowledge, and abilities. These programs also include the historical and biographical study of eminent leaders (Clark 1992a; Sisk 1993; Smith, Smith, and Barnette 1991).

DESIGNING INDIVIDUAL PROGRAMS

The previous section described a wide range of possible program components for any student who is gifted and talented. Designing an appropriate program for any one student entails considerable care and attention to the student's characteristics and needs. Traditionally, the field of education for gifted students has employed the atypical-learner model of special education as a structure for program development, particularly with regard to identifying and assessing students, selecting and training staff as well as running and evaluating the programs (Alberta Education 1986, 1989, 1995a, 1995b). Use of the atypical-learner model has significantly expanded programs for students who are gifted and talented (VanTassel-Baska 1992a, 1992b). The model highlights the need of students who are gifted and talented for modifications in regular education programs that will optimally develop their potential and that are comparable with modifications made for other exceptional learners.

Individualized Education Programs

From the special education perspective, the unique learning needs of atypical students can best be met through an IEP that acknowledges the students' strengths and needs and explains how the school's program will address these areas. Although a number of models exist for developing IEPs, all approaches include consideration for the strengths and needs, interests, and style preferences of students who are gifted and talented. The following section outlines some of the models that have been developed for designing IEPs for students who are gifted and talented. Other models of interest include Clark's (1992a) Integrated Education Model and Treffinger's (1986a, 1986b) Individualized Program Planning Model.

Alberta's Individualized Program Plan

A mandatory requirement of education for gifted students in Alberta, the Individualized Program Plan (IPP) refers to a special document designed to meet the identified strengths and needs of students who are gifted and talented (Alberta Education 1989). Similar to the Individualized Education Program in the United States, the IPP includes the following information:

- Assessed level of educational performance, strengths, and areas of need along with the assessment procedures that were used
- Long-term goals and short-term objectives

- Specialized education and related services to be provided, including any required modifications in curriculum content, instructional techniques, process and product development, evaluation strategies, materials and resources, facilities, or equipment
- Provision for parent involvement
- Names of people involved in the development, implementation, and evaluation of the IPP
- Relevant medical and background information
- Review dates
- Results and recommendations

School administrators are required to ensure that IPPs are developed, implemented, and evaluated. The development of these plans is expected to be a collaborative effort that may involve parents, teachers, other professionals, and the students themselves (Alberta Education 1995a, 1995b; Delaney and Yewchuk 1985; Renzulli 1994a; Renzulli and Smith 1979). IPPs are reviewed formally every year with parents and, when appropriate, with students.

Total Talent Model

Developing IPPs by applying the approach delineated in the popularized School-wide Enrichment Model (Renzulli and Reis 1985), which in its revised form has been termed the Total Talent Model (Renzulli 1994a, 1994b), involves considering assessment information to identify strengths, interests, and preferred learning conditions. Assessment information is collected from such sources as student product portfolios; cumulative record files; teacher, parent, peer, and self ratings; intelligence tests; achievement tests; subject grades; interest inventories; and style preference ratings of instructional methods, learning environments, intellectual modes, and forms of expression. This information is used to clarify which subject areas or assignments can be compacted and how curriculum is to be differentiated, accelerated, and enriched. The curriculum model used in this plan emphasizes content, process, original inquiry, and interdisciplinary activities.

Enrichment Matrix Model

Tannenbaum's (1986) Enrichment Matrix Model is based on the assumption that the provisional characteristics of many education programs for talented and gifted students insufficiently meet students' needs for extensive programmatic intervention. This model invites consideration of higher-level thinking skills including values clarification as well as futuristics and careers. Its use also requires that techniques for differentiation in curriculum be identified, especially in the areas of language arts, mathematics, science, social studies, music, art and literature. In addition, the model encourages a telescoped common core, skills expansion, programmatic augmentation, and enrichment activities in these curriculum areas. Finally, supplementary content areas (anthropology, geopolitics, leadership, and psychology) and interdisciplinary content areas (aesthetics and humanities) also should be considered.

Integrated Curriculum Model

The Integrated Curriculum Model presented by VanTassel-Baska (1994, 1995) is accomplished through the incorporation of interdisciplinary themes in advanced content areas as well as in higher-order thinking and processing skills. This model depends on extensive pretesting both in specified subject areas and with regard to the cognitive, affective, social, aesthetic, and psychomotor dimensions of high-ability or high-achieving students. The model features methods for differentiating curriculum in terms of concept, content, and process in the areas of language arts, science, mathematics, social studies, art, humanities, multicultural education, thinking skills, affective development, and leadership.

DESIGNING SCHOOLWIDE PROGRAMS

The previous section provided overviews of four models for designing IEPs for students who are gifted and talented. These models indicate the complexity in any one plan. Planning a schoolwide program for gifted and talented students can be particularly challenging given that the program should provide individual differentiated learning experiences, meet parental expectations, fit with existing school philosophy, effectively use community resources, and fall within the range of the professional expertise of the school's teaching and support staff. Consequently, considerable attention has been given to the processes and purposes of program development for these programs.

A coherent structure for a program for gifted and talented students should clearly discern and show congruence of goals, purposes, methods, and benefits. The design of a coherent program structure depends on clarifying beliefs about how students who are gifted and talented are actually defined; how their gifts and talents are identified; what goals are held for these students; how they are selected for participation; what specifically designed services should be provided; who should deliver the services; and how the continuum of services should be delivered, organized, and managed.

To emphasize the importance of a systematic approach to this education innovation, Goh (1993) has proposed the Recursive Procedural Model for developing and improving these programs. This five-stage model includes

- Visioning (ideation)
- Initializing (conceptualization, steering, climatization)
- Planning (assessment of needs, formulation of goals, program design)

- Implementing (preparation, application, observation, evaluation)
- Institutionalizing (program maintenance through thoughtful revision and planned improvement)

The model as a whole emphasizes concern for efficacy, structure in organization, and the interpersonal process dimensions of program implementation.

The views of all stakeholders or participants are very important in the successful development of a program for gifted and talented students. Whatever program model is selected or developed should be seen as the best choice to provide what members of the school community believe to be important (Cohen, Jeffcott, and Swartz 1991; Goh 1993). If a coordinated effort between regular education and education for gifted students is desired, then those factors of a program for gifted students that would render it acceptable to pertinent stakeholders in the community should also be considered (Berger 1991; Goh 1993; Haughey and Rowley 1991; Heck 1991; Holdaway and Ratsoy 1991; Van-Tassel-Baska 1994). Maker (1993) has identified a large number of organizational dimensions that must be clarified for a program for gifted students to be successfully carried out. Within this list, she includes not only adequate resources but also communication between teachers in programs for both gifted and regular students, between teachers and administrators, and between the school and the community.

Orenstein (1984) provided an overview of organizational dimensions that are fundamental for a gifted education program:

- Physical facilities
- Staff allocation and authority for management of the program (budgetary control, staff development, teacher selection and training)
- Type of program in terms of location and time spent in the program (regular classroom, gifted classroom, charter school, community-based program, full- or part-time)
- Organizational structure of the program (scheduling for flexible ability grouping, cooperative learning, acceleration, enrichment, independent study, computer technology, mentorship, counseling, leadership)
- Scope of the program (systematic student identification, program activities)
- Curriculum (inventory of materials, resources and equipment assigned to the program)
- Parent and community involvement and evaluation

This section on the development of gifted and talented programs offers a brief sketch of a small amount of the intensive and extensive work that has been undertaken to clarify the needs of students who are gifted and talented as well as the programming possibilities for addressing their education. The complexity and richness of the many models and materials that have been developed suggest that inclusive schooling, which attempts to meet the needs of all students including those who are gifted and talented, is an ambitious project.

THE FUTURE OF GIFTED AND TALENTED PROGRAMS IN INCLUSIVE SCHOOLS

Visions of inclusive schools tend to be complex. In Stainback and Stainback's (1990) articulation, the focus in inclusive schooling is on how to develop school and classroom communities that fit, nurture, and support the inter- and intrapersonal needs (social, familial, emotional, psychological, intellectual, creative-intuitive, economic, political, cultural, religious, gender, sexual, and physical) of every student in attendance. The more simply stated goal of "educational excellence for all" can underrepresent the multidimensionality of the inclusive schools' mission in this articulation. The question about the future of programs for gifted and talented students is not about the merit of inclusive schools' visions but about whether the momentum of development work in education for gifted and talented students will be lost within the larger project.

VanTassel-Baska (1994) and others have clarified that an emphasis on excellence for all students does not mean that all students will get the same services. All students are entitled to educational experiences that are appropriately enhancing, and some of those experiences that are appropriate for students who are gifted and talented will be unique or specialized. When public funds are dedicated to specialized provisions, policy and public rationale are typically prerequisite.

One of the perennial issues in education for gifted and talented students has been finding ways to provide services to groups who have been historically underrepresented, including economically disadvantaged students, culturally different students, female underachievers, students with limited English proficiency, students with disabilities, students enrolled in vocational and technical schools, and students who are talented in the arts (Renzulli, Reid, and Grubbins 1994). Without strong advocacy for the education of students who are gifted and talented, efforts to identify and serve these students may evaporate. In schools with large numbers of economically disadvantaged students, the energies of school staff members can be consumed by meeting a variety of students' needs other than those of identifying and addressing their gifts and talents in educational programming.

In their research on long-running talent development programs, Renzulli and Reis (1991a) have identified the key role of a catalyst teacher who assumes a leadership role of coordinator. If the notion of education for gifted and talented students is to lose valence within inclusive schooling, how likely is it that any coordinator or catalyst person will direct ongoing attention to the many diverse functions that have been part of programs for these students?

On a more promising note, we must consider the more radical possibilities of inclusive schools. Ross (1991) has identified current initiatives that hold promise for students who are gifted and talented and that are aimed at improving learning for all students. These include ungraded schools where students are grouped for instruction according to their ability; incorporation of problem-solving and thinking skills into the general curriculum; authentic assessment involving the use of portfolios for collections of student work to serve as a record of accomplishment; and curriculum revision that incorporates technology and interdisciplinary study featuring broad themes that emphasize real-life experimentation and problem solving.

Such initiatives should be only the tip of the iceberg. Many creative visionaries can be found among our educators. Many administrators are creative and know a great deal about the strengths and interests of the professionals employed at their schools. And many teachers possess gifts that are untapped or no longer used because they are in mismatched teaching assignments. To serve all students well, including students who are gifted and talented, inclusive schools will need room to maneuver as they reconceptualize the structures of schools and rethink the support teachers need to contribute effectively to educational programs. If schools wish to develop the students' gifts, they must begin by providing space and support for the teachers to use and develop their own gifts.

REFERENCES

Alberta Education. 1986. *Educating students who are gifted and talented in Alberta: A resource manual for teachers.* Edmonton, Alberta: Special Education Services.

———.1989. *Individualized Program Plans: A reference for teachers.* Edmonton, Alberta: Alberta Education Response Centre.

———.1991. *Vision for the nineties . . . A plan of action.* Edmonton, Alberta: Special Education Services.

———. 1995a. *Alberta education policy, regulations, and forms manual.* Edmonton, Alberta: Communications Branch.

———. 1995b. *Guide to education for students with special needs.* Edmonton, Alberta: Special Education Services.

Andreani, O. D., and A. Pagnin. 1993. Nurturing the moral development of the gifted. In *International handbook of research and development of giftedness and talent,* ed. K. A. Heller, F. J. Monks, and A. H. Passow, 539–53. New York: Pergamon.

Bacto, M., C. Milan, F. Litton, A. Rotatori, and J. Carlson. 1991. The gifted and talented. In *Understanding students with high incidence exceptionalities: Categorical and noncategorical perspectives,* ed. J. O. Schwenn, A. F. Rotatori, and R. A. Fox, 205–48. Springfield, Ill.: Thomas.

Batton, J., and J. Rogers. 1993. Response to "Mentoring: Extending learning for gifted students." In *Critical issues in gifted education: Programs for the gifted,* vol. 3, ed. C. J. Maker, 331–41. Austin: Pro-Ed.

Belcastro, F. P. 1987. The gifted in elementary school. *Roeper Review* 9:208–12.

Berger, S. 1991. *Differentiating curriculum for gifted students.* Reston, Va.: U.S. Department of Education, Office of Educational Research and Improvement. (ERIC Document No. ED 334 806, ERIC Digest No. E510).

Betts, G. D. 1985. *Autonomous learner model for the gifted and talented.* Berkeley, Calif.: Autonomous Learning Publications and Specialists.

Borland, J. H. 1986. IQ tests: Throwing out the bathwater, saving the baby. *Roeper Review* 8:163–67.

Brown, B., and S. Harper. 1987. Mentoring: How retired adults in your school's community can enhance students' learning. *The Canadian School Executive* (September):19–21.

Brown, L. L. 1993. Special considerations in counselling gifted students. *The School Counsellor* 40:184–90.

Burns, F. D. 1993. Independent study: Panacea or palliative? In *Critical issues in gifted education: Programs for the gifted,* vol. 3, ed. C. J. Maker, 381–99. Austin: Pro-Ed.

Canadian Charter of Rights and Freedoms, Part I of the Constitution Act, 1982, being Schedule B to the Canada Act 1982 (U.K.), 1982, c. 11.

Clark, B. 1992a. *Growing up gifted: Developing the potential of children at home and at school.* 4th ed. Toronto: Maxwell Macmillan.

———. 1992b. The need for a range of program options for students who are gifted and talented. In *Controversial issues confronting special education,* ed. W. Stainback and S. Stainback, 57–67. Boston: Allyn and Bacon.

Cohen, L. M., G. Jeffcott, and E. Swartz. 1991. Recent trends in gifted education. *Gifted International* 7 (1):13–78.

Conroy, J. 1993. Classroom management: An expanded view. In *Critical issues in gifted education: Programs for the gifted,* vol. 3, ed. C. J. Maker, 227–52. Austin: Pro-Ed.

Daniel, N., and J. Cox. 1989. *Meeting the needs of able flexible learners through flexible pacing.* Reston, Va.: U.S. Department of Education, Office of Educational Research and Improvement. (ERIC Document No. ED 314 916, ERIC Digest No. E464).

Delaney, D., and C. Yewchuk. 1985. Individualizing education for gifted students. *The ATA [Alberta Teachers' Association] Magazine* (November/December):4–7.

Douthitt, V. L. 1992. A comparison of adaptive behavior in gifted and nongifted children. *Roeper Review* 14:149–51.

Evans, D. W. 1995/1996. From the editor. *Case in Point* 9:iv.

Evans, K. M., and J. A. King. 1993. Outcome-based and gifted education: Can we assume continued support? *Roeper Review* 16:260–64.

Feldhusen, J. F. 1995. Talent development: The new direction in gifted education. *Roeper Review* 18:92.

Freeman, J. 1985. Emotional aspects of giftedness. In *The psychology of gifted children,* ed. J. Freeman, 247–64. New York: Wiley.

Friedman, R. C., and T. J. Gallagher. 1993. Reaction to "Independent study." In *Critical issues in gifted education: Programs for the gifted,* vol. 3, ed. C. J. Maker, 400–412. Austin: Pro-Ed.

Gallagher, J. J. 1991a. Educational reform, values, and gifted students. *Gifted Child Quarterly* 35:12–19.

————. 1991b. Programs for gifted students: Enlightened self-interest. *Gifted Child Quarterly* 35:175–76.

Goguen, L. J. 1993. Right to education for the gifted in Canada. In *International handbook of research and development of giftedness and talent,* ed. K. A. Heller, F. J. Monks, and A. H. Passow, 771–77. New York: Pergamon.

Goh, B. E. 1993. Administrative issues in organizing programs for the gifted. In *International handbook of research and development of giftedness and talent,* ed. K. A. Heller, F. J. Monks, and A. H. Passow, 569–83. New York: Pergamon.

Harris, D. M., and D. W. Evans. 1994. Integrating school restructuring and special education reform. *Case in Point* 8:7–19.

Harvey, D. 1996. A progressive model for gifted programming in regular classrooms. *AGATE: Journal of the Gifted and Talented Education Council of the Alberta Teachers' Association* 10:25–33.

Haughey, M., and D. Rowley. 1991. Principals as change agents. *The Canadian Administrator* 30:1–9.

Heck, R. H. 1991. Towards the future: Rethinking the leadership role of the principal as philosopher–king. *Journal of Educational Administration* 29:67–79.

Hickey, M. G. 1995. More drill and practice: Selecting software for learners who are gifted. *Teaching Exceptional Children* 27:48–50.

Holdaway, E., and E. Ratsoy. 1991. Preparation of principals for their emerging role. *The Canadian Administrator* 30:1–9.

Johnston, P. 1991. Concerns regarding mainstreaming and segregating gifted children in elementary school. *AGATE: Journal of the Gifted and Talented Education Council of the Alberta Teachers' Association* 5:57–63.

Jones, G. 1990. *Personal computers help gifted students work smart.* Washington, D.C.: U.S. Department of Education, Office of Educational Research and Improvement. (ERIC Digest No. E483).

Jones, P. R. 1991. Cost of special education: Is mainstreaming really cheaper? *Case in Point* 6:40–43.

Keating, D. P. 1990. Charting pathways to the development of expertise. *Educational Psychologist* 25:243–67.

Lupart, J. 1992. Gifted, special, and inclusive education: Past, present, and future promise. Paper presented at the Third Annual Conference of the Society for the Advancement of Gifted Education: Images in Transition, September 1992, Calgary.

Maker, C. J., ed. 1993. *Critical issues in gifted education: Programs for the gifted in regular classrooms,* vol. 3. Austin: Pro-Ed.

Marland, S. P. Jr. 1972. *Education of the gifted and talented: Report to the Congress of the United States by the Commission on Education.* Washington, D.C.: U.S. Government Printing Office.

McCluskey, K. W., and K. D. Walker. 1986. *The doubtful gift: Strategies for educating gifted children in the regular classroom.* Kingston, Ontario: Frye.

McDaniel, T. R. 1993. Education of the gifted and the excellence–equity debate: Lessons from history. In *Critical issues in gifted education: Programs for the gifted,* vol. 3, ed. C. J. Maker, 6–21. Austin: Pro-Ed.

Mendaglio, S. 1995. Sensitivity among gifted persons: A multi-faceted perspective. *Roeper Review* 17:169–72.

Myers, R., and H. Sobehart. 1994/1995. Creating a unified system: The road less travelled. *Case in Point* 9:1–9.

Nash, W. R., P. A. Haensly, V. J. S. Rodgers, and N. L. Wright. 1993. Mentoring: Extending learning for gifted students. In *Critical issues in gifted education: Programs for the gifted*, vol. 3, ed. C. J. Maker, 313–29. Austin: Pro-Ed.

Nelson, S. M., J. J. Gallagher, and M. R. Coleman. 1993. Cooperative learning from two different perspectives. *Roeper Review* 16:117–21.

Nikiforuk, A. 1993. When will they ever learn? *Western Living* 30 (September):64–67.

O'Neil, J. 1994/1995. Can inclusion work? A conversation with Jim Kauffman and Mara Sapon-Shevin. *Educational Leadership* 52:7–11.

Orenstein, A. J. 1984. What organizational characteristics are important in planning, implementing, and maintaining programs for the gifted? *Gifted Child Quarterly* 28:99–105.

Parke, B. N. 1989. *Gifted students in regular classrooms*. Boston: Allyn and Bacon.

———. 1990. Gifted students in regular classrooms. *AGATE: Journal of the Gifted and Talented Education Council of the Alberta Teachers' Association* 4:25–29.

Passow, A. H. 1993. National/state policies regarding education of the gifted. In *International handbook of research and development of giftedness and talent*, ed. K. A. Heller, F. J. Monks, and A. H. Passow, 29–46. New York: Pergamon.

Passow, A. H., and R. A. Rudnitski. 1994. Transforming policy to enhance educational services for the gifted. *Roeper Review* 16:271–75.

Reis, S. M., and G. D. Schack. 1993. Differentiating products for the gifted and talented: The encouragement of independent learning. In *Critical issues in gifted education: Programs for the gifted*, vol. 3, ed. C. J. Maker, 161–86. Austin: Pro-Ed.

Renzulli, J. S. 1994a. *Schools for total talent development: A practical plan for total school improvement*. Mansfield Center, Conn.: Creative Learning Press.

———. 1994b. *Schools for total talent development: A practical plan for total school improvement: Executive summary*. Mansfield Center, Conn.: Creative Learning Press.

———. 1994/1995. Teachers as talent scouts. *Educational Leadership* 52:75–81.

Renzulli, J. S., B. D. Reid, and E. J. Grubbins. 1994. *Setting an agenda: Research priorities for the gifted and talented through the year 2000*. Storrs: University of Connecticut, National Research Center on the Gifted and Talented.

Renzulli, J. S., and S. M. Reis. 1985. *The schoolwide enrichment model: A comprehensive plan for educational excellence*. Mansfield Center, Conn.: Creative Learning Press.

———. 1991a. Building advocacy through program design: Student productivity and public relations. *Gifted Child Quarterly* 35:182–87.

———. 1991b. The reform movement and the quiet crisis in gifted education. *Gifted Child Quarterly* 35:26–35.

Renzulli, J. S., and L. H. Smith. 1979. *A guidebook for developing Individualized Educational Programs (IEPs) for students who are gifted and talented*. Mansfield Center, Conn.: Creative Learning Press.

Robinson, A. 1991. *Cooperative learning and the academically talented student: Executive summary* [Research Monograph No. 9105]. Storrs: University of Connecticut, National Research Center on the Gifted and Talented.

Rogers, K. B. 1991a. Grouping the gifted and talented. *Roeper Review* 16:8–12.

———. 1991b. *The relationship of grouping practices to the education of the gifted and talented learner.* Storrs: University of Connecticut, National Research Center on the Gifted and Talented.

———. 1991c. *The relationship of grouping practices to the education of the gifted and talented learner: Executive summary.* Storrs: University of Connecticut, National Research Center on the Gifted and Talented.

Rosenstein, P. D., and P. Dettmer. 1991. Advocacy for gifted programs: An interview with NAGC Executive Director Peter D. Rosenstein. *Gifted Child Quarterly* 35:179–81.

Ross, P. O. 1991. Advocacy for gifted programs in the new educational climate. *Gifted Child Quarterly* 35:173–76.

Sapon-Shevin, M. 1992. Including all children and their gifts within regular classrooms. In *Controversial issues confronting special education,* ed. W. Stainback and S. Stainback, 69–81. Boston: Allyn and Bacon.

———. 1994/1995. Why gifted students belong in inclusive schools. *Educational Leadership* 52:64–68, 70.

Saskatchewan Education. 1989. *Special education policy manual.* Regina, Saskatchewan: Saskatchewan Education.

Schiever, S. W., and C. J. Maker. 1991. Enrichment and acceleration: An overview and new directions. In *Handbook of gifted education,* ed. N. Colangelo and G. Davis, 99–110. Boston: Allyn and Bacon.

Silverman, L. K. 1989. It all began with Leta Hollingworth: The story of giftedness in women. *Journal for the Education of the Gifted* 12:86–98.

———. 1996. The emotional needs of the gifted. *AGATE: Journal of the Gifted and Talented Education Council of the Alberta Teachers' Association* 10:2–15.

Silverman, L. K., ed. 1993. *Counselling the gifted and talented.* Denver: Love Publishing Co.

Sisk, D. A. 1987. Counselling and guiding the gifted. In *Creative teaching of the gifted,* ed. D. A. Sisk, 259–87. New York: McGraw-Hill.

———. 1993. Leadership education for the gifted. In *International handbook of research and development of giftedness and talent,* ed. K. A. Heller, F. J. Monks, and A. H. Passow, 491–505. New York: Pergamon.

Smith, J. L., L. J. Smith, and J. Barnette. 1991. Exploring the development of leadership. *Roeper Review* 14:7–12.

Southern, W. T., E. D. Jones, and J. C. Stanley. 1993. Acceleration and enrichment: The context and development of program options. In *International handbook of research and development of giftedness and talent,* ed. K. A. Heller, F. J. Monks, and A. H. Passow, 387–409. New York: Pergamon.

Sowa, C. J., J. McIntire, K. M. May, and L. Bland. 1994. Social and emotional adjustment themes across gifted children. *Roeper Review* 17:95–98.

Stainback, S., and W. Stainback. 1990. Inclusive schooling. In *Support networks for inclusive schooling: Interdependent integrated education*, ed. W. Stainback and S. Stainback, 3–24. Baltimore, Md.: Paul H. Brookes.

Sullivan, M. 1991. The role of cross-age groupings in accommodating student differences. *AGATE: Journal of the Gifted and Talented Education Council of the Alberta Teachers' Association* 5:8–11.

Tannenbaum, A. J. 1986. The enrichment matrix model. In *Systems and models for developing programs for the gifted and talented*, ed. J. S. Renzulli, 391–428. Mansfield Center, Conn.: Creative Learning Press.

———. 1993. History of giftedness and "gifted education" in world perspective. In *International handbook of research and development of giftedness and talent*, ed. K. A. Heller, F. J. Monks, and A. H. Passow, 3–27. New York: Pergamon.

Terman, L. M. 1925. *Genetic studies of genius: Mental and physical traits of a thousand gifted children*, vol. 1. Stanford, Calif.: Stanford University Press.

Thorkildsen, T. A. 1994. Some ethical implications of communal and competitive approaches to gifted education. *Roeper Review* 17:54–57.

Tomlinson, C. A. 1993. The easy lie and the role of gifted education in school excellence. *Roeper Review* 16:258–59.

———. 1994/1995. Gifted learners too: A possible dream? *Educational Leadership* 52:68–69.

Treffinger, D. J. 1986a. *Blending gifted education with the total school program*, 2d ed. New York: D.O.K.

———. 1986b. Fostering effective, independent learning through individualized programming. In *Systems and models for developing programs for the gifted and talented*, ed. J. S. Renzulli, 429–60. Mansfield Center, Conn.: Creative Learning Press.

———. 1991a. Future goals and directions. In *Handbook of gifted education*, ed. N. Colangelo and G. Davis, 441–49. Boston: Allyn and Bacon.

———. 1991b. School reform and gifted education: Opportunities and issues. *Gifted Child Quarterly* 35:6–11.

———. 1995. School improvement, talent development, and creativity. *Roeper Review* 18:93–97.

VanTassel-Baska, J. 1991. Gifted education in the balance: Building relationships with general education. *Gifted Child Quarterly* 35:20–25.

———. 1992a. *Developing learner outcomes for gifted students*. Reston, Va.: U.S. Department of Education, Office of Educational Research and Improvement. (ERIC Digest No. E514).

———. 1992b. *Planning effective curriculum for gifted learners*. Denver: Love Publishing Co.

———. 1994. *Comprehensive curriculum for gifted learners*. 2d ed. Denver: Love Publishing Co.

———. 1995. The development of talent through curriculum. *Roeper Review* 18:98–102.

Vialle, W. 1993. "Termanal" science? The work of Lewis Terman. *Roeper Review* 17:32–38.

Webb, J. T. 1993. Nurturing social-emotional development of gifted children. In *International handbook of research and development of giftedness and talent,* ed. K. A. Heller, F. J. Monks, and A. H. Passow, 525–37. New York: Pergamon.

Willis, S., ed. 1995. Mainstreaming the gifted. *Education Update: Association for Supervision and Curriculum Development* 37:1, 4–5.

Yewchuk, C., and S. Jobagy. 1991. The neglected minority: The emotional needs of gifted children. *Education Canada* (Winter):8–13.

———. 1992. Counselling needs of gifted children and youth. *Alberta Counsellor* 20:14–20.

Zirkel, P. A., and P. L. Stevens. 1987. The law concerning public education of gifted students. *Journal for the Education of the Gifted* 10:305–22.

Zorman, R. 1993. Monitoring and role modeling programs for the gifted. In *International handbook of research and development of giftedness and talent,* ed. K. A. Heller, F. J. Monks, and A. H. Passow, 727–41. New York: Pergamon.

8

The Education of Students with Emotional or Behavioral Disorders

Timothy J. Landrum   *Melody Tankersley*

erhaps no issue in education can raise the anxiety of teachers—particularly those in regular education—more than the prospect of teaching and working with students with emotional or behavioral disorders (E/BD).[1] By definition, students identified with E/BD present what are easily the most disturbing rule- and norm-violating behaviors that teachers have identified. As reform efforts carry us into the next century, we must acknowledge both the effect of students with behavioral disorders on our educational system—whatever form that may hold or evolve into—and our responsibility to provide quality educational services to our students regardless of their learning or behavioral characteristics.

In this chapter, we provide a brief overview of issues that demand our attention as the field of special education for students with emotional or behavioral disorders continues to grow and evolve. Many of these issues are not new, but they may require a new look as reform efforts, the inclusive schools

---

1. Because the National Mental Health and Special Education Coalition prefers the label of "emotional or behavioral disorders" and its definition, we use this term throughout this chapter instead of the federal terminology, *serious emotional disturbance*.

movement, and disciplinary issues gain the attention of educators, parents, and policymakers. A driving theme behind these issues seems to be this question: Where should we educate students with E/BD? Although pertinent in this form, we cast the question a bit more broadly in this chapter: How should we educate students with E/BD?

THE ISSUE: WHERE AND HOW TO EDUCATE STUDENTS WITH EMOTIONAL OR BEHAVIORAL DISORDERS

In it simplest form, the issue to be addressed involves a choice between two options: integrated classrooms or segregated classrooms. Should students with E/BD be educated alongside their peers without disabilities, or should they receive educational services in segregated settings with other students who have presumably similar disabilities? This question seems basic to much of the inclusion debate and rhetoric that has been around for more than a decade (e.g., Stainback and Stainback 1984). Closer scrutiny reveals some fundamental flaws in this forced choice, of course, and finer logical analysis suggests some even more troubling oversimplifications.

According to Hallahan and Kauffman (1997), the choices of regular classroom settings or special classroom settings are but two points along a continuum of placement options that includes such arrangements as intermittent help from itinerant teachers, resource help for parts of the day, and consultative or collaborative teaching. Indeed, they delineate no fewer than nine separate options along the continuum of alternative placements that have become a hallmark of special education. At a basic level, the notion that we must choose between regular classroom and special class placement is erroneous. Thus, despite the arguments of some who espouse inclusion as an alternative to segregated, separate class placement, the theme that should drive our integration efforts should be movement along this continuum toward less restrictive placements instead of a simple choice between two options.

We find arguments about how to educate E/BD students to be much more important than discussions of placement options. In other words, features such as effective, intensive, individualized instruction and behavior management; appropriate support services; specifically targeted social skills instruction; and consistent, positive approaches to discipline are probably essential elements of an appropriate educational program for students with E/BD. This question faces school child-study teams: In what setting (or settings) can these identified services be provided? Although the law clearly indicates that students may be removed from a regular education setting only when an appropriate education cannot be achieved in that regular setting—even with supplemental aids and services—current literature seems equally clear that the regular education system is generally unprepared to provide appropriate services for many students with E/BD (Lewis, Chard, and Scott 1994).

Current Parameters of the Issue: Placement and Teacher Preparation

The arguments surrounding inclusion of the student with behavioral disorders involve at least two separate factors that we must consider. The first is whether students with behavior disorders benefit from placement in regular classrooms. Do students with behavioral disorders, for example, benefit from observing positive, peer role models that may be found in regular classrooms? Conversely, are students with behavioral disorders likely to learn even more antisocial behavior patterns if they are isolated from nondisabled students in segregated classrooms that may include a number of negative models?

The second issue is quite separate. Physical placement aside, are regular classroom teachers prepared to work effectively with the student with behavioral disorders? Moreover, if we find that they are not, are we prepared to provide the support and assistance needed to ensure that students with behavioral disorders benefit from their educational programs?

Although our current knowledge base in special education does not allow us to answer either question definitively, the extant literature may offer some guidance as policymakers forge new relationships among educational entities. In the following sections, we consider several ideas related to placement and personnel preparation issues.

Placement

The controversy surrounding placement is surely the most divisive aspect of the inclusion debate and includes attention to two elements of the settings in question. First, do integrated settings more appropriately meet the unique educational needs of students with E/BD? Second, do integrated settings offer more in terms of prosocial peer models and support of appropriate social skills than do segregated settings? On the one hand, proponents argue that integrated settings mirror the "real world," that only in integrated placements can students with disabilities observe and master the appropriate skills that typical students display, and that students without disabilities must also learn to accept students who may be different from themselves. On the other hand, the evidence for these assertions is limited at best, and with regard to students who display behavioral difficulties, arguments toward placement as an end in itself may be premature.

In their chapter on the diversity of restrictive environments, Kauffman and Hallahan (1997) describe the complexity of social systems that exist and that continuously emerge in various social contexts. They note, for example, that if observational learning were all that is required for students to develop appropriate social skills, then those we identify with E/BD would certainly have developed appropriate social behavior already. They add that the chance for students with E/BD to benefit from the appropriate peer models they may encounter in regular education environments depends far more on the extensive forethought, planning, and explicit instruction on the part of teachers in those environments than on the mere exposure to positive models. The question as to whether regular education teachers are currently prepared to provide this type of intensive, protracted, and individualized training remains an area in need of further study.

At a more fundamental level, the ability of integrated settings to effectively meet the diverse educational needs of students with disabilities must be paramount. The debate over the effectiveness of special class placement has remained controversial for decades, and a review of this topic is well beyond the scope of this chapter. Instead, we highlight only three points. First, although some early studies suggested that special class placement may actually be harmful to children with disabilities, this conclusion has been widely criticized (e.g., Kauffman and Hallahan 1992). One major flaw in these early studies, for example, was the reliance on comparison groups that were not equivalent. In other words, if the natural events of schooling resulted in some students with disabilities being placed in more segregated settings than others, might it not be expected that the segregated students' difficulties with learning or behavior were greater than those of their counterparts who remained in the regular classroom? Comparisons of the achievement or other measures of functioning between such groups would be highly suspect.

A second limitation of this early research, which addresses our purposes here, was that most of it compared the placement outcomes for students with mild mental retardation. As Forness, Kavale, Blum, and Lloyd (1997) point out in their meta-analysis, however, the apparent negative effects of special class placement are not apparent in studies of students with learning disabilities or emotional and behavioral disorders. Indeed, Forness and colleagues suggest that modest, positive effect sizes are found for special class placement.

Finally, despite the controversy it has generated, the body of literature on special class placement seems to offer relatively little guidance for practice. We conclude that special class placement in itself is inherently neither positive nor negative. The services students receive should be based on the needs, strengths, and weaknesses that individual assessments have identified, and students should be placed in the least restrictive environment in which those services can be delivered. What troubles us more—and what should be the focus of much more attention than issues of placement or inclusion—is the training and preparation of teachers who will work with students who display challenging behavior.

Teacher Preparation

Unfortunately, the current pessimism regarding the ability of regular education programs to deal with students who display emotional or behavioral disorders is predictable given the disappointing results that are obtained even when students with E/BD are served by special education programs. Kauffman (1997) notes that few of the promising interventions that have emerged have produced satisfactory results. In addition, few of the problems facing educators of students with E/BD have been resolved. Indeed, the "new" issues facing our field are virtually the same as those faced a century ago. Although we believe that education in inclusive settings should be the ultimate goal for most students with disabilities, for those who work with and advocate for students with E/BD, inclusion presents an exceptional challenge. We must conclude from the available literature that regular education environments and personnel are not presently equipped to provide appropriate services to the majority of students with E/BD. What do these observations mean for teacher education? A number of ideas have been generated, but few solutions have emerged.

First, teachers of students with E/BD must be highly skilled in the art of instruction, particularly, instruction that is specifically targeted to individuals' strengths and needs. Surveys suggest that many educators still perceive programs for students with E/BD as being dominated by a curriculum of control (Bullock, Ellis, and Wilson 1994)—a curriculum in which teachers' efforts focus heavily on the reduction of problem behavior. Although reducing problem behavior is certainly a laudable goal, the implication in a curriculum of control is that teachers act as watchdogs, policing students' behavior and intervening whenever problems occur, but unfortunately, they offer relatively little active, positive instruction in academic skills and prosocial behavior. We would prefer to see curricula and instruction for students with behavioral difficulties focus on intensive, direct instruction in basic academic skills and heavily emphasize successful learning experiences. Instructional decisions must be based on data, and progress should be monitored closely.

Webber and Scheuermann (1997) delineate several instructional competencies that E/BD teachers must possess. These competencies include direct instruction, curriculum-based assessment, learning strategies instruction, and self-management training. The authors also point out, however, that critical national shortages of special education teachers have resulted in large numbers of uncertified or under-certified teachers working with what may be the most difficult population of students.

Second, all teachers must become more competent in managing general classroom behavior and in dealing with serious behavioral difficulties. The preparation of regular education teachers is, of course, becoming more critical as schools move toward more inclusive programming for students with disabilities. But even where inclusion is not the norm, the imperative for regular educators to develop competencies in behavior management remains paramount. Consider the currently accepted professional estimates of the prevalence of emotional or behavioral disorders: Although schools in the United States have typically served just under 1 percent of the school-aged population under the category of severe emotional disturbance, or SED, Kauffman (1997) has put the range of reasonable professional estimates at least 6 times and as much as 10 times higher than this figure. Thus a regular education teacher may expect to encounter six or more students with serious behavioral problems for every student with E/BD they might be asked to teach.

As education becomes more inclusive, one logical prediction might be that the sheer number of behavior problems that regular education teachers are asked to deal with will increase. Inclusive arrangements require that teachers must be able to deal effectively with not only the routine (though often significant) behavior problems that nonidentified students display but also the behavioral difficulties that integrated students with disabilities may bring. But are teachers prepared for this challenge?

Kauffman and Wong (1991) present a compelling review of the literature on effective teaching from which they conclude that generic teaching skills may not be sufficient, even for skilled teachers, when they are asked to teach students with E/BD. Kauffman and Wong's review suggests that a number of traits and characteristics of effective teachers can be gleaned from the body of research on teaching effectiveness that has accrued but that the majority of this research has excluded students who display the intense and chronic behavior problems typical of most students with E/BD. Their own conclusions offer an even more somber tone. They concur with Lloyd, Kauffman, and Kupersmidt (1990) who suggest that the research base on training effective teachers offers little hope that the behavior of teachers will change significantly in this generation and, further, that "perhaps a more realistic goal for our generation is to work toward the day when special education teachers will routinely adopt those teaching skills and attitudes that empirical data indicate produce the most reliable positive outcomes" (Kauffman and Wong 1991, 234).

Although some have questioned the extent to which regular education teachers are prepared to deal effectively with students with E/BD, Kauffman and Wong's (1991) caveat about attending first to the skills of special education teachers is even more telling. Gunter and Denny (1996) suggest that even in classrooms for students with E/BD, teachers often fail altogether to implement management strategies that offer the most promise and, further, that when they do implement strategies that are empirically sound, they often do not use the strategies correctly. In addition, Gunter and Denny (1996) cite evidence that a substantial majority of teachers of students with E/BD claim that their college coursework did a poor job of preparing them for the challenges they currently face. Likewise, few teachers report that they had learned about the management strategies they use in their classrooms from college coursework.

We could easily cite the litany of effective practices that have substantial empirical support and then call for teacher training programs to implement true, competency-based training in these areas. Indeed, it is not beyond us to make this call; we think that all teacher trainees, including those in special and regular education programs, should become skilled in the principles of applied behavior analysis and, particularly, in applying positive contingencies. But we also recognize that change in teacher preparation does not come easily and, more importantly, that mere change in the content of teacher preparation courses does not ensure that teachers will use the strategies they learn in their coursework. An unfortunate result that often occurs when teachers fail to implement positive strategies successfully is the phenomenon that Patterson (1980) has called the "negative reinforcement trap."

168

Patterson's (1980) work with antisocial children and their families offers much to educators. Among the more telling examples is Patterson's negative reinforcement trap. In his example, a mother is dealing with a child who displays inappropriate and disturbing behavior. During this interchange, the mother nags to get the child to comply with a request (for example, to clean his room), but the child only whines and complains. To maximize her own short-term payoff by quickly eliminating the child's annoying behavior, at least for the moment, the mother engages in what amounts to a very ineffective management strategy. She merely stops asking the child to comply. The mother is negatively reinforced when the child's whining stops, while the child is negatively reinforced when the mother's demands also stop. The trap is, of course, that although both mother and child have experienced a clear example of how to eliminate annoying behavior in one another, the initial issue (cleaning one's room) remains unresolved.

We believe that much of what occurs in schools, at least in terms of discipline for troubling students, also may center around a negative reinforcement trap. Consider a school example. Suppose a student is disruptive in math class. He or she is off task to the point of distracting others and disrupting the lesson. A teacher may offer a number of verbal warnings and reminders, but as the student becomes more disruptive and the teacher becomes more frustrated, the eventual consequence is that the teacher banishes the student to the hallway. In the short run, the strategy has worked for the teacher: The disruption is gone and a more enjoyable lesson can proceed. In fact, the strategy may also have been successful from the student's perspective. Particularly if he or she did not find math enjoyable, the student has been able to eliminate two adversives: the teacher's verbal reprimands and the unpleasant math lesson.

This scenario, of course, carries with it the elements that make it a negative reinforcement trap. Both parties have been reinforced by having negatives removed. The specific behaviors that have been reinforced, however, and are thus more likely to occur in the future are anything but positive. The student may have learned that to avoid math class he or she simply needs to become sufficiently disruptive. The teacher may have learned that the easiest path to a smoothly running classroom involves removing disruptive students. Of course, the math assignment itself and any chance at academic growth have been compromised.

Landrum (1992) has argued that teachers, especially those who teach students with E/BD, may be the ultimate victims when they engage or are engaged in these types of interchanges. The chance of such coercive interactions to evolve is heightened when students who are already skilled at coercion, such as those we identify as having emotional and behavioral disorders, are in the charge of teachers who may not be trained or skilled in dealing with serious problem behavior. Punishments, in- and out-of-school suspension, and even expulsions may come to carry the properties of negative reinforcement. Students may learn to use their negative behavior and its coercive power to avoid unpleasant situations while teachers come to rely on strategies that only perpetuate this cycle. Still, the problems at the root of the conflict remain unresolved.

Our argument that the negative reinforcement trap may be prevalent in schools is underscored by data suggesting that even students' appropriate behavior does not receive positive attention (Strain et al. 1983). Perhaps more distressing, students with E/BD—who, we might argue, are in even greater need of positive response to their appropriate behavior—may also be unlikely to receive any positive statements from their teachers (e.g., Shores et al. 1993). Kauffman (1997) has noted that this disdain toward positives has become fashionable throughout education and has pointed out that credible reviews of the evidence suggest that a move away from positive consequences for appropriate behavior is completely without empirical foundation. Nonetheless, one can see the potential convergence of forces at work as teachers become less likely to engage in positive approaches to discipline at a time when they are more frequently called on to teach students with challenging behavior.

PREDICTIONS FOR THE FUTURE

The adage that "those who forget the past are destined to repeat it" applies as readily to education reform as to world history. Educators, Kauffman (1997) notes, have wrestled with such issues as placement options and similarities between regular and special education for at least half a century. And remarkably, many of the interventions we use today have their roots in the work of psychologists and special educators in the early 1800s. At that time, teaching techniques that were used for students with mental retardation and behavioral disorders were often individualized, highly structured, systematic, and based on frequent positive reinforcement. With regard to our most challenging students—particularly those with behavioral disorders—we think it would be wise to attend to Kauffman's analysis: Many of the issues we face today and, indeed, many of the solutions that we have proposed or implemented have been around for decades.

The optimism and promise associated with the work of many educators in the early nineteenth century was replaced by disillusionment and regression in the quality of treatment provided to difficult students in the latter half of that century. This deterioration occurred in large part because the promising treatments that educators had believed (perhaps unreasonably) could cure the problems of the most difficult students remained unfulfilled. As we move into the twenty-first century, we must take great care to avoid a similar cycle in our thinking and intervention efforts. Many treatment options show great promise for ameliorating the problems of students with emotional or behavioral disorders. Early intervention, even for students with some of the most substantial behavioral disabilities, may be a particularly promising avenue for further research. Kamps and Tankersley (1996) offer an overview of the current status of prevention efforts that also highlights the important distinction between true prevention ("primary" prevention) and early intervention.

The term *prevention* suggests that emotional or behavioral disorders can be stopped from ever truly emerging. Such preventive efforts carry significant pitfalls, of course, such as relying on the inexact science of prediction to decide whom to serve with our preventive efforts. However, as Kamps and Tankersley (1996) point out, in practice, efforts to prevent behavioral or conduct disorders is essentially early intervention. Because research on the development of antisocial behavior has yielded overwhelming evidence that key signs of risk are evident early in life, early intervention efforts can be better targeted. Kamps and Tankersley delineate the following five elements as key to preventive efforts: using parents as key interventionists; cross-setting, intervening proactively; involving teachers and peers as intervention agents; increasing students' self-management skills; and encouraging collaboration among families, schools, and community service providers. Clearly, the overarching principles of early intervention mirror those described by advocates who argue for comprehensive systems of care.

Another promising line of research on early intervention has been contributed by Hill Walker and his colleagues (Walker et al. 1998). Their First Step to Success program has shown promise in reducing the development of antisocial behavior patterns in kindergarten students who are identified as being at high risk because of their high rates of aggressive, oppositional behavior. The First Step program includes three key components: universal screening of all kindergarten students so that emerging problems are detected at the earliest possible stage; school-based interventions that actively involve the target students and their peers and teachers; and intensive training for parents or caregivers (Walker et al. 1998). Although their initial work suggests that treatment gains are realized and maintained into the early primary grades, Walker and colleagues caution that, even with such promise, the true measure of these interventions will come only with longer-term follow-up on students and families who participate in these early intervention efforts.

It is perhaps simplistic but nonetheless true, we believe, that truly appropriate services for children with E/BD should imply commitment to both early and long-term intervention. When signs of risk are evident, early intervention that is done by parents and families, schools, and other agencies to ameliorate the development of serious behavioral difficulties is imperative. Equally important, however, should be our commitment to sustain the intensity of service efforts when our early intervention efforts do not seem to be successful.

Although much of the emerging evidence on early intervention and prevention shows promise, we find that the most realistic and professionally responsible outlook includes both (1) substantial efforts at preventing emotional and behavioral disorders and (2) acceptance that many children with troubling behavior will continue to experience problems into adolescence and adulthood. We argue, in fact, that to expect that students who display chronic, serious, and versatile antisocial behavior can be cured—to expect that their disability can be made to go away—is to do them as great a disservice as was done a hundred years ago.

For us to capitalize on the gains that have been made in a way that enhances the treatment potential for students with behavior disorders, we need a more parsimonious approach to their education and treatment. The ideas of Wolf, Braukmann, and Ramp (1987), who question the appropriateness of treatment goals that are based on short-term treatment and expectations of a permanent cure, may be especially important as reform efforts wax and wane. Wolf and colleagues suggest that the education of students who have developed patterns of antisocial behavior may be best conceptualized as long-term, perhaps life-long, supportive treatment for both those students and their families. Even in their review of treatment components that have shown great promise, these authors conclude that short-term cures generally have not been realized. We agree that a view toward long-term care that includes potentially life-long services is wise, and we hope that a movement toward this view is coupled with greatly enhanced education and training for teachers in both general and special education and for other professionals who will be called on to provide these services.

This view is echoed by those who approach treatment of students with E/BD from a systems perspective (e.g., Epstein et al. 1993). "Systems of care" has become a common phrase in the literature on how to adequately cope with the diverse and intensive service needs of youth with emotional and behavioral disorders and their families. An early observation from research in this area was that many children and youth were receiving services from multiple agencies (e.g., Landrum et al. 1995) but, often, with little or no coordination among these agencies. A growing consensus seems to be that schools—even when they provide the appropriate and intensive educational services students need—cannot adequately address the varied needs of students and families without the collaborative support of other community providers, including mental health, juvenile justice, and social service agencies. We believe that a systems-of-care approach, coupled with a life-span view of the service needs of children and families, may offer the most promise for children who experience emotional and behavioral disorders.

CONCLUSION

The education of students with emotional or behavioral disorders, including both those identified under this category of disability and those in regular education who display consistent patterns of problem behavior, will continue to be the greatest challenge our educational system faces. And despite programs that show great promise and treatment research that has guided us to many effective practices, a permanent "cure" for many students with the most serious behavioral difficulties remains an unrealistic goal (Wolf et al. 1987). Given this backdrop, how should we approach the education of these students? Are regular education teachers and environments prepared to deal with these chronically disabled students? Indeed, are special education teachers and environments prepared to deal appropriately and effectively with these students?

The recent thinking of some scholars within special education (Kauffman 1997; Wolf et al. 1987) suggests that, despite our best efforts, cures are not imminent, and long-term supportive treatment may be the most efficacious approach. To suggest simultaneously that regular education environments may be the most appropriate setting in which to serve all students with behavioral difficulties seems paradoxical. Inclusion, no matter how one defines it, involves educating students with disabilities in regular education environments with their nondisabled peers. But we must move away from discussions of place and focus instead on programs and services. If regular education environments are able to provide the sustained, intensive, individualized treatment that students with behavioral disorders demand, then appropriate inclusion is not only possible but also preferable. Indeed, we hope that appropriate inclusion will, at some time in our future, become the norm. If, however, we expect that students will be cured of their behavioral disabilities, if we claim that regular education teachers are presently equipped to deal with the extreme range of behavioral characteristics that students with E/BD evince, if we demand that they consistently display behavior that is within the normal range in regular education environments, and if we move to exclude them from these environments when their behavior falls outside this acceptable range, then we will regress rather than progress. In fact, as we move into the twenty-first century, we will be following a pattern remarkably similar to that which characterized the nineteenth century. Most certainly, if we forget the past, we, too, are destined to repeat it.

REFERENCES

Bullock, L. M., L. L. Ellis, and M. J. Wilson. 1994. Knowledge/skills needed by teachers who work with students with severe emotional/behavioral disorders: A revisitation. *Behavioral Disorders* 19:108–25.

Epstein, M. H., C. M. Nelson, L. Polsgrove, M. Coutinho, C. Cumblad, and K. Quinn. 1993. A comprehensive community-based approach to serving students with emotional and behavioral disorders. *Journal of Emotional and Behavioral Disorders* 1:127–33.

Forness, S., K. Kavale, I. Blum, and J. W. Lloyd. 1997. Mega-analysis of meta-analyses: What works in special education and related services. *Teaching Exceptional Children* 29:4–9.

Gunter, P. L., and R. K. Denny. 1996. Research issues and needs regarding teacher use of classroom management strategies. *Behavioral Disorders* 22:15–20.

Hallahan, D. P., and J. M. Kauffman. 1997. *Exceptional learners: Introduction to special education.* 7th ed. Boston: Allyn and Bacon.

Kamps, D. M., and M. Tankersley. 1996. Prevention of behavioral and conduct disorders: Trends and research issues. *Behavioral Disorders* 22 (1): 41–48.

Kauffman, J. M. 1997. *Characteristics of emotional and behavioral disorders of children and youth.* 6th ed. Upper Saddle River, N.J.: Merrill.

Kauffman, J. M., and D. P. Hallahan. 1992. Deinstitutionalization and mainstreaming exceptional children. In *Encyclopedia of educational research,* vol. 1, 6th ed., ed. M. C. Aiken, 299–303. New York: Macmillan.

———. 1997. A diversity of restrictive environments: Placement as a problem of social ecology. In *Issues in educating students with disabilities,* ed. J. W. Lloyd, E. J. Kameenui, and D. Chard, 325–42. Mahwah, N.J.: Lawrence Erlbaum Associates.

Kauffman, J. M., and K. L. H. Wong. 1991. Effective teachers of students with behavioral disorders: Are generic teaching skills enough? *Behavioral Disorders* 16:225–37.

Landrum, T. J. 1992. Teachers as victims: An interactional analysis of the teacher's role in educating atypical learners. *Behavioral Disorders* 17:135–44.

Landrum, T. J., N. N. Singh, M. S. Nemil, C. R. Ellis, and A. M. Best. 1995. Characteristics of children and adolescents with serious emotional disturbance in systems of care, part II: Community-based services. *Journal of Emotional and Behavioral Disorders* 3:141–49.

Lewis, T. J., D. Chard, and T. M. Scott. 1994. Full inclusion and the education of children and youth with emotional and behavioral disorders. *Behavioral Disorders* 19:277–93.

Lloyd, J. W., J. M. Kauffman, and J. Kupersmidt. 1990. Integration of students with behavior disorders in regular education environments. In *Advances in learning and behavioral disabilities,* vol. 6, ed. K. D. Gadow, 225–64. Greenwich, Conn.: JAI Press.

Patterson, G. R. 1980. Mothers: The unacknowledged victims. *Monographs of the Society for Research in Child Development,* vol. 45, no. 5.

Shores, R. E., S. L. Jack, P. L. Gunter, D. N. Ellis, T. J. DeBriere, and J. H. Wehby. 1993. Classroom interactions of children with behavior disorders. *Journal of Emotional and Behavioral Disorders* 1:27–39.

Stainback, W., and S. Stainback. 1984. A rationale for the merger of special and regular education. *Exceptional Children* 51:102–11.

Strain, P. S., D. L. Lambert, M. M. Kerr, V. Stagg, and D. A. Lenker. 1983. Naturalistic assessment of children's compliance to teacher's requests and consequences for compliance. *Journal of Applied Behavior Analysis* 16:243–49.

Walker, H. M., K. Kavanaugh, B. Stiller, A. Golly, H. Severson, and E. G. Feil. 1998. First step to success: An early intervention approach for preventing school antisocial behavior. *Journal of Emotional and Behavioral Disorders* 6:66–80.

Webber, J., and B. Scheuermann. 1997. A challenging future: Current barriers and recommended action for our field. *Behavioral Disorders* 22:167–78.

Wolf, M. M., C. J. Braukmann, and K. A. Ramp. 1987. Serious delinquent behavior as part of a significantly handicapping condition: Cures and supportive environments. *Journal of Applied Behavior Analysis* 20:347–59.

9

From Tolerance to Acceptance to Celebration: Including Students with Severe Disabilities

Deborah Peters Goessling

tudents with severe disabilities frequently have been marginalized and segregated by school administrators, teachers, classmates, and society in general. This chapter discusses many of the issues regarding students with severe disabilities and the characteristics of students labeled with "severe and profound, multiple disabilities." Why have these students been excluded from traditional general education classrooms? When they have been included with their peers, has it been a successful experience? For whom was it a successful experience—the student with severe disabilities, the parents, the peers, the teachers, the administrators? What dilemmas does inclusion of the most severe students present to schools and to society in general? What are the hidden messages about tolerating difference, accepting diversity, and learning to celebrate disability? Is that celebration possible in the schools of the twenty-first century?

DEFINING STUDENTS WITH SEVERE DISABILITIES

The definition of a severe disability varies according to state regulations, federal guidelines, and medical interpretations. In this chapter, the definition of the Association of Persons with Severe Handicaps is used: "Students with severe disabilities are defined as the intellectually lowest 1 percent of the school-age population or students with delays of three or more standard deviations in two or more areas of development" (TASH 1986). This 1 percent includes learners who may have labels such as multiply handicapped, physically handicapped, deaf-blind, autistic, trainable mentally retarded, or moderately or profoundly retarded (Meyer, Peck, and Brown 1991; Snell 1993). Students with severe disabilities require extensive ongoing support in more than one major area (mobility, communication, self-care, learning) to participate in school and community.

DEFINING INCLUSION

Inclusion has been defined in many ways during the past twenty years. Distinctions have been made among the terms mainstreaming (i.e., "visiting"), integration (i.e., "physical presence"), and inclusion. As defined by Stainback and Stainback (1996), inclusion is about belonging to a school community of typical peers. Inclusion means that the general education teacher (or teachers) takes ownership of the students with severe disabilities and that the student with severe disabilities experiences student membership. One of the most accepted definitions of inclusion in terms of students with severe disabilities was articulated by Sailor (1991), who stated that inclusion can be defined by six components:

1. Home school or neighborhood-school placement. All students receive education in the school they would attend if they had no disability. This school provides the benefit of greater opportunities for social inclusion and support as well as more connection to neighborhood peers. It allows students with severe disabilities to have friends in their community. This approach is opposite to having a "clustered" system where students with severe disabilities are placed in a designated school within the community and their services are clustered for ease of delivery.

2. Natural proportion at each school. The population of students with disabilities at the school must represent the number of students with disabilities in the community. If, in general, approximately 10 percent of students have a disability and if an average-sized class consists of twenty-four students, then one could expect two or three students with disabilities in each classroom. Distributing students with disabilities across all classrooms equalizes the opportunity that all students might have to interact with each other.

3. Zero reject philosophy. This belief states that all children should be educated in the home community initially. All should be welcomed and provided the opportunity to be included in neighborhood schools. No young children should start their school careers segregated from the children and adults in their community.

4. Same-age or same-grade placements. Students with severe disabilities should be placed with their peers in the same grade they would be placed in if they did not have a disability. Students need to be with peers of the same age for social role modeling and friendship development. Placement should not be based on academic achievement but on chronological age.

5. Cooperative learning. This method of learning in small groups (Johnson and Johnson 1987) is frequently found in inclusive classrooms and facilitates student interaction and learning.

6. A collaborative spirit. Schools that have a history of collaborating across grade levels and disciplines have a head start on inclusion. When teachers believe that instruction is enhanced through planning, implementing, and evaluating instruction that is done together and when teachers act on the philosophy that "two heads are better than one," then general educators and special educators will more likely be able to collaborate effectively.

How much time in general education classes is enough time to be called inclusion? Lou Brown and his colleagues asked this question in 1991, and it is still asked today. That is, can you have inclusion if the students with severe disabilities are in the classroom only 50 percent of the school day? Does 80 percent of the school day spent in a general education classroom count as quality inclusion? Can a child be fully included if he or she is in a general education classroom 30 percent of the total school day? Is inclusion about the quantity of time or the quality of time?

These questions about inclusion have been debated for the past twenty years. Determining how much time a student with severe disabilities should spend in the general education classroom to achieve successful inclusion is difficult. Usually, a minimum of 50 percent of the school day is necessary, but each classroom that includes a child with a severe disability is different than the next classroom. The culture and climate of the general education classroom will dictate if a student with severe disabilities will have ownership and membership—in other words, if the student will be accepted or rejected and have an opportunity to learn.

Currently in the United States, there are 99,114 students, ages 6 to 21, classified as having severe or multiple disabilities. These data are from the *Twentieth Annual Report to Congress on the Education of the Handicapped Act* (U.S. Department of Education 1998) and use information from the 1995–96 school year. These figures do not include students classified as having physical disabilities, deaf-blindness, autism, or mental retardation although, sometimes, some students with those labels are also considered severely disabled.

The same document reports that 5,235,952 total students were classified in need of special education services in the United States. Fifty-one percent of these students were classified as having learning disabilities. These data indicate that the percentage of school-age children with intensive severe and profound disabilities is less than 10 percent of the special education population. Currently, approximately 9 percent of the school-age population in the United States is classified as having a disability, and less than a quarter of 1 percent of all school-age students are classified as having severe or multiple disabilities. Clearly, through inclusion, this small number of students can have a big effect on a school.

Table 1 shows the 1994–95 educational placements of U.S. students from the ages of six to twenty-one years.

HISTORICAL BACKGROUND

"A history of the way society has cared for people with disabilities can be captured in four words: ignorance, isolation, insulation, and integration," wrote Ysseldyke, Algozzine, and Thurlow (1992, 14). An important hurdle for students with severe disabilities has been access to education. The following provides a brief chronological sketch of this quest for access.

Ignorance: The Nineteenth Century

Many students with severe disabilities in the nineteenth century were rejected by their families and society and were "put away" in state-supported institutions and asylums to protect society from those "afflicted" with mental retardation. Negative attitudes toward people labeled with mental retardation significantly increased institutional populations. However, many people viewed "specialized" institutional care as better treatment. New England witnessed the opening of the American Asylum for the Education and Instruction of the Deaf and Dumb in 1817 in Hartford, Connecticut; the New England Asylum for the Education of the Blind in 1832 in Watertown, Massachusetts; and the Experimental School for Teaching and Training Idiotic Children in 1846 in Barre, Massachusetts.

These institutions, however, served a very small proportion of students with

Table 1.

Educational Placements in the United States during 1994–95

	Percentage of Students with Special Needs	Percentage of Students with Severe Disabilities
Regular Class	45.0	9.0
Resource/Pullout	29.0	14.0
Separate Class	22.0	49.0
Separate Day School	3.0	22.0
Residential School	.7	3.0
Home/Hospital	.6	2.0

Note: Numbers have been rounded and may not equal 100 percent. Source: Twentieth Annual Report to Congress *(U.S. Department of Education 1998).*

severe disabilities. Even with the passage of compulsory school attendance laws in the early 1900s, many children with disabilities continued to be excluded from public schools (Karagiannis, Stainback, and Stainback 1996).

Isolation: The First Half of the Twentieth Century

The concept of special public school classes with special curricula as well as special training for teachers of students with severe handicapping conditions came about first in the urban school systems. The growth of these classes was substantial: Scheerenberger reported that "in 1922, 133 cities in 23 states had enrollments of 23,252 pupils in some type of special education" (1983, 166). The initial purpose of these classes was primarily to remove the most difficult students from the regular classroom. After the completion of schooling, most of these students labeled with mental retardation spent their adult years in state institutions.

Increasing school enrollments caused many school systems to redefine who was eligible for special classes. By the late 1920s, an IQ above 50 was necessary to be eligible for a public school education (Sheerenberger 1983). This criteria continued to exclude students who were labeled with severe mental retardation.

The majority of students with severe disabilities continued to be placed in state institutions or kept at home. They were not enrolled in public school classes. Even enrollment in the preferred private residential special schools was denied to students with multiple disabilities, who were considered uneducable because they were labeled severely and profoundly mentally retarded (Karagiannis, Stainback, and Stainback 1996).

With the development of special classes and special private schools, a critical problem was locating educators qualified to teach students labeled with mental retardation. The common practice was to recruit teachers from among those with training in kindergarten and primary education. Schools also encouraged teachers to attend summer training sessions at private institutions (e.g., Vineland, Elwyn, and Fernald) that were led by noted physicians and psychologists. These programs were not universal and existed in small pockets throughout the country.

Most institutions serving people labeled mentally retarded implemented a "medical model" that called for the institution's director to be a physician. This model created the need for programs involving nursing, recreation, and social work. Educators worked under the guidance of the medical community, and the primary goal of the institution was seen as maintaining physical health and safety (Scheerenberger 1983), not providing education.

Isolation Continues: The 1950 and 1960s

In the 1950s, states began passing legislation related to public special education services for those students labeled with moderate mental retardation. A "trainable child" was defined as "an individual who, because of retarded mental development, would not profit from public school special education classes for educable mentally handicapped but who possesses potentialities for learning self-care; social adjustment in the home and neighborhood; and economic usefulness in the home under supervision" (Goldstein 1956, 226–27).

Scheerenberger (1983) suggests several reasons why schools began to provide an education for trainable children: longer life expectancy rates for people labeled moderately mentally retarded, a stronger sense of the nuclear family, parental concerns about sending a child to an institution with a deplorable reputation, the emergence of the Association for Retarded Citizens, the growing right of taxpayers to demand services for their children, and the redirection of educational policymaking from local school boards to state agencies. However, states continued to legislate that the child must be able to benefit from such school experiences and be able to participate in the educational environment. Access was still denied to most students with severe disabilities.

By 1953, certification standards for teaching in special education classes existed in thirty-five states and the District of Columbia. However, with only 30 percent of the positions filled with trained special education teachers, schools continued to face a severe shortage of qualified, trained personnel. This personnel shortage remained until federal support programs to higher education began to become available in the early 1960s.

After the horrors of Hitler and the hardships of World War II, the American people seemed ready to develop an increased recognition and respect for the dignity of all citizens, regardless of their individual differences. Some of this change was in response to the vast number of people who had been exposed to diverse cultures during World War II and during the Korean conflict. People were ready for a new openness (Scheerenberger 1983).

In 1954, Chief Justice Warren ruled in the *Brown v. Board of Education* decision that separate education is not equal education. The Court found that segregating children in public schools solely on the basis of race—even where the physical facilities, quality of teachers, and other tangible factors may be equal—deprives minority children of equal educational opportunities in violation of the Equal Protection Clause of the Fourteenth Amendment to the Constitution (Mills 1993). This ruling led the way toward more reflection and study on exclusionary tendencies in American society (Karagiannis, Stainback, and Stainback 1996).

During his first year in office, John F. Kennedy formed a special President's Panel on Mental Retardation to provide "an intensive search for solutions to the problems of the mentally retarded." Many people believe he created this panel partly because of his experience of having a sister labeled with mental retardation. The final 1962 report presented 112 recommendations for research, preventive health measures, strengthened educational programs, comprehensive medical and social services, a new legal and social concept of "the retarded," programs of education and information to overcome negative public opinion, and help to overcome the personnel shortages in all fields of services to those with mental retardation (Scheerenberger 1983).

One other important event in the 1960s related to people with severe disabilities was the publication of the photographic essay, *Christmas in Purgatory*

(Blatt and Kaplan 1966). The poignant photographs and accompanying narrative visually detailed the gross inadequacies and dehumanizing conditions found at state institutions. The institutional lives of people with severe disabilities were brought to the nation's consciousness.

Insulation: The 1970s and Early 1980s

During the 1970s and early 1980s, tremendous changes affected the manner in which students with severe disabilities could receive an education. These changes were influenced by important writers of the time period as well as by court decisions and sweeping legislation.

In the early seventies, Wolfensberger wrote about "normalization" in his book, *The Principle of Normalization in Human Services* (1972). The idea of normalization was that children and adults labeled with severe disabilities should have life experiences paralleling the normal patterns of the culture and should be drawn into the mainstream of society. Housing, daily routines, clothing, social activities, sexuality, and opportunities for choice should be as close as possible to the norms and patterns of a mainstream society. These concepts implied that it would be best for a person labeled mentally retarded to live in the society's mainstream. They also implied that every effort should be made to assist the person to attain his or her maximum level of independence regardless of the degree of retardation or the extent of physical limitations (Sheerenberger 1983).

Two landmark court cases opened the possibility of access to education for all students, irrespective of the level of disability. In 1972, the Federal District Court upheld a consent agreement between the Pennsylvania Association for Retarded Citizens and the Commonwealth of Pennsylvania, guaranteeing every child labeled with mental retardation in the state the right to a free public education. The decision was supported and expanded by *Mills v. Board of Education* in 1972. This judgment contended that no child in that district could be denied a public education because of mental, behavioral, physical, or emotional handicaps. This decision set in motion the concept of "zero reject," meaning that no student could be denied access to a free and appropriate education based on the severity of disability (Turnbull and Turnbull 1998).

Subsequently, because of pressure from the courts, advocates, and parents, the Education for All Handicapped Children Act (PL 94–142) was passed in 1975 and enacted in 1978 (it was renamed the Individuals with Disabilities Education Act, or IDEA, in 1990). This federal legislation clearly mandated that all those students labeled as handicapped, including those with severe disabilities, were entitled to an appropriate education in the least restrictive environment (LRE). It gave their parents and guardians strong due process rights if the child's Individualized Education Program (IEP) did not meet the child's needs (Turnbull and Turnbull 1998).

By 1976, all states had passed laws financially subsidizing public school programs for students with disabilities. Many states began requiring new types of teacher certification (i.e., certification for teaching those with severe disabilities or multiple handicaps) and coursework to prepare teachers for the needs of students with severe disabilities who would be entering the public schools for the first time.

Since 1975, students with severe disabilities have been educated in separate private schools, public day schools, or regional collaborative programs at the expense of local school districts. Public school administrators and educators believed that this segregated education provided the only method for delivery of services. They reasoned that by providing a separate system of service delivery, education for students with severe disabilities could be provided more intensively and efficiently (Skrtic 1991). Thus, two different, parallel educational systems were set up and carried out (Gartner and Lipsky 1987).

During this time period, most special education teachers worked in separate special needs classrooms or schools. Classrooms usually had from four to ten students and two or three assistant teachers or paraprofessionals. Physical, occupational, and speech therapy services were provided several times a week. For these therapies, students were often taken out of their classrooms and educated in small therapeutic rooms—even more separation from the already separate classroom. This approach was the pervasive model of educational services for students with severe disabilities twenty years ago. However, in many places throughout the country this segregated education model is still the norm. Table 2 describes the five states with the least number of students with severe or multiple disabilities in inclusive settings.

Integration: The 1980s and Early 1990s

In 1986, the U.S. Office of Special Education and Rehabilitative Services (OSERS) issued the Regular Education Initiative (Will 1986), which required school systems to find ways to serve in regular classrooms those students classified as having mild and moderate disabilities. Madeline Will, then assistant sec-

Table 2.

States with the Lowest Percentage of Students with Severe Disabilities Taught in General Education Classrooms

	Regular Class	*Resource Room*	*Separate Class*	*Separate School*	*Residential School*	*Home/Hospital*
Mississippi	.50	4	58	16	17	4
Rhode Island	.51	9	58	28	4	0
Hawaii	.78	1	94	3	0	0
South Carolina	.96	31	51	16	0	1
Louisiana	1.00	1	75	7	8	7

Note: Numbers have been rounded and may not equal 100 percent. Source: Twentieth Annual Report to Congress (U.S. Department of Education 1998).

retary of OSERS, envisioned a partnership between regular and special education that would enable students with special needs to receive services within the regular classroom and to be educated through the merged efforts and collaboration of general and special educators.

At the same time, the literature in the field began questioning whether segregated education was the best model for students with disabilities (Wang and Walberg 1988), including students with severe and profound disabilities (Biklen 1985; Brown et al. 1991; Brown, Long, Udavri-Solner, Davis et al. 1989; Thousand and Villa 1990). Many new successful educational strategies had emerged in the field of severe disabilities. These strategies included concepts of generalization (Horner, McDonnell, and Bellamy 1986), community-referenced instruction and social skills training (Falvey 1989), and supported employment (Wehman and Kregel 1985).

Educators of students with severe disabilities began to believe that these new educational strategies were more effective when taught in the community or general education settings (Falvey 1989; Snell 1993). They also thought that social skills training could be more generalized in a school community with peers who were not disabled than in a school with only peers who were disabled. The generalization of basic concepts to various environments had more meaning when discussed in the broader context of the whole school than when taught in one small classroom isolated in the basement. Suddenly, students with severe disabilities understood that the concept of "cup" was more than just the set of red plastic cups by the sink in the separate classroom. Cups were also the cone cups at the water cooler in the principal's office and the Styrofoam cups in the cafeteria and the real glass cups in home economics class. In addition, the concept of cup was also the bright red large paper cup for Coke at McDonalds across the street from the school. The literature in the field of special education began reporting these teaching successes, and parents also noticed improvement in the social skills of their children (Forest and Lusthaus 1989).

Students with severe disabilities who had shown very limited attempts at initiating any type of communication became more interested in their nonsegregated environments. Students who had previously been educated only with other nonverbal, non-ambulatory students began to have increased eye contact, vocalizations, and increased formal and informal communication (sign language, gestures, pictures, and so on) when learning in integrated settings. Peers who were not disabled were stimulating for students with severe disabilities and were excellent models for appropriate social skills (Giangreco and Putnam 1991). Some educators and families believed that a quality education for students with severe disabilities could not be delivered in segregated education settings (Biklen 1992).

Educators and families came to understand that when a student with a severe disability completes school and goes out into the community to live and work with supports, the student's level of social skills are the prime indicator of success (Chadsey-Rusch 1990). The research began to indicate that social skills are best learned in the environment of the neighborhood public school, where friendships can be established (Brown, Long, Udavri-Solner, Davis et al. 1989; Strully and Strully 1989) with local children and where principles of normalization are practiced.

This increased knowledge about teaching strategies combined with the concerns of parents pushed the integration movement forward. Many parents began to wonder about the benefits of segregated learning. They began using the basic principles of Public Law 94–142—least restrictive placement and the IEP—to demand entry into the local public school for their children with severe disabilities. Parents felt it was not enough to bring segregated classes into the public school building and have the students share only a home economics class and a lunch period with their peers who were not disabled (Brown et al. 1991). Generally, such practices are not considered integration but, rather, mainstreaming (Sailor, Gee, and Karasoff 1993). With mainstreaming, students with severe disabilities do not have enough consistent opportunities to develop friendships, and students who are not disabled do not have enough opportunities to develop an understanding of the unique qualities and strengths of students with severe disabilities (Brown, Long, Udavri-Solner, Schwartz et al. 1989).

Schnorr (1990) emphasized problems with the mainstreaming concept. First graders discussed their perceptions of a student with severe disabilities (Peter), who was mainstreamed for one to two hours per day in their classroom. Peter was not accepted as a member of the class; he was seen as a nice but unusual child passing through the class once or twice a day. The first graders did not perceive Peter as a first grader. He was an outsider.

With encouragement from a few model programs like Vermont's Homecoming Model (Thousand et al. 1986), some risk-taking administrators, educators, and parents of students with severe disabilities began to believe in inclusive education. Full-time placement in a general education classroom created ample learning opportunities. The teaching of instructional objectives (how to signal for help, how to write one's first name, how to count objects) could be conducted in regular classrooms with enough support, a willing general educator, and a helping principal.

In some inclusive schools, teachers of students with severe disabilities began to bring their teaching techniques into general education classrooms, making modifications along the way. In a few school districts, parents and school administrators supported the notion of full inclusion for all students, and gradually, the special education classroom became nonexistent or rarely used because students with severe disabilities were being taught full-time in general education classrooms (Villa et al. 1992). And then, slowly, related services staff members also began to work with students in the general education classroom (Rainforth, York, and MacDonald 1992). This sharing of space, resources, and students created new models of delivering education to students with severe disabilities in general education classrooms.

CURRENT DEBATES RELATED TO THE INCLUSION OF STUDENTS WITH SEVERE DISABILITIES

Including students with severe disabilities in general education classrooms continues to be controversial (Fuchs and Fuchs 1994; Kauffman 1993; Kliewer 1998). It is difficult to find a single school district where families of children with severe disabilities totally agree on how best to educate their children. In the past ten years, legal cases seeking inclusive education and requesting specialized, segregated education have been initiated (Newcomer and Zirkel 1999). Educators themselves (e.g., Chesley and Calaluce 1997; Giangreco et al. 1993; Shanker 1994) are often in disagreement about whether inclusion is appropriate for students with severe disabilities. Federal grants and state grants continue to support inclusionary efforts at local school districts while state and federal monies continue to fund private, residential schools and institutions for students with severe and profound disabilities. At the end of the century, inclusion is finally a choice on the continuum of services for many students with severe disabilities, but it is not always the first choice of educators, families, and the federal government.

Some of the current debates about educating students with severe disabilities are shaped by recent court decisions as discussed below. Another debate focuses on determining the best placement for transition to postsecondary life for adolescents and young adults with severe disabilities (Agran, Snow, and Swaner 1999). A third issue is the rapidly increasing number of paraeducators (sometimes called aides, instructional assistants, paraprofessionals, tutors, teacher assistants, and educational technicians) in our schools for students with severe disabilities and their need for role clarification, supervision, training, and support (Giangreco et al. 1997; Pickett and Gerlach 1997). A fourth concern is the best way to create caring, competent special education teachers who are trained in the complex skills of working with students with severe disabilities and who are grounded in the general education curriculum (Fox and Williams 1992; Goessling 1998). Educating a student with severe disabilities in an inclusive classroom will remain a viable option for families if we as educators can better understand some of these inclusion challenges.

Recent Court Decisions

During the past ten years, legal decisions in the United States have assisted school districts and families in interpreting the meaning of inclusive education for students with severe disabilities. Three important legal cases from different geographic regions of the United States were related to students with significant mental retardation and complex health care needs. These three examples helped the nation understand that the inclusive classroom is a placement option for students with severe disabilities.

In 1993, the case of Rafael Oberti, an eight-year-old with Down syndrome, from a small New Jersey town, was settled in the third circuit court (*Oberti v.*

Board of Education of Clementon School District 1993). After Rafael completed his kindergarten education in a developmental kindergarten, his IEP team decided that an out-of-district, self-contained, special education class would be the appropriate placement. He had both academic and social success in kindergarten, but he had also developed some disruptive and aggressive behaviors. No behavioral plans or provisions for support staff members had been incorporated into his IEP.

Rafael's parents objected to the segregated placement, and the district agreed to explore mainstreaming possibilities. The parents requested mediation a second time to reiterate their demands for placement in a general education classroom in the neighborhood school. In 1993, the U.S. Court of Appeals affirmed the ruling of the lower court and stated that the Clementon, New Jersey, school district had violated the LRE requirement of the Individuals with Disabilities Education Act (IDEA). The court said that the school district had made only negligible efforts to include Rafael in the general education classroom and that it had failed to provide a clear curriculum plan, a behavior management plan, and adequate special education support and consultation to the general education teacher. The current IEP also contained no goals or provisions for supplementary aids and services. The court stressed that, although it was not embracing the full inclusion concept of placing all students with disabilities in inclusive classrooms, this specific case showed that the school district had not made an adequate attempt to educate Rafael in the general education classroom because it had made no plans or efforts to address his behavioral problems (Yell 1995). Rafael's case was important because it delivered a strong message that IEP teams cannot judge who is appropriate and not appropriate for inclusive education and that school districts must try to make an inclusive placement successful for the student with severe disabilities and not sabotage inclusion for the district's own benefit.

In 1994, the U.S. Court of Appeals for the Ninth Circuit affirmed a lower court's decision related to Rachel Holland, an eleven-year-old girl with moderate mental retardation, from Sacramento, California (*Sacramento City Unified School District v. Rachel H.*). From 1985 through 1989, Rachel attended a number of special education programs. In 1989, her parents requested that Rachel be placed in a general education classroom for the entire school day. The district contended that Rachel was too disabled to benefit from this placement. The parents went through due process, and the hearing officer held for the parents, stating that the school district had failed to make an adequate effort to educate Rachel in a general education classroom. The school district continued to appeal the decision (Yell 1995).

The court determined that Rachel's right to an inclusive education was based on four factors to help determine an appropriate placement. The first factor was related to the educational benefits of a general education placement: was it possible for a student with severe disabilities to receive even minimal academic benefit from the general class placement? The placement need not be "the best academic placement" but only one in which some academic gains might be made. In addition, the school district must provide supplementary aids and services to assist with academic goals. The second factor to be considered was the nonacademic benefits to the student from interactions with peers who were not disabled. In Rachel's case, the inclusive classroom provided opportunities for her to increase her communication, self-help skills, and social-behavioral skills. Another nonacademic benefit was the potential for developing friendships with typical peers.

The third factor considered the potential negative effects of Rachel's presence in the general education classroom on her peers. Would she be "unreasonably" disruptive or take too much of the classroom teacher's time? Would her presence be a detriment to her classmates? The court ruled that the school must take all necessary steps to ensure a successful learning experience not only for Rachel but also for her classmates. This support might include supplementary aids and services, including a paraeducator to assist Rachel or a consultant-special education teacher to support the general education teacher.

The final factor was related to the costs of the inclusive placement. The court stated that each school district must balance the needs of each student with a disability with the needs of the other students in the district. However, there was no indication that the cost of educating Rachel in an inclusive setting was prohibitively more expensive than educating her in a special education class. Thus, the cost factor was not relevant to Rachel's case (Turnbull and Turnbull 1998; Yell 1995).

Weighing these factors, the court determined that the inclusive placement with supplementary aids and services was the appropriate placement for Rachel. These four factors continue to be important guideposts for school districts in making educational placement decisions for students with severe disabilities.

In 1999, the U.S. Supreme Court ruled in favor of the right to an inclusive education for an adolescent with severe disabilities and complex health care needs (*Cedar Rapids Community School District v. Garret F.* 1999). Garret Frey, age sixteen, had requested nursing help to make it possible for him to attend general education classes. Since the age of four when he was paralyzed in a motorcycle accident, Garret has required, during school hours, a ventilator for breathing, periodic catheterization, suctioning of his tracheotomy once a day, and constant monitoring for any trouble with his breathing (Walsh 1999).

The Cedar Rapids School District argued that one-on-one nursing care was not a related service but an excluded medical service not covered under IDEA. The majority opinion ruled that the care necessary for Garret to attend school was a related service because it did not require the full-time participation of a physician. Justice Stevens also stated that the case is about whether meaningful access to public schools will be ensured for students with severe disabilities (Walsh 1999).

Each of these three legal cases that relate to inclusion of students with severe disabilities demonstrates the complexity of deciding how to interpret the law and of determining which placement provides the optimum educational benefit. Clearly, the decisions related to Rafael, Rachel, and Garret were difficult ones, but they continued to allow the inclusive classroom to be a placement option for students with severe disabilities.

Functional Skills versus Social and Academic Skills

Many educators support the inclusive placement of students with severe disabilities but worry about the location and quality of functional life skills instruction (Billingsley 1993; Chesley and Calaluce 1997). Instruction in the areas of functional math skills (telling time, calendar use, money management, vending machine use); literacy skills (reading maps, menus, newspapers; writing notes, lists; completing application forms, tax forms, rebates); mobility skills (using public transportation, using lockers, following both written and verbal directions); and other basic life skills (personal hygiene, nutrition and cooking skills, shopping skills, telephone skills, the development of leisure and recreational interests) is necessary for every student with severe disabilities to be a participating member in his or her community (Gaylord-Ross and Holvoet 1985; Snell 1993).

Although some of the skills that are mentioned above can be learned in the home or the community with friends and family, many skills require systematic instruction that is repeated over time, with opportunities for practice in generalized settings. The school community is an excellent setting to practice many of these skills (Hamre-Nietupski, Nietupski, and Strathe 1992; Kliewer 1999). However, many educators and parents believe that as students with severe disabilities become older, they need to spend some time in potential work environments in the community and some time in segregated placements learning basic skills for adult life (Brown et al. 1991; Sandler 1999). Others argue that the development of functional skills for life in the community is not an either–or issue (either the adolescent with severe disabilities pursues instruction outside of school in a community work setting or the adolescent with severe disabilities is included in seven sections of high school academics). Some educators (e.g., Jorgensen 1998; Sage 1997) believe that many factors must be considered in planning the last years of a student's education plan, factors that must take into account the learning goals of both the student and his or her family as well as the environment of both the school and community (Vandercook, York, and Forest 1989; Wehman 1992).

Sage (1997) reports that only one-third the number of students with severe disabilities who are included in the elementary years remain included in the secondary years. Does the academic content become too difficult to adapt for students with severe cognitive disabilities? Do students with severe disabilities continue to receive educational services through age twenty-one, as stated in IDEA, while their typical peers graduate at age seventeen or eighteen? Can task analysis and the direct instruction of specific functional skills that are necessary for independence in the community be taught in the secondary general education classroom? Do parents pursue community instruction and school-to-work programs with the hope that their son or daughter with severe disabilities will have a "real" job when he or she transitions from high school to postsecondary life? These are difficult questions to answer and they continue to be debated. However, we do know that friendships as well as community connections and networks that start in elementary schools can help sustain social contacts for students with severe disabilities into adulthood (Hendrickson et al. 1996; Kennedy, Shukla, and Fryxell 1997). We also know that some high school courses (e.g., chorus, drama, home economics, consumer math, band) are authentic ways of teaching many communication, social, and functional skills to young adults with severe disabilities (Ferguson et al. 1992).

As the dialogue about the acquisition of functional life skills and community-based instruction (Falvey 1989; McDonnell 1997) continues into the new century, we must remember that this dialogue may not be in conflict with inclusive practice. The challenge is to determine how all these potential learning opportunities can best be used (or not used) based on the students' needs. Dymond (1997) suggested that if we have learned anything in education, it is that no one best way exists to educate all students. Opting for total participation in an inclusion program or, similarly, community instruction is justified only if such programming is resonant with the student's needs, wishes, and interests (Agran, Snow, and Swaner 1999).

Roles and Responsibilities of Paraeducators in Inclusive Classrooms

Paraeducator is a term suggested by Pickett, Faison, and Formanek (1993) and is similar to the concept of paralegal, one who assists lawyers and paramedic, one who assists doctors. Paraeducators support general education or special education teachers in their teaching efforts by supporting the learning, emotional, and physical needs of students with severe disabilities in schools. The challenge to provide quality inclusive education to students with severe disabilities is directly linked to the ability to provide quality training, supervision, and support to the paraeducators in general education classrooms (Doyle 1997; Giangreco et al. 1997).

Since 1990, the number of paraeducators working in the nation's public schools has doubled. Some educators believe this growth is attributed to cost-saving measures by school districts to hire fewer certified special education teachers and specialists and more noncertified, less expensive staff members. Others believe that as students with severe disabilities move from self-contained classrooms to various general education classrooms, more teacher assistants are needed to provide one-to-one or small-group support. Another consideration is the fact that, in many schools, general education students have more needs for assistance because of their language backgrounds, cultural backgrounds, or family situations. During the past decade, school districts, for a variety of reasons, have come to rely on an increased supply of paraeducators (Pickett and Gerlach 1997).

What are the challenges facing paraeducators who support students with severe disabilities in inclusive classrooms? Michael Giangreco and his colleagues

(1997) identify several areas of concern related to the proximity of paraeducators to instruction in general education classrooms:

- Paraeducators could interfere with the instruction in the classroom by removing the responsibility of the students with severe disabilities from the general education teacher.

- Paraeducators could interfere with interactions that the student with severe disabilities may have with his or her classmates.

- Paraeducators could foster dependence on adults, especially when a student has the same one-to-one support paraprofessional every day.

- Paraeducators could create ineffective instructional plans and evaluation systems because of their limited training and experience in working with students with severe disabilities.

- Paraeducators could limit the personal control that students with severe disabilities struggle to develop in their lives.

- Paraeducators could limit the development of gender identity (e.g., when a male student is taken into a women's bathroom by a female paraeducator).

- Paraeducators could create interference with instruction for typical students in the class.

These challenges for paraeducators are not their concern alone. Teachers, administrators, and families need to specify clear roles and responsibilities for paraeducators and clarify how the support, supervision, and training needs of paraeducators will be met (French and Pickett 1997). For many schools, the inclusion of students with severe disabilities is a new phenomenon, and learning to work with paraeducators in general education classrooms is a new experience (Marks, Schrader, and Levine 1999). Also, many educators have not had training in how to work with paraeducators, and their inappropriate decisions about the use of instructional assistants are not necessarily rational but, rather, driven by their fear of difference or of change, their adherence to customary routines, their reluctance to add another substantial task to what many perceive as an already extensive set of responsibilities, or their lack of knowledge or support for teaching the student with disabilities (Giangreco et al. 1997, 15).

Sometimes the students with the most challenging behaviors in inclusive classrooms are left to be the primary responsibility of paraeducators. General education teachers are trying to teach the curriculum in the classroom, and the special educator's attention is frequently divided among consulting and co-teaching in a variety of classrooms, paperwork, and meetings. Therefore, the paraeducator is left to instruct, monitor, and modify learning processes and behavioral objective issues (Marks, Schrader, and Levine 1999).

Paraeducators are frequently concerned about who their supervisor is, who evaluates their job performance, and who guides them with difficult students and situations. Is it the general education teacher with whom they spend most of their day? Is it the special education teacher with whom they meet several times a week? What if the paraeducators are working with more than one teacher—where does their allegiance lie? Who, then, becomes "expert" about the student with a severe disability? Confusion about roles and responsibilities can be decreased by ongoing collaborative meetings for discussing and clarifying areas of responsibility; by training for both teachers and paraeducators on the goals of inclusive practices; and by modeling and guidance related to the need to fade assistance and to increase opportunities for students with severe disabilities to experience independence and participation (Marks, Schrader, and Levine 1999). These areas of role confusion are important inclusion challenges because, without the presence of the paraeducator, the educational benefits for the included students would be minimal (Janney and Snell 1997).

Preparing Teachers of Students with Severe Disabilities for Inclusive Classrooms

Successful inclusion for students with severe disabilities demands skilled teachers in both general education and special education. Specifically, schools need teachers with competence in educating students with severe disabilities, including students with complex heath care needs that are similar to the needs of Garret Frey. More students with physical and health disabilities are entering our public schools and inclusive settings (Heller et al. 1999). Some families of students who are assisted by ventilators believe that the lack of skilled special educators who are capable of teaching in general education classroom has prevented the inclusion of their children in general education classrooms (Jones et al. 1996). Clearly, a challenge for the next decade will be to prepare teachers who can competently serve students with complex health care needs and other severe disabilities in the inclusive classroom (Izen and Brown 1991).

Heller and her colleagues state the need for competent special educators (more specifically, those certified in severe, intensive, and multiple disabilities) to work on instructional teams for inclusive education:

> If the teacher lacks knowledge and skill in augmentative communication and assistive technology, the student will lack appropriate access to educational material and instruction as well as formal and social communication. If the teacher is not well trained in teaching reading to nonverbal students, the student may not learn to read. If the teacher does know how to analyze students' behaviors to determine if they are communicative, students' efforts to communicate may be ignored, and the student may either stop trying to communicate or increase undesirable behaviors. When the teacher lacks strategies to work with chronically ill and terminally ill students and their families, the result can be feelings of isolation, helplessness, and increased emotional stress. (1999, 232)

As schools restructure themselves for the inclusion of students with severe disabilities, traditional approaches to personnel preparation and ongoing professional development also must undergo significant reforms. The implications that truly inclusive educational practices raise for teacher education and certification are numerous and complex. Some of the concerns for the next decade are listed here:

- The need for merged teacher education programs and for dual certification in both general and special education
- The need for additional teacher preparation coursework and skills in organizational change, conflict resolution, and collaboration
- The challenge to find enough quality inclusive field placements for student teachers
- The struggle for teacher educators to cross disciplines and to model collaboration and risk taking
- The need for future teachers of students with severe disabilities to have both in-depth technical skills in teaching students with severe disabilities and broad knowledge of the general curriculum (Goessling 1998)

Educators also need to be knowledgeable about issues related to inclusion and the general education curriculum. They should be familiar with instructional strategies for students with physical disabilities, severe cognitive disabilities, and complex health care needs.

CELEBRATING DIFFERENCES IN THE FUTURE

The education of students with severe disabilities has changed dramatically in many ways during the past 100 years. Students like Rafael, Rachel, and Garret have won the legal right to be educated with their peers in general education classrooms. However, the courts cannot mandate attitudinal change and move students, teachers, and parents from tolerating students with severe disabilities to accepting them into their schools and classrooms. In some school communities, the presence of a student with severe disabilities is a genuine reason for celebration. A student who communicates in nontraditional ways and who does not walk challenges each individual classmate and teacher to broaden their understanding of diversity and to find the hidden strengths and attributes in each individual. When the participation of a student with severe disabilities is welcomed and celebrated, then the inclusion will have been successful.

The new century presents many challenges for the inclusive education of students with severe disabilities. The students not only must feel accepted and celebrated but also must be educated by collaborative teams of competent, caring general educators, special educators, and paraeducators. Debate will continue about the best methods and approaches for individual students, especially during the adolescent years. However, research is beginning to document that authentic learning and social gains for students with severe disabilities are taking place (Hunt and Goetz 1997). A future of acceptance and celebration appears possible not only in the schools of tomorrow but also, possibly, in society.

REFERENCES

Agran, M., K. Snow, and J. Swaner. 1999. A survey of secondary level teachers' opinions on community-based instruction and inclusive education. *Journal of the Association for Persons with Severe Handicaps* 18:61–63.

Association of Persons with Severe Handicaps. 1986. Definition of the people TASH serves. In *Critical issues in the lives of people with severe disabilities*, ed. L. Meyer, C. Peck, and L. Brown, 19. Baltimore: Paul H. Brookes.

Biklen, D. 1985. *Achieving the complete school.* New York: Teachers College Press.

———. 1992. *Schooling without labels.* Philadelphia: Temple University Press.

Billingsley, F. F. 1993. In my dreams: A response to some current trends in education. *Journal of the Association for Persons with Severe Handicaps* 24:58–62.

Blatt, B., and F. Kaplan. 1966. *Christmas in Purgatory.* Boston: Allyn and Bacon.

Brown, L., E. Long, A. Udavri-Solner, L. Davis, P. Van Deventer, C. Ahlgren, F. Johnson, L. Gruenwald, and J. Jorgensen. 1989. The home school: Why students with severe intellectual disabilities must attend the schools of their brothers, sisters, friends, and neighbors. *Journal of the Association for Persons with Severe Handicaps* 14:1–7.

Brown, L., E. Long, A. Udavri-Solner, P. Schwartz, P. Van Deventer, C. Ahlgren, F. Johnson, L. Gruenwald, and J. Jorgensen. 1989. Should students with severe intellectual disabilities be based in regular or special education classrooms in home schools? *Journal of the Association for Persons with Severe Handicaps* 14:8–12.

Brown, L., P. Schwas, A. Solner, F. Johnson, and J. Jorgensen. 1991. How much time should students with severe intellectual disabilities spend in regular education classrooms and elsewhere? *Journal of the Association for Persons with Severe Handicaps* 16:39–47.

Brown v. Board of Education, 347 U.S. 483 (1954).

Cedar Rapids Community School District v. Garret F. (96-1793) 106 F. 3d 822 (U.S. 1999).

Chadsey-Rusch, J. 1990. Social implications of secondary-aged students with severe handicaps: Implications for facilitating transition from school to work. *Journal of the Association of Persons with Severe Handicaps* 15:69–78.

Chesley, G. M., and P. D. Calaluce, Jr. 1997. The deception of inclusion. *Mental Retardation* 35:488–90.

Doyle, M. B. 1997. *The paraprofessional's guide to the inclusive classroom.* Baltimore: Paul H. Brookes.

Dymond, S. K. 1997. Community living. In *Functional curriculum for elementary, middle, and secondary-age students with special needs*, ed. P. Wehman and J. Kregel, 197–226. Austin: Pro-Ed.

Falvey, M. 1989. *Community-based curriculum: Instructional strategies for students with severe handicaps.* 2d ed. Baltimore: Paul H. Brookes.

Ferguson, D., G. Meyer, L. Jeanchild, L. Juniper, and J. Zingo. 1992. Figuring out what to do with the grownups: How teachers make inclusion "work" for students with disabilities. *Journal of the Association for Persons with Severe Handicaps* 17:218–26.

Forest, M., and E. Lusthaus. 1989. Promoting educational equality for all students: Circles and maps. In *Educating all students in the mainstream of regular education*, ed. S. Stainback, W. Stainback, and M. Forest, 43–57. Baltimore: Paul H. Brookes.

Fox, L., and D. G. Williams. 1992. Preparing teachers of students with severe disabilities. *Teacher Education and Special Education* 15:97–107.

French, N. K., and A. L. Pickett. 1997. Paraprofessionals in special education: Issues for teacher educators. *Teacher Education and Special Education* 20:61–73.

Fuchs, D., and L. Fuchs. 1994. Inclusive schools' movement and the radicalization of special education. *Exceptional Children* 60:294–309.

Gartner, A., and D. K. Lipsky. 1987. Beyond special education: Toward a quality system for all students. *Harvard Educational Review* 57:367–90.

Gaylord-Ross, R. J., and J. F. Holvoet. 1985. *Strategies for educating students with severe handicaps.* Boston: Little Brown.

Giangreco, M. F., R. Dennis, C. Cloninger, S. Edelman, and R. Schattman. 1993. "I've counted Jon": Transformational experiences of teachers educating students with disabilities. *Exceptional Children* 59:359–72.

Giangreco, M. F., S. W. Edelman, T. E. Luiselli, and S. Z. C. MacFarland. 1997. Helping or hovering? Effects of instructional assistant proximity on students with disabilities. *Exceptional Children* 64:7–18.

Giangreco, M. F., and J. Putnam. 1991. Supporting the education of students with severe disabilities in regular education environments. In *Critical issues in the lives of people with severe disabilities*, ed. L. Meyer, C. Peck, and L. Brown, 245–70. Baltimore: Paul H. Brookes.

Goessling, D. P. 1998. Inclusion and the challenge of assimilation for teachers of students with severe disabilities. *Journal of the Association of Persons with Severe Handicaps* 23:238–51.

Goldstein, H. 1956. Lower limits of eligibility for classes for trainable children. *Exceptional Children* 22:226–27.

Hamre-Nietupski, S., J. Nietupski, and M. Strathe. 1992. Functional life skills, academic skills, and friendship/social relationship development: What do parents of students with moderate/severe/profound disabilities value? *Journal of the Association of Persons with Severe Handicaps* 17:53–58.

Heller, K. W., L. D. Fredrick, M. K. Dykes, S. Best, and E. T. Cohen. 1999. A national perspective of competencies for teachers of individuals with physical and health disabilities. *Exceptional Children* 65:219–34.

Hendrickson, J. M., M. Shokoohi-Yekta, S. Hamre-Nietupski, and R. Gable. 1996. Middle and high school students' perceptions on being friends with peers with severe disabilities. *Exceptional Children* 63:19–28.

Horner, R., J. McDonnell, and G. T. Bellamy. 1986. Teaching generalized skills: General case instruction in simulation and community settings. In *Education of learners with severe handicaps: Exemplary services strategies*, ed. R. H. Horner, L. H. Meyer, and H. D. B. Fredericks, 289–314. Baltimore: Paul H. Brookes.

Hunt, P., and L. Goetz. 1997. Research on inclusive educational programs, practices and outcomes for students with severe disabilities. *Journal of Special Education* 31:3–29.

Izen, C. L., and F. Brown. 1991. Education and treatment needs of students with profound, multiply handicapping, and medically fragile conditions: A survey of teachers' perceptions. *Journal of the Association of Persons with Severe Handicaps* 16:94–103.

Janney, R. E., and M. E. Snell. 1997. How teachers include students with moderate and severe disabilities in elementary classes: The means and meaning of inclusion. *Journal of the Association of Persons with Severe Handicaps* 22:159–69.

Johnson, D. W., and R. T. Johnson. 1987. *Learning together and alone: Cooperation, competition, and individualization.* 2d ed. Englewood Cliffs, N.J.: Prentice Hall.

Jones, D. E., C. C. Clatterbuck, J. Marquis, H. R. Turnbull, and R. L. Moberly. 1996. Educational placements for children who are ventilator assisted. *Exceptional Children* 63:47–57.

Jorgensen, C. M. 1998. *Restructuring high schools for all students: Taking inclusion to the next level.* Baltimore: Paul H. Brookes.

Karagiannis, A., W. Stainback, and S. Stainback. 1996. Historical overview of inclusion. In *Inclusion: A guide for educators,* ed. S. Stainback and W. Stainback, 17–28. Baltimore: Paul H. Brookes.

Kauffman, J. 1993. How we might achieve the radical reform of special education. *Exceptional Children* 60:6–16.

Kennedy, C., S. Shukla, and D. Fryxell. 1997. Comparing the effects of educational placement on the social relationships of intermediate school students with severe disabilities. *Exceptional Children* 64:31–47.

Kliewer, C. 1998. The meaning of inclusion. *Mental Retardation* 36:317–22.

———. 1999. Seeking the functional. *Mental Retardation* 37:151–54.

Marks, S. U., C. Schrader, and M. Levine. 1999. Paraeducator experiences in inclusive settings: Helping, hovering or holding their own? *Exceptional Children* 65:315–28.

McDonnell, J. 1997. Participation in content-area classes and community-based instruction in secondary schools: Isn't it about achieving a balance? *TASH [Association of Persons with Severe Handicaps] Newsletter* 23:23–30.

Meyer, L., C. Peck, and L. Brown. 1991. *Critical issues in the lives of people with severe disabilities.* Baltimore: Paul H. Brookes.

Mills, C. D. 1993. Important education-related U.S. Supreme Court decisions (1943–1993). In *Challenges and achievements of American education,* ed. G. Cawelti, 187–92. Alexandria, Va.: Association for Supervision and Curriculum Development.

Mills v. District of Columbia Board of Education, 348 F. Supp. 866 (D.D.C. 1972), contempt proceedings, EHLR 551:643 (D.D.C. 1980).

Newcomer, J., and P. Zirkel. 1999. An analysis of judicial outcomes of special education cases. *Exceptional Children* 65:469–80.

Oberti v. Board of Education of Clemonton School District, 995 F. 2d 1204 (3rd Cir. 1993).

Pennsylvania Association for Retarded Children v. Pennsylvania, 334 F. Supp. 1257 (E.D. Pa. 1971); 343 F. Supp. 279 (E.D. Pa. 1972).

Pickett, A. L., K. Faison, and J. Formanek. 1993. *A core curriculum and training program to prepare paraeducators to work in inclusive classrooms serving school age students with disabilities.* New York: National Resource Center for Paraprofessionals in Education and Related Services, Center for Advanced Study in Education, City University of New York.

Pickett, A. L., and K. Gerlach. 1997. *Supervising paraeducators in school settings: A team approach.* Austin: Pro-Ed.

Rainforth, B., J. York, and C. MacDonald. 1992. *Collaborative teams serving students with severe disabilities: Integrated therapy in educational programs.* Baltimore, Md.: Paul H. Brookes.

Sacramento City Unified School District v. Rachel H., F. 3d 1398 (9th Cir. 1994).

Sage, D. D., ed. 1997. *Inclusion in secondary schools: Bold initiatives challenging change.* Port Chester, N.Y.: National Professional Resources.

Sailor, W. 1991. Special education in the restructured school. *Remedial and Special Education* 12:8–22.

Sailor, W., K. Gee, and P. Karasoff. 1993. Full inclusion and school restructuring. In *Instruction of students with severe disabilities,* 4th ed., ed. M. Snell, 1–30. New York: Macmillan.

Sandler, A. G. 1999. Short-changed in the name of socialization? Acquisition of functional skills by students with severe disabilities. *Mental Retardation* 37:48–50.

Scheerenberger, R. S. 1983. *A history of mental retardation.* Baltimore, Md.: Paul H. Brookes.

Schnorr, R. 1990. "Peter? He comes and goes …": First graders' perspectives on a part-time mainstream student. *Journal of the Association of Persons with Severe Handicaps* 15:231–340.

Shanker, A. 1994. Full inclusion is neither free nor appropriate. *Educational Leadership* 52:18–21.

Skrtic, T. M. 1991. *Behind special education.* Denver: Love Publishing Co.

Snell, M. 1993. *Instruction of persons with severe handicaps.* 4th ed. New York: Macmillan.

Stainback, S., and W. Stainback. 1996. *Inclusion: A guide for educators.* Baltimore: Paul H. Brookes.

Strully, J., and C. Strully. 1989. Friendship as an educational goal. In *Educating all students in the mainstream of regular education,* ed. S. Stainback, W. Stainback, and M. Forest, 59–68. Baltimore: Paul H. Brookes.

Thousand, J., T. J. Fox, R. Reid, J. Godek, W. Willams, and W. L. Fox. 1986. *The Homecoming Model: Educating students who present intensive educational challenges within regular education environments.* Burlington: University of Vermont, Center for Developmental Disabilities.

Thousand, J., and R. Villa. 1990. Strategies for educating learners with severe disabilities within their local home schools and communities. *Focus on Exceptional Children* 23:1–24.

Turnbull, H. R., and A. P. Turnbull. 1998. *Free appropriate public education: The law and children with disabilities.* 5th ed. Denver: Love Publishing Co.

U.S. Department of Education. 1998. *Twentieth annual report to Congress on the implementation of the Education of the Handicapped Act.* Washington, D.C.: Department of Education, Office of Special Education Programs.

Vandercook, T., J. York, and M. Forest. 1989. The McGill action planning system (MAPS): A strategy for building the vision. *Journal of the Association of Persons with Severe Handicaps* 14:205–15.

Villa, R., J. Thousand, W. Stainback, and S. Stainback. 1992. *Restructuring for caring and effective education: An administrative guide to creating heterogeneous schools.* Baltimore, Md.: Paul H. Brookes.

Walsh, M. 1999. *Education Week* 10 (March):1, 22.

Wang, M. C., and H. J. Walberg. 1988. Four fallacies of segregationism. *Exceptional Children* 55:128–37.

Wehman, P. 1992. *Life beyond the classroom: Transition strategies for young people with disabilities.* Baltimore, Md.: Paul H. Brookes.

Wehman, P., and J. Kregel. 1985. A supported work approach to competitive employment of individuals with moderate and severe handicaps. *Journal of the Association for Persons with Severe Handicaps* 10:3–11.

Will, M. C. 1986. Educating children with learning problems: A shared responsibility. *Exceptional Children* 52:411–16.

Wolfensberger, W. 1972. *The principle of normalization in human services.* Toronto: National Institute on Mental Retardation.

Yell, M. L. 1995. Least restrictive environment, inclusion, and students with disabilities: A legal analysis. *Journal of Special Education* 28:389–404.

Ysseldyke, J. E., B. Algozzine, and M. Thurlow. 1992. *Critical issues in special education.* Boston: Houghton Mifflin.

10

Inclusion of Infants, Toddlers, and Preschoolers with Disabilities

Shavaun M. Wall

For more than twenty years, the education system in the United States has devoted considerable effort to "mainstreaming" children with disabilities. The primary focus of this effort has been the placement of school-age children into regular elementary and secondary school classrooms. Recently, however, appreciation has been growing for the importance of "inclusion," a broader concept that calls for "full integration of individuals with disabilities in all aspects of home, school, and community life" (Guralnick et al. 1995, 359). Inclusion reaches beyond traditional mainstreaming in two important regards. First, inclusion encompasses not only school-age children but also the very youngest members of society—infants, toddlers, and preschoolers. Second, and correspondingly, inclusion extends beyond formal educational settings to a wide variety of family, child care, and community activities (Gemmel-Crosby and Hanzlik 1994; Turnbull and Turbiville 1995). In general terms, the goal of the inclusion movement is to ensure that even the youngest children with disabilities are

Preparation of this chapter was supported in part by the Administration for Children and Families, U.S. Department of Health and Human Services, Early Head Start Local Grant # 90YF0003, with ACF Project Officer Esther Kresh.

woven tightly into the educational and social fabric of the community (Hanline and Galant 1993).

An extensive body of research deals with the integration of school-age children with special needs into the regular education classroom. Both the efficacy of such programs and the elements essential to their success have been widely debated. However, many of the important issues surrounding the inclusion of infants, toddlers, and preschoolers have been addressed only recently and preliminarily, if at all. As a result, crucial conceptual, policy, and empirical questions that relate to the inclusion of very young children remain unanswered. This chapter addresses the most significant of these issues.

This discussion begins with an analysis of the contemporary legislative and attitudinal parameters that frame the debate regarding the inclusion of infants, toddlers, and preschoolers. The discussion is followed by an analysis of the research concerning the effect of inclusive programs on young children and the factors that are most important to the effectiveness of such programs. Because training, continuing consultation, and family support have been identified as crucial to inclusion for this age group, current practices and future needs in these areas are discussed in detail. The final portion of this chapter addresses the likely future direction of the inclusion movement as it affects young children.

The fundamental premise of this chapter is that inclusion of young children with special needs, if properly funded and supported, is both a desirable social value and an effective educational strategy. Indeed, inclusion is now widely supported, in general terms, by policymakers, educators, and parents. Nevertheless, increasingly difficult and controversial issues will arise as inclusion is extended to younger children in a wider range of community settings. These controversies, together with concern for the cost of making inclusion a reality in these new settings, could endanger congressional and public support for inclusion. In the long run, the only effective response to this threat is to ensure that inclusive programs for young children actually work, that is, benefit both children with special needs and their nondisabled peers. Among the most important factors in making inclusion more effective for this age group will be better conceptualization and articulation of program methods and expectations; improved training and support for providers, interventionists, and family members; and well-conceived, empirically based research to document the effect of inclusion and the factors most important to its success in preschools, child care programs, and other programs serving the very young.

LEGISLATIVE PARAMETERS

The first legislative step toward inclusion in the public schools was Public Law 94–142, enacted in 1975. PL 94–142 amended the Education of the Handicapped Act (subsequently renamed the Individuals with Disabilities Education Act, or IDEA) to ensure that each child with disabilities would receive a "free appropriate public education" (FAPE) in the least restrictive environment (LRE) consistent with the needs of the child. Congress also provided that "to the maximum extent appropriate," children with special needs must be "educated with children who are not handicapped." Educational agencies were required to prepare an Individualized Education Program (IEP) for each child with disabilities and to identify in the IEP the extent to which that child would be able "to participate in regular educational programs." Parents were guaranteed the right to participate in the assessment, IEP development, and placement of their child as well as to challenge any disputed recommendations in court.

PL 94–142 was a major step forward in the education of children with special needs and has served as a focal point of the mainstreaming and inclusion movements with regard to school-age children. However, PL 94–142 was far from comprehensive. The youngest and most vulnerable of the disabled, that is, children under six years old, remained beyond the scope of mandatory federal requirements (unless state law provided for public education of nondisabled children of the same age). Moreover, the federal mandates applied only to educational institutions and not to family or community settings.

Not until 1986 did Congress bring preschoolers (from three through five years old) firmly within the scope of federal inclusion requirements. As a result of PL 99–457 (codified in Part B of IDEA), educational agencies that receive federal funding under IDEA must serve all preschoolers with a diagnosed disability or developmental delay. As with school-age children, these services must be provided in the LRE consistent with the needs of the child. These provisions have remained much the same since 1986. However, because each state may establish its own definition of the term "delay," and because there is no federal requirement that services be provided to preschoolers who are "at risk" (but who are not yet experiencing a delay), eligibility requirements for services to preschoolers have varied significantly from state to state.

PL 99–457 also authorized the states to develop and implement a comprehensive program of "early intervention services" for infants and toddlers (from birth through two years of age) with developmental delays or with conditions that create a high probability of developmental delay. Among the services covered by this provision (codified as Part H of PL 99–457) are speech pathology, audiology, physical therapy, occupational therapy, psychological services, and early assessment. States that receive funds for early intervention services under Part H may choose to also serve infants and toddlers who are at risk of developmental delay. However, at-risk infants and toddlers are provided early intervention services in only eleven states, although several other states provide services to very young children who show a combination of risk factors (National Early Childhood Technical Assistance System [NEC–TAS] 1995).

PL 99–457 also marked the first legislative recognition of the importance of serving the parents and families of children with disabilities. The Part H early intervention program was intended to "enhance the capacity of families to meet the special needs of their infants and toddlers," and consequently, state agencies are encouraged to provide family counseling, training, and home visits. Indeed, all Part H services must be based on an individual family services plan (IFSP). Like the IEP that was mandated in PL 94–142, an IFSP must identify the child's level of development, the anticipated results of early intervention, and the specific services needed to reach those results. Unlike an IEP, an IFSP must also identify the family's strengths and needs related to enhancing their child's development, the services to be provided to the family, and the expected effect of these services.

Congress has subsequently reaffirmed and expanded the family support services available under IDEA. In 1991, PL 102–119 authorized states to provide early intervention services to families of preschoolers rather than solely to families of infants and toddlers. In 1994, Congress provided one-time grants to assist in modifying statewide support systems to better serve families of children with disabilities, including children from birth to six years old (Title III, section 315, of PL 103–382). This legislation was intended, in part, to promote "integration and inclusion" so that children with disabilities could use "the same community resources that are used by and available to other individuals and families."

IDEA was amended most recently in 1997 with PL 105–17. Part C of these amendments provides financial support for comprehensive statewide systems for the delivery of early intervention services. These amendments also call for "family-directed" needs assessments, transition services for children moving from early intervention to preschool programs, and comprehensive staff training in early intervention. Further, state agencies are encouraged to expand services to infants and toddlers who are at risk for experiencing developmental delay. Most important, as a result of the 1997 amendments, all early intervention programs must ensure, to the maximum extent appropriate, that services are provided in "natural environments, including the home and community settings in which children without disabilities participate." As defined by the Council for Exceptional Children (1996), a natural environment is one in which the child would spend time had he or she not had a disability. This definition includes the family and home environments as well as "play groups, child care, nursery schools, Head Start programs, kindergartens, and neighborhood school classrooms." As a result, occupational and physical therapy, speech and language therapy, nutritional consultations, adaptive feeding, and similar services for infants, toddlers, and preschoolers must ordinarily be provided in inclusive settings. Specific justification is required if these services are to be delivered outside such natural environments.

Thus, IDEA establishes a firm legal framework that supports inclusion for even the youngest children with disabilities. For this reason, the current primary focus of the inclusion movement is not on further legislative change, but on giving practical meaning to IDEA's requirements that educational services must be provided in the "least restrictive environment" (preschoolers) while early intervention services must be provided in "natural settings" (infants and toddlers).

ATTITUDES TOWARD INCLUSION

Whether the broad provisions of IDEA are translated into effective inclusion programs for very young children depends largely on the preschool teachers, parents, and children involved in these programs. The following discussion reviews the available research concerning the attitudes of teachers, parents, and young children toward inclusion.

Preschool Teachers

The attitudes of preschool teachers toward inclusion can have a great effect on the availability of inclusive options and the effectiveness of classroom integration (Eiserman, Shisler, and Healy 1995). Although the research is limited (NEC–TAS 1991), existing studies suggest that the attitudes of preschool teachers toward inclusion correspond closely to the extent of the teachers' experience with inclusive programs and to the training and support they have received.

A survey of preschool teachers in Colorado found that their feelings toward inclusion were more positive if they were satisfied with their training and support and felt that they had been adequately prepared (Gemmel-Crosby and Hanzlik 1994). Although the teachers in this survey worked only with children with mild to moderate disabilities, the available evidence suggests that teachers also would respond favorably to inclusion of children with severe disabilities if they were provided adequate support (Giangreco et al. 1993). Following their exposure to an inclusive program, the teachers involved in this study (at the elementary school level) became less skeptical regarding inclusion and more confident in their ability to work effectively with children who were severely disabled. Overall, the respondents felt they had become better teachers because of inclusion—more reflective, more aware of the needs of all children, and more flexible.

Conversely, teachers who have no personal experience with inclusion are likely to be less attuned to inclusion issues and to express greater reservations about their own ability to manage an inclusive classroom. A 1995 survey of 220 Florida preschool and Head Start teachers and administrators revealed that they knew little about the statutory protections afforded children with disabilities and had no significant experience with such children (Eiserman, Shisler, and Healey 1995). Although these educators had moderately positive attitudes toward the idea of inclusion, they drew more distinctions based on the type of disability and the location in which the children could be served. They also showed greater anxiety regarding the availability of special equipment, reference materials, training, consultation, and classroom assistance.

Thus, the existing research suggests that if a preschool teacher feels adequately trained and supported, personal experience with an inclusive program is likely to result in greater self-confidence and a more favorable attitude toward inclusion. Nevertheless, even teachers with extensive experience in inclusive classrooms report continuing difficulty in finding the time for planning and for coordination with other service providers (Stoneman 1993).

The availability and effectiveness of inclusive programs for infants and toddlers will, correspondingly, be heavily influenced by the attitudes of childcare providers. Although it seems reasonable to assume that the attitudes of child care providers would parallel those of preschool teachers, little or no empirical research has been done on this issue except as a side product in training studies (Jones and Meisels 1987; Kontos 1988; Magliocca et al. 1993; Rule et al. 1985, 1987).

Parents

Parental attitudes toward inclusion might be expected to correspond to whether the parent has a child with special needs. In fact, the research indicates that most parents, both with and without disabled children, generally favor inclusion. Parents also recognize, however, that inclusion usually involves a range of potential benefits and drawbacks (see reviews and research by Guralnick 1994; Lamorey and Bricker 1993; Stoneman 1993; Tari, Hancock, and Brophy 1989).

Parents of children with disabilities often believe that inclusion can offer their child greater exposure to the "real world," positive social contacts, opportunities to learn from nondisabled children, a wider variety of activities, and greater community acceptance. Correspondingly, many parents of typically developing children feel that an inclusive classroom will enable their child to develop a greater awareness of others' needs, become more accepting of individual differences, and grow comfortable being with people with disabilities. Parents and teachers surveyed in 1992 observed that nondisabled preschoolers in inclusive classrooms improve in their understanding of others and display less prejudice as well as fewer stereotypes (Peck, Carlson, and Helmstetter 1992).

Moreover, parents of children with special needs often feel that inclusion benefits them in their role as parents. Greater interaction with nondisabled children can assist the parents of a child with disabilities to better understand their child's development and behavior (Tari, Hancock, and Brophy 1989). There are also indications that parents of children with special needs may receive valuable support from parents of other children who are part of the same inclusive setting. However, the research is divided on this issue, with some studies suggesting that little interaction occurs between the two groups of parents even in an inclusive setting (Lamorey and Bricker 1993; Winton 1993).

Parents also perceive potential drawbacks to inclusive programs for young children (Guralnick 1994; Tari, Hancock, and Brophy 1989; Stoneman 1993). Not surprisingly, parents of children with special needs fear that their children will meet rejection, teasing, or stigmatization. These parents often question the adequacy of the staff training and wonder whether their children will receive adequately individualized instruction. Whether or not these anxieties are well founded in any particular case, it is clear that the burden of gathering information on and making decisions about inclusive programs can be a source of significant uncertainty and stress. Parents may experience additional pressures as their child with disabilities adjusts to a new peer group and to a new environment within the inclusive program and as the parents themselves become familiar with other parents and new administrators (Tari, Hancock, and Brophy 1989). In some cases the additional stress associated with participation in an inclusive program can require intervention (Stoneman 1993).

Young Children

Little research has been done that attempts to determine how infants, toddlers, and preschoolers conceive of disabilities or whether they show a preference for peers without disabilities (Stoneman 1993). The existing data suggest that although young children do not have a clear or comprehensive understanding of disabilities, disability is an important factor in friendships and other peer relationships. Preschool children with disabilities ordinarily have a restricted network of peer relationships both in and out of school. Even among classmates, three- and four-year-olds seem to prefer peers without disabilities as playmates (Diamond, Le Furgy, and Blass 1993). Only rarely do children with special needs have contact with their typically developing classmates outside of school (Stoneman 1993).

These studies indicate that there is good reason to believe that even very young children notice and take into consideration the disabilities of others. This behavior often increases the social distance between children with disabilities and their peers. If such social distancing is undesirable (as most teachers and parents believe it is), then we must determine whether inclusion programs could ameliorate this problem. Consequently, the following sections of this chapter review the research findings that concern the effect of inclusion in the preschool and in child care settings.

THE EFFICACY OF INCLUSION IN PRESCHOOLS

The research strongly suggests that a preschool child with disabilities will develop at least as well in an inclusive setting as in a segregated special education setting (see a comprehensive review by Buysse and Bailey 1993). Moreover, preschoolers without disabilities develop as well in inclusive settings as in preschool programs that serve only nondisabled children (Diamond, Hestenes, and O'Connor 1994; Wolery et al. 1993). Further, typically developing preschoolers rarely acquire inappropriate behaviors from classmates with special needs (Wolery et al. 1993).

Most studies have found clear and positive social behavioral outcomes among young children with disabilities who participate in inclusive preschool programs (see Buysse and Bailey 1993; Diamond, Hestenes, and O'Connor 1994; Lamorey and Bricker 1993). Preschoolers with special needs generally have more positive interactions with peers in an inclusive setting. This finding means that they are more likely to initiate interactions, have appropriate interactions, and play at higher social levels if taking part in a regular education program. This effect may be attributed to the more intense social demands generated by the typically developing peers (Guralnick et al. 1995). One of the most encouraging research findings is that the disabled child's attempts at interaction are responded to consistently and positively by typically developing peers (Strain 1984).

Despite these overall positive findings, inclusion alone does not eliminate the social deficiencies of many preschoolers with disabilities. Even in a fully inclusive setting, young children with disabilities are more often unoccupied or isolated (Buysse and Bailey 1993; Diamond, Hestenes, and O'Connor 1994; Kopp, Baker, and Brown 1992) and their play is often less mature and less social (Gottlieb, Levy, and Gottlieb 1986; Kopp, Baker, and Brown 1992; O'Connell 1984). This tendency may occur, in part, because of the attitudes of others who may not fully accept preschoolers with disabilities (Guralnick et al. 1995). But the less satisfactory social integration of many preschoolers with disabilities occurs sometimes because these children's own peer-related social skills are deficient (e.g., Guralnick and Groom 1987; Odom and Brown 1993). Young children with special needs may not attempt to elicit peer interactions as frequently (Beckman 1983) or may be less responsive to peer initiations (Strain 1984). Some may even elicit negative reactions, making more disruptive entries and maintaining a less positive affect than their typically developing peers (Kopp, Baker, and Brown 1992). Overall, preschoolers with special needs interact more frequently with adults and less often with peers than do their nondisabled classmates (Burstein 1986).

Timely intervention is often needed to support and to encourage the rewarding of social interaction between children with disabilities and their classmates. The literature identifying the types of intervention that can address the social deficits of young children with disabilities in an integrated setting is growing (see review by Odom and Brown 1993). For example, well-planned environmental arrangements can be effective in easing social integration. Special efforts can also be made to teach fundamental social skills such as greeting, sharing, helping, and complimenting. Likewise, prompts and reinforcements by the preschool teacher can increase positive peer social interactions. Indeed, four- and five-year-old peer "mediators" have, at times, been trained to persist in social overtures to engage children with disabilities.

Most of the existing research concerning the efficacy of inclusion in preschools has been conducted in high-quality, federally funded demonstration programs at universities (Buysse and Bailey 1993; File and Kontos 1993). Further study will be required to determine whether inclusion will produce equally positive results in community-based preschool programs.

Early on, Guralnick (1981) identified numerous programmatic factors likely to affect the results of inclusion on social and developmental outcomes: teacher-children ratio; the ratio in the group of children with and without disabilities; the types of disabilities involved; the mix of ages; the suitability of the developmental match between children with disabilities and their classmates;

the adequacy of teacher training; the degree to which the children were prepared for entry into an inclusive program; the quality of the intervention regime; and the availability of resource specialists. For example, it is well documented that better teacher training and a lower teacher-to-student ratio can encourage children's play behavior (File and Kontos 1993). Similarly, group size can significantly affect the type of play and the level of aggression among preschool children with special needs (Gottlieb, Levy, and Gottlieb 1986). These factors suggest that inclusion may be less effective in marginal preschool programs unless accompanied by broad programmatic improvements.

In summary, inclusive preschool programs, when operating with appropriate resources and intervention capacities, can be of substantial developmental and social benefit to preschoolers with disabilities while also assisting in the social development of nondisabled students. However, additional research is required before it is clear that the success experienced in "ideal" settings can be duplicated in community-based preschool programs and in preschools that include children with severe disabilities.

INCLUSION IN CHILDCARE PROGRAMS

High-quality personal care and attention is of great importance for the appropriate development of infants, toddlers, and preschoolers (see Howes and Olenick 1986; Howes and Stewart 1987; Howes, Phillips, and Whitebook 1992). Because so many parents of young children work outside the home, there is a tremendous need for quality child care (Landis 1992). Yet the availability of competent, affordable child care has not kept pace with the demand (Kontos and File 1993). Parents of children with disabilities find it particularly difficult to locate suitable child care facilities (Morgan and Madsen 1994). Expansion of inclusive child care options would provide invaluable support to these families.

Moreover, inclusive child care programs may have a positive effect on the development of young children with disabilities. The only significant empirical study of inclusive child care (the federally funded Social Integration Project) evaluated the integration of children with disabilities into child care programs in Utah (Rule et al. 1985, 1987). The project provided workshops for the day care staff, a part-time special education resource teacher, access to consulting specialists, a social skills curriculum, and parent education. The children with disabilities made developmental, educational, and social advancement that was equal to similar children participating in segregated special education programs. Both parents and the staff expressed satisfaction with this program. Moreover, the child care center was less expensive than special education programs and met the parents' employment needs by offering longer hours.

As child care programs become more inclusive, there will be more opportunities for research concerning their effectiveness. Firm conclusions regarding the effect of inclusive child care programs must await that research. However, the preschool findings give us good reason to expect that inclusive child care programs have the potential to offer significant benefits to both children with disabilities and nondisabled children.

ELEMENTS OF EFFECTIVE INCLUSION FOR YOUNG CHILDREN

If infants, toddlers, and preschool children are to be served successfully in "natural environments," certain elements are critical. The professionals who work with these children must receive inclusion training and on-site consultation. Support networks must also be available to the children's families.

Inclusion Training

If infants, toddlers, and preschool children are to be served successfully in "natural environments," teachers, child care staff members, and early intervention specialists must be provided well-conceived training and support. Unfortunately, this support appears to be the exception rather than the rule. Several studies have found that few preschool teachers or day care staff members who serve children with disabilities in an inclusive setting receive significant support from a special educator or other appropriate professional (McDonnell, Brownell, and Wolery 1997; Wolery et al. 1993; Wolery, Martin et al. 1994; Wolery, Venn et al. 1994).

This lack of training and support cannot be justified by claiming that it is not needed. Many preschool teachers and day care providers have not completed an early childhood education program, much less a program focusing on young children with special needs. Combined training in both regular and special education is rare, even in programs that are accredited by the National Association for the Education of Young Children (McDonnell, Brownell, and Wolery 1997). Consequently, an urgent need exists for broad, in-service professional development for preschool teachers and child care providers.

Moreover, a large percentage of early intervention workers also lack specialized professional training (Kontos and File 1993). Many need training in such early intervention areas as naturalistic intervention, collaboration with parents, and problem solving with staff members (Gallagher 1997; Kontos and File 1993). This training should be oriented around the "consulting" role that many intervention professionals will be expected to fulfill. Because children with special needs move each day through a variety of settings, intervention professionals must often accomplish their work indirectly through day care and preschool teachers rather than by working directly with the children.

A substantial body of literature addresses how inclusion training can best be provided (Deiner and Whitehead 1988; Giovinazzo and Cook 1995; Jones and Meisels 1987; Kontos 1988; Magliocca et al. 1993). The training projects reviewed in these studies are based on the premise that early intervention should be provided in the child's "natural environment." Consequently, in each project, an effort was made to train providers to deliver early intervention services in the context of inclusive child care. This approach conforms not only to IDEA but

also to the evidence showing that interventions are most effective when conducted within the framework of the child's daily routines (Dunst et al. 1987) and
in ways that meet family needs (Deutsch 1983; Dunst, Trivette, and Deal 1988).

Two training projects in Delaware (Bruder, Deiner, and Sachs 1990; Deiner
and Whitehead 1988) provided from sixteen to twenty hours of general training to in-home child care providers who were willing to serve infants with special needs. The topics addressed in the training included typical and atypical
development, special considerations in teaching infants and toddlers with disabilities, and the importance of supporting families. Six additional hours of
training focused on the care of a particular infant with special needs who was
then placed with the in-home provider. Subsequently, the provider received biweekly visits from an early childhood special educator. Comparable training
has also been described in demonstration projects in Connecticut (Bruder,
Deiner, and Sachs 1990) and Colorado (Colorado Department of Education
1991). This "general to specialized" training regime is compelling, but the actual effect on young children with special needs requires further empirical
evaluation.

Other research has described training and has evaluated its effect on
providers' knowledge, skills, and attitudes. The Family Day Care project in
Michigan (Jones and Meisels 1987) trained in-home child care providers to care
for twenty-seven children with disabilities, ranging in age from three months to
six years. The training was intended to teach caregivers about child development
generally and children with special needs in particular. The year-long project included workshops, assistance in locating books and equipment, toy lending, and
biweekly consultation. Follow-up study showed that, following the training program, the child care providers had significantly greater knowledge of special
needs and provided a higher-quality, in-home environment.

Project Neighborcare offered consultative services to eight providers in the
Midwest who were serving preschoolers with special needs (Kontos 1988). This
project started with assessment of the quality of the child care environment and
the caregivers' skills. The providers were then given a three-hour workshop each
week for six weeks. These workshops focused on special needs, program planning,
progress tracking, instructional strategies, behavior management, and working
with parents. Individual consultation plans were then developed, based on the
needs of the caregiver and the child. The providers reported that this training increased their early intervention skills, although they requested further support.
The evaluators noted improvements in the quality of care following the training.

A program in Maryland, referred to as Project Together (Giovinazzo and
Cook 1995), provided training regarding developmentally appropriate practices
and inclusion to seventy-seven in-home child care providers. Parents and their
children with special needs were included in the training. This training enabled
the child care providers to develop support networks and to receive credits for
Child Development Associate credentials. Following the training, the providers
were more confident in their ability to care for children with disabilities and to
provide family support.

Finally, an Ohio program referred to as the Early Intervention Training Project (Magliocca et al. 1993) offered a fifteen-hour, multidisciplinary training program to more than 1,000 child care providers, parents, early interventionists, and special educators in connection with the inclusion of children from birth to five years old. The training emphasized individualization and a family-centered approach. Post-training evaluation showed that parent participation in the training increased the professionals' understanding of family needs.

Although they are far from conclusive, these evaluations not only demonstrate that training for inclusion can be effective but also they suggest how this training should be accomplished. There appear to be at least three "training factors" that are particularly important for successful inclusion training at the child care and preschool levels.

First, the training must take into consideration the "developmental stages" in staff members' attitudes toward disabilities and toward their own competence to operate a successful inclusion program (Volk and Stahlman 1994). The training regime must encourage teachers and staff members to shift their focus, over time, from their own needs and fears to the needs of the children in their program or preschool. Volk and Stahlman (1994) have identified six distinct stages in their developmental approach to inclusion training:

1. Identification of the similarities between caring for young children with disabilities and caring for those without disabilities so the trainees will recognize that they already have skills that will be valuable in an inclusive program

2. Observation of inclusive programs in action and discussions with confident and successful staff members

3. Identification of the existing abilities of the child with special needs who is to be served so staff members can note what already applies from their program

4. Identification of the new skills that are needed by the staff members to serve children with special needs, with emphasis on how these new skills may be helpful in dealing also with nondisabled children

5. Acknowledgment of the trainees' feelings toward disabilities generally and inclusive programs in particular, with emphasis on the special competencies of providers serving in such programs

6. Identification of the supportive resources that are available to assist staff members on a continuing basis, including parents, special educators, and early interventionists

Second, staff training should be designed to develop collaborative and problem-solving skills. To do this training well, trainers should bring together all those who will be involved in the inclusive program, including teachers, interventionists, and parents. Because inclusion requires a family-centered approach, parental participation is crucial (Magliocca et al. 1993). Collaboration and problem solving should be practiced throughout the training and during on-site consultations. Central to this collaborative approach is the notion that all participants value each other's expertise (Kontos and File 1993).

Finally, effective training programs for child care staff members and preschool teachers should devote substantial time and resources to analysis of developmentally appropriate practices. This training should cover normal and exceptional development, early intervention terminology, systems for delivering early intervention services, developmentally appropriate environments, procedures for setting goals and tracking progress, use of naturalistic interventions, and behavioral strategies. The training should also provide guidance regarding practices that are necessary to meet the developmental needs of infants and toddlers with disabilities. Such accommodations include appropriate adaptations to the physical environment, scheduling strategies, preferred modes of communication, opportunities to improve gross motor coordination, and feeding considerations (Vergara et al. 1993).

Continuing Consultation

Effective inclusion programs must also provide ongoing, on-site consultation after the conclusion of staff training. Collaborative consultation in the field permits shared problem solving in ways that can be tailored to the staff member and individual child (Klein and Sheehan 1987). This collaboration should be "an interactive process which enables people with diverse expertise to generate creative solutions to mutually defined problems" (Idol, Paolucci-Whitcomb, and Nevin 1986, ix).

Although a number of the programs discussed above offered ongoing consultation, the Infant-Toddler Care Project at the University of North Carolina has been particularly influential in this area (Wesley 1994). In this project, on-site consultation is the main support to providers who care for infants and toddlers with disabilities along with typically developing young children. The consultant observes and gives feedback to the provider in the child care center or home. The consultant also demonstrates techniques and shares information (including readings, audiovisual materials, and referrals to resources such as toy-lending programs). In addition, the consultant incorporates information about accommodating disabilities with overall program improvements.

Support to Families

The quality of personal interactions within the family and the immediate neighborhood crucially affect the satisfactory development of most infants, toddlers, and preschoolers (Bronfenbrenner 1989; Turnbull, Turnbull, and Blue-Banning 1994). However, families with young children with disabilities face extraordinary challenges as they attempt to maintain a stimulating family and community environment while also obtaining needed services. One of these challenges is the social isolation that often accompanies a disability. If the child with disabilities attends a segregated special education program, especially one not located in the community, the absence of local friends can be a significant problem for parents and child alike (Winton 1986). Conversely, an inclusive local child care or preschool program with an effective family support capacity can provide crucial connections to other parents and children in the community.

Parents of children with special needs may also require support in dealing with the bureaucratic maze surrounding services for people with disabilities. This support is particularly needed by families in poverty. The Carnegie Task Force on the needs of young children (Carnegie Corporation 1994) and the Surgeon General's Conference (1992) both found that parents in poverty face major barriers as they seek appropriate health care, education, and other social services, even for their nondisabled children. Some of these hurdles are presented by poverty itself (e.g., lack of funds for transportation) whereas others are bureaucratic (excessive paperwork and limited hours) or are rooted in cultural differences and communication problems (Jasluski 1993). Parents of a child with a physical, mental, or emotional disability routinely face additional obstacles. For example, the tumultuous feelings of fear and confusion that parents may experience when they learn that their child has a disability can interfere with their effort to secure appropriate services (Pearl 1993; Smith 1997). Of course, these problems are compounded for single parents (Vadasy 1986).

Inclusive child care and preschool programs can provide significant support for such families. The research indicates that by building a supportive network, parents can reduce stress, enhance their perceptions of themselves and their children and, in some circumstances, reduce the incidence of mental and physical illnesses (Bronfenbrenner 1979; Carnegie Corporation 1994; Smith 1997). Improvements like these are likely to enhance the development of the child with disabilities because that development depends heavily on the extent to which the parents "believe in the child's capacity to develop and in their own power to influence the child's development" (Bronfenbrenner 1995, 18).

Moreover, providing support to the entire family is crucial because family-centered intervention is more effective than intervention that is directed solely to the child (Dunst, Trivette, and Deal 1988, 1994). Best practices in early intervention now call for working with the needs and priorities identified by the family, using family strengths, mapping the family's networks for potential supports, and linking the family with support in a way that empowers the family to mobilize these resources independently in the future (Dunst, Trivette, and Deal 1988, 1994). As discussed above, practices for supporting families in relation to their enhancement of their child's development are now legal requirements under IDEA for programs receiving federal funds.

Nevertheless, the research indicates that many child care and preschool programs have not yet developed successful family support capacities. This failure is attributed, in part, to the continuing tendency of early intervention specialists to focus solely on the child. For example, a survey of early intervention providers serving young children in six states revealed that most providers still focus on child-centered, clinical goals, with 40 percent of the interventionists spending no time with families (Mahoney and O'Sullivan 1990). Few of the interventionists surveyed used family preferences as a basis for identifying service objectives but, instead, based the objectives solely on the provider's evaluation of the child's needs. This low level of family support appeared to be tied to a lack of training.

Similar findings emerged from a survey of speech and language pathologists affiliated with 117 hospitals providing early intervention services for infants and toddlers (Weitzner-Lin, Chambers, and Sierpierski 1994). Although the pathologists recognized the importance of communicating with families, they felt they had not been provided with adequate training in this area. They had little confidence in their ability to work as part of an interdisciplinary team (an important vehicle for assessment of the child and the family) and requested more training in early intervention.

Family support efforts are also compromised by structural flaws in the delivery of services. In a recent study of California's Part C early intervention services under IDEA, parents reported significant difficulty obtaining early intervention services (Montgomery et al. 1997). They also reported frustrations in making the transition to Part B services when their children turned three years old. Despite the legal requirement that a comprehensive IFSP be prepared for each family, more than one-third of the IFSPs reviewed in this study focused only on the needs of the child and omitted any discussion of family resources. Further, there was little evidence that early intervention was occurring in inclusive settings. Few IFSPs (12 percent) even mentioned the possibility that services could be delivered in an inclusive environment.

Significant additional effort will be required before early interventionists, preschool teachers, and child care providers are routinely providing effective family support. Although improvement is required on many fronts (Winton 1993), probably the most critical need is improved training.

FUTURE DIRECTIONS

During the next decade, there will be continuing pressure to expand and extend inclusive services for young children with disabilities. This pressure will stem, in part, from the greater number of infants, toddlers, and preschoolers who will be eligible for early intervention services in natural environments. Several factors will contribute to this increase, including medical advances that improve the survival rate of premature infants, more aggressive efforts by the states to identify young children who need services, and greater willingness among the states to address the at-risk population. These developments are likely to be particularly important among groups that have been underrepresented in the past, for example, low-income, minority, inner-city, and rural populations.

Moreover, child care, preschool, and community programs will be asked to serve a broader range of children with special needs. To date, young children with severe disabilities have rarely been fully integrated into inclusive programs. There will be pressure to reduce this barrier as the benefits and feasibility of inclusion are better documented. Likewise, a greater percentage of young children with emotional and behavioral problems will seek services within inclusive programs.

Inclusion will also expand into new settings. Families, neighborhoods, and communities will struggle to resolve how to best serve children with disabilities in a variety of public and private settings, including libraries, recreation centers, parks, child care homes, church-affiliated nurseries, and other locations well beyond the classroom.

Expansion along these lines is likely to lead to difficult and sensitive challenges for the inclusion movement. In some cases, the fundamental value and legitimacy of inclusion will be questioned, at least, as the concept is applied to very young children outside the school context. In other instances, resistance will be based on financial concerns or on arguments regarding equity and fairness ("We shouldn't spend so much on such a small group of the population"). Advocates of inclusion must be prepared to respond thoughtfully to these challenges, always remembering the great importance of public support for future legislation and funding.

In the long term, however, public and legislative support for inclusive programs that serve infants, toddlers, and preschoolers are likely to depend largely on whether advocates can show convincingly that such programs "work," that is, provide real and demonstrable benefits to both children with disabilities and their nondisabled peers. Thus, to better serve young children in existing inclusive programs and to prepare for the challenges to new efforts at inclusion, the primary focus for the foreseeable future should be on ensuring that inclusive programs function as effectively as possible. This focus will require comprehensive and well-conceived efforts in three areas.

First, inclusive programs must better articulate their basic philosophy, educational methods, and anticipated results. Early childhood programs generally have not sufficiently articulated their guiding developmental principles and goals. Often, as a result, no unifying theme and purpose tie program activities together. Some progress has been made recently on this issue by the National Association for the Education of Young Children (NAEYC) and the Division for Early Childhood of the Council for Exceptional Children. Traditionally, many early childhood educators were oriented toward child development issues whereas special educators drew more from learning theories, particularly behaviorism. A deliberate effort was made to integrate these approaches in the revised guidelines to *Developmentally Appropriate Practice*, issued by NAEYC (Bredekamp 1997). These guidelines retain the original orientation toward active learning and child-directed activities but now also feature ongoing assessment, individualized goals, and adaptations for special needs. Each inclusive child care and preschool program should make use of these guidelines in articulating its educational philosophy and establishing specific, measurable expectations.

A second step toward improving inclusion programs for very young children would be to make available more comprehensive training for child care providers, preschool teachers, and interventionists. This training should be tied to the articulated principles, methods, and expectations of the programs involved. Crucial training factors and examples of successful training regimes have been discussed above. Early childhood teachers and providers should also become more integral participants in assessment, decision making, and planning for young children with special needs. This type of practical experience is likely to enhance the providers' self-confidence and strengthen their commitment to inclusion. In addition, professional preparation programs should be revised to recognize the growth and importance of inclusive programs. Indeed, preservice training for regular and special education should be integrated, parallel to the integrated classroom, and should include field experience in inclusive programs (Volk and Stahlman 1994).

Similarly, because special educators are likely to provide fewer direct services to children and to deal more often with parents, regular education teachers, and child care providers, the training of interventionists should include development of greater collaborative and consultative skills.

Finally, more emphasis must be placed on systematic study and documentation of the factors that are essential to successful inclusion and the developmental and social effect of inclusive programs. Some of this work can and should be undertaken by the child care and preschool programs themselves. As a practical matter, however, only the federal government has the resources to support comprehensive, long-term studies in this area. Two major programs sponsored by the federal government are currently under way.

The Early Childhood Research Institute on Inclusion (Odom 1995) consists of researchers from five universities working with at least sixteen inclusive preschool, child care, Head Start, and public school early childhood programs. Researchers will attempt to identify the specific type and degree of inclusion that are desired by the families involved as well as favored by the providers, interventionists, and policymakers. The researchers will then identify the factors that impede or facilitate different types and degrees of inclusion. Family and community inclusion will be addressed along with inclusion in child care or preschool programs. This project is expected to result in new inclusion strategies.

The second extended federal research project dealing with inclusion is Early Head Start (EHS). This program (the younger sibling of the Head Start Program) was first funded in 1994 by the Administration on Children, Youth, and Families of the U.S. Department of Health and Human Services. The framework for the new program was described in a statement in 1995 by the Advisory Committee on Services for Families with Infants and Toddlers that was established by the Health and Human Services Secretary ("The Statement of the Advisory Committee" 1995). Early Head Start serves infants and toddlers from low-income families as well as the families themselves. The program enrolls pregnant women or parents of young infants and serves the children and families until the child reaches the age of three years. At least 10 percent of enrolled infants and toddlers in each program must have special needs. Although they are based on different service models, all Early Head Start programs seek to produce outcomes in four areas (or "cornerstones"):

- Child development (health, attachment, cognitive and language development as well as social competence)
- Family development (parenting, family health, financial self-sufficiency, family functioning)
- Staff development
- Community building (developing quality child care options, collaborating with the community, and integrating services)

A national longitudinal evaluation involving seventeen sites and 3,400 children and their families will measure the effect of Early Head Start across different types of programs (Mathematical Policy Research 1996). Local research studies have also been funded at fifteen of these sites to identify the factors most important to the outcomes achieved at those programs. Catholic University's local research (conducted with the Early Head Start program administered by United Cerebral Palsy of Washington and Northern Virginia) focuses on the experiences of families who have an infant or toddler with special needs.

Because enrollment in Early Head Start occurs during pregnancy or the child's infancy, the program offers an excellent opportunity for research regarding the factors affecting the age at which children in low-income families receive early intervention services. The research will also examine whether earlier intervention, coupled with appropriate services in a natural environment, can prevent or mitigate more serious disabilities. Because Early Head Start programs establish collaborative relationships with service agencies in the community, researchers will also find opportunities to study the emergence of partnerships between community-based child care programs and early interventionists.

The work of the Early Childhood Research Institute and the Early Head Start program is an important step toward building a body of empirical knowledge regarding the factors most important to effective inclusion for young children. Nevertheless, the issues yet to be addressed reach far beyond the scope of even these broad studies. Because the long-term viability of inclusive programs for young children is likely to depend heavily on whether these programs can be shown to be effective, this subject offers manifold opportunities for timely and important research efforts.

CONCLUSION

The frontier of the inclusion movement has shifted from elementary and secondary school classrooms to childcare programs, preschools, and informal community activities for the very young. Although the literature concerning the effect of these inclusive programs on infants, toddlers, and preschoolers is encouraging, many questions remain. Likewise, more work must be done to identify how providers and interventionists can systematically revise and improve inclusive programs for this age group. Even while this research is being conducted, however, the demand for inclusive programs for young children will continue to grow. For these reasons, inclusion for young children with disabilities promises to be one of the most stimulating and challenging fields in education and human services during the next decade.

REFERENCES

Beckman, P. J. 1983. The relationship between behavioral characteristics of children and social interaction in an integrated setting. *Journal of the Division for Early Childhood* 7:69–77.

Bredekamp, S., ed. 1997. *Developmentally appropriate practice in early childhood programs serving children from birth through age 8*. Washington, D.C.: National Association for the Education of Young Children.

Bronfenbrenner, U. 1979. *The ecology of human development: Experiments by nature and design*. Cambridge, Mass.: Harvard University Press.

———. 1989. Ecological systems theory. In *Annals of child development*, ed. R. Vasta, 6. New York: JAI Press.

———. 1995. Toward a research design for Early Head Start: Assessing intervention under siege. Unpublished manuscript, Cornell University, Ithaca, New York.

Bruder, M. B., P. Deiner, and S. Sachs. 1990. Models of integration through early intervention/child care collaboration. *Zero to Three* 10:14–17.

Burstein, N. D. 1986. The effects of classroom organization on mainstreamed preschool children. *Exceptional Children* 52:425–34.

Buysse, V. and D. B. Bailey, Jr. 1993. Behavioral and developmental outcomes in young children with disabilities in integrated and segregated settings: A review of comparative studies. *Journal of Special Education* 26:434–61.

Carnegie Corporation. 1994. *Starting Points: Meeting the needs of our youngest children: The report of the Carnegie task force on meeting the needs of young children*. New York: Carnegie Corporation.

Colorado Department of Education, Early Childhood Special Education Unit. 1991. *Douglas County Pilot Integration Project*. Denver: Colorado Department of Education, Early Childhood Special Education Unit.

Deiner, P., and L. Whitehead. 1988. Levels of respite care as a family support system. *Topics in Early Childhood Special Education* 8:51–61.

Deutsch, F. 1983. *Child services: On behalf of children*. Belmont, Calif.: Brooks/Cole.

Diamond, K. E., L. L. Hestenes, and C. E. O'Connor. 1994. Integrating young children with disabilities in preschool: Problems and promise. *Young Children* 49:68–75.

Diamond, K. E., W. Le Furgy, and S. Blass. 1993. Attitudes of preschool children toward their peers with disabilities—a year-long investigation in integrated classrooms. *Journal of Genetic Psychology* 154:215–21.

Dunst, C. J., J. Lesko, K. Holbert, L. Wilson, K. L. Sharpe, and R. Liles. 1987. A systematic approach to infant intervention. *Topics in Early Childhood Special Education* 7:19–37.

Dunst, C. J., C. M. Trivette, and A. G. Deal. 1988. *Enabling and empowering families: Principles and guidelines for practice.* Cambridge, Mass.: Brookline Books.

———, eds. 1994. *Supporting and strengthening families: Vol. 1. Methods, strategies and practices.* Cambridge, Mass.: Brookline Books.

Eiserman, W. D., L. Shisler, and S. Healey. 1995. A community assessment of preschool providers' attitudes toward inclusion. *Journal of Early Intervention* 19:149–67.

File, N., and S. Kontos. 1993. The relationship of program quality to children's play in integrated early intervention settings. *Topics in Early Childhood Special Education* 13:1–18.

Gallagher, P. G. 1997. Teachers and inclusion: Perspectives on changing roles. *Topics in Early Childhood Special Education* 17:363–86.

Gemmel-Crosby, S., and J. R. Hanzlik. 1994. Preschool teachers' perceptions of including children with disabilities. *Education and Training in Mental Retardation and Developmental Disabilities* 29 (4):279–90.

Giangreco, M., R. Dennis, C. Coninger, S. Edelman, and R. Schattman. 1993. "I've counted Jon": Transformational experiences of teachers educating students with disabilities. *Exceptional Children* 59:359–72.

Giovinazzo, C., and D. Cook. 1995. Project together: Family child care providers' commitment to continuing education and inclusion. *Infants and Young Children* 8:26–36.

Gottlieb, J., L. Levy, and B. W. Gottlieb. 1986. The play behavior of mainstreamed disabled children. In *Mainstreaming handicapped children: Outcomes, controversies, and new directions,* ed. C. J. Meisel, 95–109. Hillsdale, N.J.: Lawrence Erlbaum Associates.

Guralnick, M. J. 1981. Programmatic factors affecting child-child social interactions in mainstreamed preschool programs. *Exceptional Education Quarterly* 1:71–93.

———. 1994. Mothers' perceptions of the benefits and drawbacks of early childhood mainstreaming. *Journal of Early Intervention* 18:168–83.

Guralnick, M. J., R. T. Connor, M. Hammond, J. M. Gottman, and K. Kinnish. 1995. Immediate effects of mainstreamed settings on the social interactions and social integration of preschool children. *American Journal on Mental Retardation* 100:359–77.

Guralnick, M. J., and J. M. Groom. 1987. The peer relations of mildly delayed and non-handicapped preschool children in mainstreamed playgroups. *Child Development* 58:1556–72.

Hanline, M. F., and K. Galant. 1993. Strategies for creating inclusive early childhood settings. In *Implementing early intervention: From research to effective practice,* ed. D. M. Bryant and M. A. Graham, 216–32. New York: Guilford.

Howes, C., and M. Olenick. 1986. Family and child care influences on toddler's compliance. *Child Development* 57:202–16.

Howes, C., D. A. Phillips, and M. Whitebook. 1992. Thresholds of quality: Implications for the social development of children in center-based child care. *Child Development* 63:449–60.

Howes, C., and P. Stewart. 1987. Child's play with adults, toys, and peers: An examination of family and child-care influences. *Developmental Psychology* 23:423–30.

Idol, L., P. Paolucci-Whitcomb, and A. Nevin. 1986. *Collaborative consultation.* Austin: Pro-Ed.

Jasluski, T. 1993. *Building cultural competence in the disability community: A resource for Developmental Disabilities Councils.* Washington, D.C.: National Association of Developmental Disabilities Councils.

Jones, S. N., and S. J. Meisels. 1987. Training family day care providers to work with special needs children. *Topics in Early Childhood Special Education* 7:1–12.

Klein, N., and R. Sheehan. 1987. Staff development: A key issue in meeting the needs of young handicapped children in day care settings. *Topics in Early Childhood Special Education* 7:13–27.

Kontos, S. 1988. Family day care as an integrated early intervention setting. *Topics in Early Childhood Special Education* 8:1–14.

Kontos, S., and N. File. 1993. Staff development in support of integration. In *Integrating young children with disabilities into community programs: Ecological perspectives on research and implementation,* ed. C. A. Peck, S. L. Odom, and D. D. Bricker, 169–86. Baltimore: Paul H. Brookes.

Kopp, C. B., B. L. Baker, and K. W. Brown. 1992. Social skills and their correlates: Preschoolers with developmental delays. *American Journal on Mental Retardation* 96:357–66.

Lamorey, S., and D. D. Bricker. 1993. Integrated programs: Effects on young children and their parents. In *Integrating young children with disabilities into community programs: Ecological perspectives on research and implementation,* ed. C. A. Peck, S. L. Odom, and D. D. Bricker, 249–70. Baltimore: Paul H. Brookes.

Landis, L. J. 1992. Marital, employment, and childcare status of mothers with infants and toddlers with disabilities. *Topics in Early Childhood Special Education* 12:496–507.

Magliocca, L. A., D. J. Sykes, M. T. Anketell, and R. B. Tyree. 1993. *The early integration training project.* Final Report. Columbus: Ohio State University. (ERIC Document Reproduction Service No. ED 356 575).

Mahoney, G., and P. O'Sullivan. 1990. Early intervention practices with families of children with handicaps. *Mental Retardation* 28:169–76.

Mathematical Policy Research. 1996. Overview of the Early Head Start research and evaluation project. Unpublished manuscript, Mathematical Policy Research, Princeton, N.J.

McDonnell, A. P., K. L. Brownell, and M. Wolery. 1997. Teaching experience and specialist support: A survey of preschool teachers employed in programs accredited by NAEYC. *Topics in Early Childhood Special Education* 17:263–85.

Montgomery, D., T. Parrish, K. Hebbeler, and R. Cook. 1997. Successes and challenges in implementing California's Early Start Program. Paper presented at the International Early Childhood Conference on Children with Special Needs, November 20–23, New Orleans, Louisiana.

Morgan, R. L., and K. Madsen. 1994. *Child care for young children with disabilities.* Chadron, Nebr.: Chadron State College. (ERIC Document Reproduction Service No. ED 369 593).

National Early Childhood Technical Assistance System (NEC–TAS). 1991. *NEC–TAS Resource packet: Least restrictive environment for infants, toddlers, and preschoolers.* Chapel Hill, N.C.: Frank Porter Graham Child Development Center.

————. 1995. Helping our nation's infants and toddlers with disabilities and their families: A briefing paper on Part H of the Individuals with Disabilities Education Act (IDEA) 1986–1995. Chapel Hill, N.C.: Frank Porter Graham Child Development Center.

O'Connell, J. C. 1984. Preschool integration and its effects on the social interactions of handicapped and nonhandicapped children: A review. *Journal of the Division for Early Childhood* 8:38–48.

Odom, S. L. 1995. Inclusion of preschool children with disabilities in typical settings. *Kennedy Center News* 31:1–4.

Odom, S. L., and W. H. Brown. 1993. Social interaction skills interventions for young children with disabilities in integrated settings. In *Integrating young children with disabilities into community programs: Ecological perspectives on research and implementation,* ed. C. A. Peck, S. L. Odom, and D. D. Bricker, 39–64. Baltimore, Md.: Paul H. Brookes.

Pearl, L. F. 1993. Developmental follow-up of at-risk infants. In *Family-centered intervention with infants and toddlers: Innovative cross-disciplinary approaches,* ed. W. Brown, S. K. Thurman, and L. F. Pearl, 211–45. Baltimore, Md.: Paul H. Brookes.

Peck, C. A., P. Carlson, and E. Helmstetter. 1992. Parent and teacher perceptions of outcomes for typically developing children enrolled in integrated early childhood programs: A statewide survey. *Journal of Early Intervention* 16:53–63.

Rule, S., J. Killoran, J. Stowitschek, M. Innocenti, S. Striefel, and C. Boswell. 1985. Training and support for mainstream day care staff. *Early Child Development and Care* 20:99–113.

Rule, S., J. J. Stowitschek, M. Innocenti, S. Striefel, J. Killoran, K. Sweezey, and C. Boswell. 1987. The social integration program: An analysis of the effects of mainstreaming handicapped children into day care centers. *Education and Treatment of Children* 10:175–92.

Smith, P. M. 1997. Parenting a child with special needs: A guide to readings and resources. *National Information Center for Children and Youth with Disabilities News Digest,* 2d edition (February 1997):2–5.

The Statement of the Advisory Committee on Services for Families with Infants and Toddlers. 1995. *Federal Register* 60 (March 17):14,571–79.

Stoneman, Z. 1993. The effects of attitude on preschool integration. In *Integrating young children with disabilities into community programs: Ecological perspectives on research and implementation,* ed. C. A. Peck, S. L. Odom and D. D. Bricker, 223–48. Baltimore, Md.: Paul H. Brookes.

Strain, P. S. 1984. Social behavior patterns of nonhandicapped and developmentally disabled friend pairs in mainstream preschools. *Analysis and Intervention in Developmental Disabilities* 4:15–28.

Surgeon General's Conference on "Healthy Children Ready to Learn: The Critical Role of Parents." 1992. Executive summary. In *Parents speak out for America's children: Report of the Surgeon General's conference* (February 9–12, 1992). Washington, D.C.: U.S. Department of Health and Human Services.

Tari, A., S. Hancock, and K. Brophy. 1989. Factors to be considered in integrated programs for young children: A review. *Early Child Development and Care* 53:37–46.

Top, B. 1997. Status of policies, procedures, and practices: State directors of special education perceptions regarding implementation of inclusion. Paper presented at the Annual Convention of the Council for Exceptional Children, April 1997, Salt Lake City, Utah.

Turnbull, A. P., and V. P. Turbiville. 1995. Why must inclusion be such a challenge? *Journal of Early Intervention* 19:200–202.

Turnbull, A. P., H. R. Turnbull, and M. Blue-Banning. 1994. Enhancing inclusion of infants and toddlers with disabilities and their families: A theoretical and programmatic analysis. *Infants and Young Children* 7:1–14.

Vadasy, P. F. 1986. Single mothers: A social phenomenon and population in need. In *Families of handicapped children,* ed. R. R. Fewell and P. F. Vadasy, 221–49. Austin: Pro-Ed.

Vergara, E. R., S. Adams, H. Masin, and D. Beckman. 1993. Contemporary therapies for infants and toddlers: Preferred approaches. In *Implementing early intervention: From research to effective practice,* ed. M. Bryant and M. A. Graham, 253–88. New York: Guilford.

Volk, D., and J. I. Stahlman. 1994. "I think everybody is afraid of the unknown": Early childhood teachers prepare for mainstreaming. *Day Care and Early Education* (Spring):13–17.

Weitzner-Lin, B., D. Chambers, and J. Sierpierski. 1994. What specialized knowledge is needed to provide early intervention services in children's hospitals? *Infant-Toddler Intervention: Transdisciplinary Journal* 4:87–104.

Wesley, P. W. 1994. Innovative practices: Providing on-site consultation to promote quality in integrated child care programs. *Journal of Early Intervention* 18:391–402.

Winton, P. J. 1986. The consequences of mainstreaming for families of young handicapped children. In *Mainstreaming handicapped children: Outcomes, controversies, and new directions,* ed. C. J. Meisel, 129–48. Hillsdale, N.J.: Lawrence Erlbaum Associates.

———. 1993. Providing family support in integrated settings. In *Integrating young children with disabilities into community programs: Ecological perspectives on research and implementation,* ed. C. A. Peck, S. L. Odom, and D. D. Bricker, 65–80. Baltimore, Md.: Paul H. Brookes.

Wolery, M., A. Holcombe-Ligon, J. Brookfield, K. Huffman, C. Schroeder, C. G. Martin, M. L. Venn, M. G. Werts, and L. A. Fleming. 1993. The extent and nature of preschool mainstreaming: A survey of general early educators. *Journal of Special Education* 27:222–34.

Wolery, M., C. G. Martin, C. Schroeder, K. Huffman, M. L. Venn, A. Holcombe, J. Brookfield, and L. A. Fleming. 1994. Employment of educators in preschool mainstreaming: A survey of general educators. *Journal of Early Intervention* 18:64–77.

Wolery, M., M. L. Venn, A. Holcombe, J. Brookfield, C. G. Martin, K. Huffman, C. Schroeder, and L. A. Fleming. 1994. Employment of related service personnel in preschool programs: A survey of general early educators. *Exceptional Children* 61:25–39.

11

Bilingual/Bicultural Education for Deaf Students

Margery S. Miller   *Donald F. Moores*

Throughout most of the twentieth century in North America, those in the education field were consistently prejudiced against Deaf children using any kind of manual communication and maintained an especially intense opposition to the use of American Sign Language. Sometimes, the opposition has consisted of a large majority of educators of Deaf children and sometimes a minority, but it was always a factor. American Sign Language has been denigrated as being too concrete, as representing merely a system of gestures, as alienating Deaf people from the hearing world, and as being animalistic. Part of this perspective, this *Weltanschauung*, is rooted in a perversion of the concept of normality, a perspective that dichotomizes the world—into good and bad, black and white, normal and abnormal, a deaf world and a hearing world—rather than addresses the infinite diversity of human existence.

Historically, proponents of such a view, almost all of whom have been hearing, forget that there is only one world and that it includes both deaf and hearing members. Those who see the world in this narrow way proclaim that their mission is to cure or prevent deafness. Failing those goals, Deaf children must be "normalized"; that is, they must learn to speak. The major criterion for success is held to be intelligible speech. Erroneously believing that signs inhibit the development of speech, proponents of oralism have dedicated themselves to the eradication of American Sign Language (fortunately, without success). In the late nineteenth century, educators argued that Deaf children could be taught to speak and speechread, thereby learning English, making signs unnecessary. Later, they argued that speech reading would bring English to the Deaf child, so signs were not necessary. In the first half of the twentieth century, the spreading use of hearing aids was seen as bringing speech to the Deaf child, so signs were not necessary. Similar claims have been made with the introduction of early education, increasingly powerful hearing aids, cochlear implants, and genetic engineering.

The prototypical oralist was Alexander Graham Bell, who devoted much of his career to the prevention, cure, and denial of deafness. Bell was the founder and financial supporter of the American Association to Promote the Teaching of Speech to the Deaf (Moores 1996). In 1883, Bell published *Memoir Upon the Formation of a Deaf Variety of the Human Race* and in 1884, he published "Fallacies Concerning the Deaf." He was troubled by what he saw as an increase of marriages among Deaf people and concluded, "The production of a defective race of human beings would be a tragedy" (1884, 41). Bell proposed that residential schools for the Deaf should be closed, Deaf teachers should be eliminated, and the "gesture language" should be discontinued. Bell later turned over data that he had gathered to E. A. Fay for analysis. Fay (1898) reached the following conclusions:

1. Deaf individuals are less likely to marry than hearing individuals, and when they do, they have fewer children. The large majority of their children are hearing, even when both parents are deaf.

2. Deaf people tend to marry other deaf people, even when their education has been completely with hearing students.

3. Deaf Americans marry more often than Deaf Europeans.

4. When both parents are deaf, the marriage is more likely to be a happy one, with a lower incidence of divorce and separation.

Although Bell accepted Fay's results, Bell's followers were unable to accept them. To some extent, perhaps, they were unable to come to terms with the information that marriages of Deaf individuals tended to be just as normal as marriages of hearing individuals. Because of this reluctance to accept Fay's conclusions, myths and misunderstandings continued throughout the twentieth century despite evidence that, from the beginnings of education of the Deaf in North America, thousands of Deaf individuals have functioned in a bilingual/bicultural environment. The first teacher of the Deaf on the continent, Laurent Clerc, was quadrilingual—French Sign Language and French in his native country as well as American Sign Language and English in America. Many Deaf individuals with excellent oral and English skills are part of Deaf culture and the Deaf community by choice. Intelligible speech for a Deaf person is a mark of success by oralists. It is not so for Deaf adults who have other criteria for success.

The acceptance of a bilingual/bicultural philosophy frees an individual from the constraints of an either-or dichotomy. One can be fulfilled in a variety of ways. This fact is something that most Deaf adults have known instinctively as they interact with hearing parents, siblings, and children or as they shop, buy gas, go to movies, buy homes, and establish IRAs. It is something that some educators of Deaf children have yet to learn.

The emergence of bilingual educational programs—programs that in some way instruct Deaf children using English and American Sign Language (ASL)—represents a logical culmination of the move away from oral-only systems of instruction that began in the 1960s. To some extent, it also represents a recapitulation of the nineteenth-century "oral-manual" controversy, which, at that time, was seen as resulting in the final victory of oralism, exemplified by the 1880 Milan Conference in which it was declared that neither signs alone nor signs coordinated with speech should be used in the instruction of Deaf children. The victory of oralism was seen as so complete that, by the end of the nineteenth century, Edward Miner Gallaudet, perhaps the leading hearing advocate of signs in instruction, published an article titled, "Must the Sign Language Go?" (1899).

Obviously, the sign language did not go. It was kept alive by the Deaf community in the face of hostility, ridicule, and oppression, and it has now witnessed both an acceptance as a legitimate language and a resurgence of use in the classroom. Today, sign language is seen as a defining characteristic of a recognizable ethnic group (Reagan 1990).

Currently, educators of Deaf and hard of hearing children use the terms "bilingual" and "bilingual/bicultural" to refer to the classroom use of two languages—ASL and English—and two cultures—Deaf culture and hearing culture. Obviously, the situation can be much more complicated than that. Many children come from families that use languages other than English and ASL, and there are numerous cultures and subcultures in our society. For purposes of consistency the authors follow the current usage, with a caveat to the reader that we refer to "bilingual" and "bilingual/bicultural" education in a very general way.

As might be expected, the educational uses of ASL have been a matter of controversy and confusion, compounded by a lack of definition of key terms and a scarcity of relevant data. This chapter is designed to provide a context for the development and possible future of bilingual education of Deaf children. Different perspectives on bilingual education will be presented, and practical suggestions for successful implementation will be given.

MODES OF INSTRUCTION FROM 1960 TO 1985

In 1960, the education of Deaf children was primarily oral only. Without exception, public school programs allowed no signs in classes. This practice was also true of all residential schools for children up to the age of twelve years. The "oral" schools maintained this policy through high school, and the "manual" schools would move their "oral failures" into classes where signs were allowed. Younger children were segregated from older children so they would not be contaminated by signs. Deaf teachers were not employed by public schools or by oral residential schools. In the manual residential schools, Deaf teachers were limited to teaching in high school and vocational departments or with children who had multiple disabilities. Not one program for deaf children in North America was led by a Deaf professional (Moores 1996). Deaf students were not accepted into the graduate program at Gallaudet College, now Gallaudet University, thus closing off teaching certification for all but a select few. In an earlier study of Gallaudet graduates, Fusfeld (1941) reported that more than half were employed as teachers or dormitory supervisors at residential schools. Most, clearly, were in dead-end jobs and were underpaid, with little opportunity to influence educational practice. This legacy of oppression should be kept in mind when considering the reactions that present-day Deaf educators express to criticism regarding the use of ASL.

The outlook in 1960 was for a continuation and strengthening of oral-only education. New, more powerful hearing aids were becoming available, and an emphasis on preschool education for Deaf children was growing. It was believed that early education programs emphasizing auditory training, sometimes called "acoupedics," would substantially reduce the number of deaf children. Some advocates (Pollack 1964; Stewart, Pollack, and Downs 1964) viewed this procedure as the final breakthrough; one advocate even claimed that her procedures would cure deafness if they were instituted before the child was eight months of age (Griffiths 1967, 42–50). Apropos of the spirit of the times, Griffiths titled her book *Conquering Childhood Deafness.*

The spirit of optimism was short-lived. In 1965, the *Report to the Secretary of Health, Education and Welfare,* by the Advisory Committee on Education of the Deaf asserted, "The American people have no reason to be satisfied with their limited success in educating Deaf children and preparing them for full participation in our society" and characterized the state of education of the Deaf as unsatisfactory (Advisory Committee, 1965, xv).

At the same time, data began to be reported on the relative ineffectiveness of oral preschool programs. In six schools, Phillips (1963) found no differences in English, math, and socialization measures between Deaf children up to age nine who had preschool training and Deaf children of the same age who did not have preschool training. Similarly, drawing from subjects in two schools, Craig (1964) found no differences in speechreading or reading skills between children with preschool experiences and those with no preschool experiences. McCroskey (1967) compared children who had gone through a home-centered preschool program to children with no preschool experience and reported that the few differences found tended to favor the children with no preschool experience. Vernon and Koh (1970) matched students at a residential school for the Deaf who had attended the three-year John Tracy Clinic (a preschool program) to students at the school who did not have preschool experiences. They found no differences in speech, speechreading, academic achievement, or reading. A third group, consisting of Deaf children of Deaf parents, was found to be superior to the other two groups in academic achievement and reading, with no differences in speech and speechreading.

The findings reported by Vernon and Koh on the relative superiority of Deaf children of Deaf parents was similar to previous reports by Meadow (1967) and by Stuckless and Birch (1966) indicating that Deaf children of Deaf parents, who were introduced to sign communication at birth, scored higher than Deaf children of hearing parents in English skills, academic achievement, reading, writing, and social maturity. Educators of Deaf children, then, were confronted with two unexpected findings. First, the effects of oral-only preschool programs appeared, at best, to be negligible. Second, children who signed at home had superior English and academic skills to matched groups of children who did not sign at home, and those who signed at home showed no negative effects on speech or speechreading. These findings came as a shock to those educators who believed that signs were detrimental to the acquisition of speech, English, and academic content.

Concurrent with the findings on oral-only education and the achievements of Deaf children of Deaf parents, several educators were developing sign systems representing English to be used in the classroom. Unlike ASL, which is a separate language, these systems were designed as codes on English. Drawing heavily on ASL vocabulary, the systems use English word order and add invented signs for bound morphemes (such as -s, -ed, -ly, -ment), some function words, pronouns, and forms of the verb *to be*. Currently, the most commonly used codes on English are Signing Exact English (Gustason, Pfetzing, and Zawolkow 1972) and Signed English (Bornstein and Saulnier 1972, 1982).

By 1975, a remarkable shift had taken place in classroom instruction modes. Approximately two-thirds of deaf children were being taught through some form of manual communication and one-third through oral-only instruction (Jordan, Gustason, and Rosen 1976, 1979). Children taught in oral-only classes tended to be younger and have more residual hearing.

The umbrella term *total communication* was used to describe the systems that were introduced in the 1970s. The term was popularized by Holcomb (1970), the first Deaf professional to head a public school program for Deaf children, who used it to describe a philosophy that would incorporate all means of communication—use of speech, speechreading, audition, reading, writing, the manual alphabet, manual codes on English, and ASL. In practice, this interpretation frequently was not the case, and the term total communication was often used interchangeably with *simultaneous communication* (or *Sim-Com*), which involves coordinated speaking and signing.

RECENT DEVELOPMENTS AND ISSUES

The use of signing in education programs has led to a general improvement in academic achievement for Deaf children (Caccamise and Blaisdell 1977; Hatfield and Brewer 1978; Delaney, Stuckless, and Walter 1984; Goppold 1988; Mitchell 1982; Moores 1985, 1996). Because it has opened up options, it may also have helped the effectiveness of oral-only programs for those children who could benefit from them. Generally, all but a minority of educators agree that the introduction of manual communication to instruction was an improvement over the inflexibility of the past, with its insistence on only one mode of instruction and communication—speech.

The development and acceptance of English-based sign systems represented significant advances. However, an element was usually missing—American Sign Language. In many cases, it was ignored. Whether this neglect was through ignorance of the nature of ASL or was deliberate is unclear.

Two questions have been raised about the effectiveness of English-based sign systems. First, can English be represented adequately through signs? Second, can coordinated signs and speech be presented and understood adequately? Kluwin (1981) reports that teachers' signing skills using Sim-Com improved over time, and as they became more fluent, they tended to incorporate elements of ASL into their signing. Studying a class of elementary school Deaf children, Supalla (1992) reports that young Deaf children who had been instructed through manual codes on English had basic problems expressing English syntax. Supulla argues that manual codes on English are not natural languages and that children exposed to them change them into more efficient systems that resemble natural languages such as ASL. His position is that manual codes on English cannot represent English adequately. In contrast, Schick and Moeller (1989), studying the expressive English usage of Deaf public school children using a manual code on English, report that the students produced English to a high degree and that they had internalized the rules of English.

For the most part, the criticisms of various manual codes on English have been that they are awkward, that they are artificial, that they do not correspond to English grammatical elements on a one-to-one basis, and that the academic achievement of Deaf children using these systems is still below that of hearing children.

The arguments concerning the use of manual codes on English and ASL are reminiscent of the nineteenth-century conflict over "methodical" signs that were designed to represent English and "natural" signs that were generated by members of the Deaf community. "Natural" signs may be considered the precursor of ASL. In a review of the literature on the nineteenth-century controversy, Stedt and Moores (1990) note that both ASL-based and English-based sign systems have survived and thrived since the beginning of education of Deaf children and will continue to do so because they fulfill important and complementary needs.

On balance, the evidence suggests that manual codes in English can be signed and understood with consistency, given that appropriate training and monitoring is provided. The sign-to-speech match for fluent signers and experienced teachers is approximately 90 percent. This level of sign-to-speech match has been reported not only for manual codes on English in North America (Luetke-Stahlman 1988; Mayer and Lowenbraun 1990) but also in Australasian Signed English (Hyde and Power 1991) and British Signed English (Savage, Savage, and Potter 1987). Still, most educators would agree that the invented sign systems lack the power and sophistication of natural sign languages.

Educators of Deaf children essentially are faced with four communication options that can be used either separately or in combination. These options are briefly presented as follows.

1. *Auditory (Acoupedic) Systems.* This unisensory approach primarily relies on hearing and is especially used with very young children. The use of vision in training is de-emphasized, thus, the term *unisensory.* The justification for this approach is that, with early identification, fitting of powerful hearing aids (or cochlear implants), and intensive training, Deaf children can be taught to use and even improve their auditory potential to the extent that they can function essentially as hearing individuals. The counterargument is that, although effective with children who have usable residual hearing, it simply does not work with most children who have severe to profound hearing losses. The impetus for this approach came from Sweden in the years following World War II and spread to Western Europe and North America. (Note that Sweden currently uses a bilingual/bicultural approach.)

2. *Speechreading.* Speechreading usually is employed with the use of residual hearing in a bimodal, visual-auditory system to produce the typical "oral" classroom instruction. While speechreading, children can use their residual hearing, but they cannot be required to depend on it entirely. Again, success has been documented for some children, but difficulties in accurately understanding speechreading increase as a function of the hearing loss.

3. *Manual codes on English.* Most commonly, manually coded systems that are used in the classroom incorporate the use of residual hearing, speechreading, speech, the manual alphabet, and signs in an effort to provide an adequate representation of English. As previously mentioned, the major criticism is that, although it represents an improvement over oral-only means of instruction, it is awkward and does not fully represent English.

4. *American Sign Language (ASL).* ASL was not officially used in classrooms throughout most of the twentieth century until the mid-1960s. It is a complete, powerful, natural language that can be used for all aspects of communication. Reservations about its classroom use stem from two facts—it does not correspond directly with English, and most parents of deaf children are hearing and so are not fluent in ASL.

BILINGUAL/BICULTURAL EDUCATION FOR DEAF CHILDREN: TWO PERSPECTIVES

Among educators of Deaf children and adults, it is commonly agreed that bilingual/bicultural education should have two languages—American Sign Language and English. They also agree that Deaf children of all ages should be exposed to Deaf adults and to cultural aspects of the Deaf community. They have differences of opinion, however, over the ways in which English and ASL should be used. In August 1990, a group of educators, administrators, and researchers met at Hofstra University in Long Island, New York, for a three-day symposium concerning issues related to the educational uses of ASL. The symposium was organized around four major issues:

1. Parent-child communication, particularly communication between hearing parents and Deaf children

2. Which language—English or American Sign Language—should be promoted as the primary language of Deaf children

3. How American Sign Language is presently being used in educational programs involving Deaf children

4. The extent to which programs designed for hearing users of English as a second language can provide insights for educators working with Deaf children (Walworth, Moores, and O'Rourke 1992)

Four of the participants wrote and disseminated chapters to provide background for the symposium (Moores 1992; Schlesinger 1992; Stewart 1995; Walworth 1992). The participants, of whom approximately half were Deaf and half hearing, generally agreed that the use of ASL would—and should—increase, but they disagreed about how this increase should occur. Bowe (1992) summarized the observations:

- The field is not yet clear on its goals with regard to using ASL in the classroom.

- We do not have good measurement tools to apply to the research on ASL in the classroom.

- We know surprisingly little about how Deaf children learn ASL or how we should teach it to them.

- The programs that are using ASL are doing little research.

- The field is experiencing a severe shortage of teachers who are fluent in ASL, especially, teachers who are deaf and fluent in ASL.

- We are finding few, if any, indications that teacher training programs will soon alleviate these shortages.

- Resistance to change is strong.

- Many of the research questions surrounding the educational uses of ASL are so complex that a long-term program of study is likely to be required.

Two basic positions were presented concerning the implementation of a bilingual/bicultural system of education for Deaf children. One position challenged that all person-to-person or "through the air" communication must involve ASL only and that ASL must be the language of instruction. In this paradigm, manual codes on English would not be used. Because ASL is a different language than English, no speech would be used. English would be taught through print after the first language, ASL, had been mastered. Hearing parents would be taught ASL by Deaf adults who were fluent in the language. Representatives from two programs following this model discussed issues concerning the small number of available Deaf teachers, biases against ASL, and interactions with hearing parents (Philip and Kuntze 1992).

The second position advocated the incorporation of ASL into an inclusive model that would involve speech, hearing, English, and ASL, depending on individual and situational need. This approach, presented by Stewart and Moores, assumes that research has demonstrated that manual codes on English can represent English adequately, either separately or in coordination with speech. The approach also assumes that hearing parents can acquire initial aspects of an English-based sign system more easily than they can master a new language that involves different structures and rules of combination. The use of English codes and spoken language can also offer access to the phonological system, a requirement for literacy. Stewart and Moores also agreed that ASL is a much more powerful and sophisticated tool than any manual code on English, and it should be featured prominently in any educational program. The key is to develop techniques and mechanisms for codeswitching to maximize educational growth.

Since the publication of the proceedings of the symposium, the educational use of ASL has grown substantially. To illustrate this growth, the authors analyzed self-reports from the *American Annals of the Deaf 1998 Directory of Services* of the twenty largest programs serving Deaf and hard of hearing children in the United States for the 1997–98 school year. Enrollment ranged from 399 to 2,455 children. These reports represented a range of comprehensive programs in our largest cities (such as New York and Los Angeles), suburban programs, countywide programs, and residential schools. The programs were asked to identify communication modes that were used in instruction. They were given four choices: auditory/oral, cued speech, sign with speech, and American Sign Language. Programs could list from only one to all four modes.

As shown in table 1, almost all programs are inclusive in their use of instructional mode. No program used auditory/oral instruction exclusively. All twenty programs had some form of manual communication, with nineteen using sign with speech and sixteen using ASL. Only one program used ASL exclusively, and only two programs used sign with speech exclusively. Fifteen of the twenty programs used both sign with speech as well as ASL. From these data, we may conclude that bilingual education already is a reality in 75 percent of the largest programs for Deaf children in the United States. By extension, we may estimate that its use is pervasive in most programs serving Deaf and hard of hearing children. Clearly, despite generations of opposition to ASL, most teachers of Deaf children readily embrace its use in the classroom.

The situation reflected in table 1 is likely to endure for the foreseeable future. The most commonly used approach at present is one that incorporates sign-with-speech, auditory/oral, and ASL components. Exclusive auditory/oral instruction is relatively rare on a programmatic basis, although it may be used in individual classrooms. Usually, it is used with hard of hearing children. The greater an individual child's hearing loss, the higher the probability that some

Table 1.

Instructional Modes in the Twenty Largest Programs Serving Deaf and Hard of Hearing Children in the United States, 1997–1998

Program	Enrollment	Auditory/ Oral	Cued Speech	ASL	Sign with Speech
Los Angeles Unified School District	2,455	x		x	x
Ingham (Michigan) Intermediate District	2,347	x		x	x
New York City Public Schools	1,893	x	x	x	x
Florida School for the Deaf and the Blind	512				x
California School for the Deaf, Fremont	510			x	x
California School for the Deaf, Riverside	507			x	x
Orange County (Florida) Public Schools	487	x	x	x	x
Maryland School for the Deaf	470			x	
Fairfax County (Virginia) Public Schools	450	x	x	x	x
Texas School for the Deaf	446			x	x
Arizona State Programs for the Deaf	445	x		x	x
San Diego Public Schools	440	x		x	x
Dade County (Florida) Public Schools	424	x		x	x
SEDOL, Illinois	408				x
Louisiana School for the Deaf	408			x	x
Dupage Region (Illinois) Public Schools	406	x			x
Lexington School for the Deaf (New York)	404	x		x	x
Pinellas County (Florida) Public Schools	400	x			x
Columbia Region (Oregon) Public Schools	399	x		x	x
South Carolina School for the Deaf	399			x	x

Source: Schools and Programs in the United States. 1998. *American Annals of the Deaf* 143 (2):122–52.

form of manual communication will be used in instruction. Even with the growing recourse to cochlear implants and impressive improvements in hearing aid technology, this tendency should remain true well into the twenty-first century.

MAJOR ISSUES

Both Canada and the United States have mandated that services for disabled children be implemented as soon as a disability is diagnosed. The services are to be family-centered, especially for families with very young children. For parents of Deaf children, more than 90 percent of whom are hearing and have had little exposure to deafness, these services involve providing information on deafness, encouraging parental acceptance, and helping parents develop communication skills and other skills that are unique to the presence of a Deaf child in a family. For most parents, the reality—documented by generations of research—is that a child with a severe or profound hearing loss, even with the best of medical procedures and hearing aids, is not likely to develop the ability to speak fluently, at least, not at an early age when clear, unambiguous communication is essential. When a child has been identified as having a severe or profound hearing loss, the parents should be informed of available bilingual options for their child, options that do not preclude the development of speech and auditory abilities but options that open up communication from the time a hearing loss is identified.

Most Deaf parents already possess the skills to provide a bilingual environment to their children. Typically, these parents are fluent in ASL, can easily codeswitch to a manual code on English, and can expose their children to print at an early age. Hearing parents, however, present a challenge. A parent whose native language is spoken English or French, for example, cannot provide an ASL environment any more than she or he can provide an environment in spoken Chinese. Kemp (1998) has documented that the learning of ASL is equivalent in difficulty to the learning of any spoken language. Kemp points out that the presence of readily understandable gestures for eating, sleeping, and drinking may lead some new signers to underestimate the sophistication of the language. It is not acquired overnight.

At this point, it is helpful to make a distinction between language and communication. Hearing parents cannot be expected to acquire either a signed language or a new spoken language easily; however, they can learn to communicate effectively with a young Deaf child while they are developing their language skills. The key is to establish effective communication as quickly as possible. From the authors' experience, parents are not overly concerned with theoretical issues or conflicts over the purity of a language. Their concerns are much more immediate and are related to questions of communication, not language. Parents want to know how to sign such everyday things as "I love you," "Give me a hug," "Eat your food," "Don't hit your brother," "Go to bed," and "Want some ice cream?" Just as important, they want their children to have the ability to immediately express their wants, needs, likes, and feelings and not have to wait for some ambiguous breakthrough sometime in the distant future. In other words, hearing parents of hearing children (and Deaf parents of all children) communicate with their children purely to communicate. They do not set out deliberately to teach the child a language or have the child learn a language. Language development is a by-product of the communicative and developmental process. The goal for Deaf children of hearing parents should be the same.

Parents have the legal and moral right to decide on the type of communication that should be used with their Deaf children, and professionals have the responsibility to provide these parents with information to help them make informed choices on the basis of a child's individual needs at a particular point of development. Especially at early ages, when services are mandated to be family-centered, parents should be the decision makers to the greatest extent possible. Although it may be difficult for some professionals to acknowledge, parents know more about their children than anyone else and are the real experts. If parents opt for a bilingual program for their children, they should be aware that a number of options are available to them. Many parents are overwhelmed by the idea of learning a totally new language such as ASL and introducing it immediately into the home.

In addition to the real difficulty that adults face in learning a new language, work and other family demands may also make such learning unfeasible. Nevertheless, some parents may be very motivated to learn ASL and may become involved in the Deaf community immediately. Both sets of parents can be accommodated. The first set of parents can be encouraged to begin learning a manual system that is based on English or another spoken language and is coordinated with speech to the extent it is comfortable. Children can be exposed to ASL through ASL-using Deaf adults and children at home, school, and elsewhere. Parents should be aware that bilingual programs for hearing children typically involve two languages at school but, often, only one language at home. For hearing parents of Deaf children, the goal should be to bring ASL into the entire environment. Respect and acceptance of both languages is important, but fluency in both is not necessary.

Regardless of the parents' fluency in sign, every effort should be made to ensure that the environment is a bilingual/bicultural one. Bilingual/bicultural environments can be nurtured in myriad ways. Deaf people should be in the home in a natural way, not just as instructors or facilitators. Deaf baby-sitters can be used, and the family can regularly attend Deaf cultural events. Religious services should be signed, either by the celebrant or by an interpreter. All family events— weddings, funerals, confirmations, bar and bat mitzvahs, funerals—should be communication accessible to the Deaf child.

The Deaf child, while at an early age, and his or her hearing family members should be exposed to the pragmatics of communication and behavioral patterns of Deaf and hearing communities. The two communities practice different communication behaviors related to turn taking, eye contact, and physical contact, and those differences should be learned.

As previously noted, very little is known about how Deaf children acquire fluency in ASL. The same may be said about the acquisition of English, whether in spoken, written, or signed forms. All of this background should be made clear to parents. A major concern expressed by parents is the fear that children who use some form of sign will not develop adequate speech and literacy skills in the home languages. Reviews of research (Goppold 1988; Moores 1996) suggest that the use of signs can facilitate literacy and has no effect, either positive or negative, on vocal skills.

Family Systems

Much previous writing has referred to "the Deaf child in a hearing family." On reflection, obviously, such terminology not only is incorrect but also makes invidious assumptions about the worth of the Deaf child. Any family with both Deaf and hearing members is not a "hearing" family. The Deaf child is a full-fledged family member, and any depiction of the family should not exclude him or her.

When parents decide they want a bilingual/bicultural environment for their child, they should be assured that they are not choosing one language or one culture over another. As the name implies, they want a child who is bilingual in English (or some other spoken language) and ASL (or some other signed language). One does not preclude the other. By the same token, the family—and, later, the child—does not have to choose one culture over another. Rather, preparing a Deaf child for participation in the Deaf community opens up exciting new possibilities and experiences. The Deaf community enjoys an endless variety of Deaf organizations at local, regional, national, and global levels. The choices include such general categories as religion, racial-ethnic identification, and sports as well as more specialized groups such as Deaf entrepreneurs and Deaf rock climbers. Again, we must emphasize that either-or dichotomies are unnecessary. The International World Games for the Deaf are one exciting option. At the same time, Deaf athletes have participated and have won medals in Olympic swimming, running, and wrestling events. In 1995, we celebrated a Miss Deaf America (Jennifer Yost) and a Deaf Miss America (Heather Whitestone). Whether it be gymnastics, dressage, karate, flower arranging, or a Dead Poets Society, options are available. The child can be truly bicultural.

Programs serving families with Deaf children should have a significant representation of Deaf professionals. If they do not, questions should be asked concerning the exclusion of individuals with unique skills. Deaf professionals provide guidance in several additional areas together with their obvious role in fostering the acquisition of signing skills. Effective interaction with the child is the most obvious role, of course. Deaf professionals can provide invaluable information on how to attract and maintain visual contact, how to use eye contact, and how to visually monitor the environment. One extremely important role is demonstrating to parents how to read with very young Deaf children, an area often overlooked by hearing parents who can be unaware that developing preliteracy skills in Deaf children is critical to their language and academic development. Deaf professionals can also introduce hearing parents to Deaf parents with similar backgrounds and interests to help smooth the hearing parents' introduction to and participation in the Deaf community, a unique community with a special language and a rich tradition that will, in all probability, include their child as a member.

One very productive support system for families can be developed during a learning vacation, such as those sponsored by the Gallaudet Family Learning Vacation Program. We recommend a total immersion version of an annual family vacation or retreat of up to two weeks in which families with Deaf children can interact with each other, Deaf adults, and Deaf and hearing professionals to exchange information, insights, and perspectives. A major component of the retreat should be dedicated to developing effective sign communication skills and integrating them into everyday family life.

Educational Considerations

Educational programs must be "Deaf friendly." The term may seem simple, but it covers some complex issues. We have already mentioned the need for Deaf teachers and other professionals to be present. In most residential schools and day schools, accommodations have already been made to meet the needs of children who are visual learners. These accommodations have not been made necessarily in those programs where Deaf children are in the minority, the situation for most Deaf children in North America today. Public schools have been established with hearing children in mind, and our habits are ingrained. For one example, consider the use of public address systems. Throughout the day, these communication systems provide information vocally about schedule changes, special activities, and events. Deaf children and Deaf teachers do not have equal access to the information. One simple and equalizing change, which many schools are doing, is to provide information through television monitors via sign, voice, and print.

For a Deaf child to be truly included in a school, that child must have equal access to communication—not only access through computers, print, and television but also to all aspects of the school environment. Communication with principals, secretaries, counselors, school psychologists, and nurses—especially nurses—should be open. Extracurricular activities from sports to dance to school newspapers should be available with the support of interpreters when necessary. Training in ASL should be offered to hearing students and staff members. Participation in the Junior National Association of the Deaf could occur through school auspices.

Schools, even those with a predominantly hearing enrollment, can offer truly bilingual/bicultural programs by adding material to the curriculum about the Deaf community, American Sign Language, and the richness of Deaf culture. The contributions that Deaf members have made to our society can be highlighted.

The need for effective communication cannot be overemphasized, especially when dealing with issues of assessment. Moores (1996) has addressed the shortage of professionals who have been trained to work as counselors or school psychologists with Deaf children. Miller (1991) has demonstrated that valid and reliable psychological testing of Deaf children, especially on verbal scales of intelligence, can be accomplished only by fluent signers who have the skill to move back and forth from English-based to ASL-based assessment depending on the needs and skills of the child. Lacking such tester flexibility, we run the risk of underestimating the academic and cognitive potential of the child.

CONCLUSION

Bilingual/bicultural education for Deaf children began to gain popularity in the last decade of the twentieth century, long after the appearance of bilingual education for hearing children. The reasons for its late arrival are complex, but include the lamentable resistance for more than a century to the legitimacy of American Sign Language and, by extension, to a flourishing Deaf community. The willingness of the general population to embrace the philosophy of diversity has brought educators of Deaf children—some enthusiastically and some reluctantly—to the point where ASL has attained its rightful position of importance in the education of young Deaf children and its traditional place of honor among the majority of Deaf adults, regardless of their educational training.

REFERENCES

Advisory Committee on the Education of the Deaf. 1965. *Report to the Secretary of Health, Education and Welfare*. Washington, D.C.: U.S. Department of Education.

Bell, A. G. 1883. *Memoir upon the formation of a deaf variety of the human race*. Washington, D.C.: U.S. Government Printing Office; reissued by the Alexander Graham Bell Association for the Deaf, 1969.

———. 1884. Fallacies concerning the deaf. *American Annals of the Deaf* 28:124–39.

Bornstein, H., and K. Saulnier. 1972. *The Signed English series*. Washington, D.C.: Gallaudet University Press.

———. 1982. Signed English: A brief follow up to the first edition. *American Annals of the Deaf* 126 (1):468–81.

Bowe, F. 1992. Radicalism vs. reason: Directions in the educational use of ASL. In *A free hand*, ed. M. Walworth, D. Moores, and T. J. O'Rourke, 182–97. Silver Spring, Md.: T. J. Publishers.

Caccamise, F., and R. Blaisdell. 1977. Reception of sentences under oral, manual, interpreted and simultaneous conditions. *American Annals of the Deaf* 109 (2):280–96.

Craig, W. 1964. Effects of preschool training on the development of reading and lip reading skills of deaf children. *American Annals of the Deaf* 109 (2):280–96.

Delaney, M., R. Stuckless, and G. Walter. 1984. Total communication effects: A longitudinal study of a school for the deaf in transition. *American Annals of the Deaf* 129 (6):481–86.

Fay, E. A. 1898. *Marriages of the deaf in America.* Washington, D.C.: Gibson Brothers.

Fusfeld, I. S. 1941. Professional preparation and advancement of deaf teachers. *American Annals of the Deaf* 86 (5):420–28.

Gallaudet, E. M. 1899. Must the sign language go? *American Annals of the Deaf* 44 (3):221–29.

Goppold, L. 1988. Early intervention for preschool deaf children: The longitudinal effects relative to methodology. *American Annals of the Deaf* 141 (4):285–88.

Griffiths, C. 1967. *Conquering childhood deafness.* New York: Exposition Press.

Gustason, G., D. Pfetzing, and E. Zawolkow. 1972. *Signing Exact English.* Rossmoor, Calif.: Modern Signs Press.

Holcomb, R. 1970. The total approach. In *Proceedings of the International Congress on Education of the Deaf,* 104–7. Stockholm.

Hyde, M. B., and D. Power. 1991. Teachers' use of simultaneous communication. *American Annals of the Deaf* 136 (5):381–87.

Jordan, I., G. Gustason, and R. Rosen. 1976. Current communication trends at programs for the deaf. *American Annals of the Deaf* 121 (5):527–31.

———. 1979. An update on communication trends at programs for the deaf. *American Annals of the Deaf* 124 (3):350–57.

Kemp, M. 1998. Why is learning American Sign Language a challenge? *American Annals of the Deaf* 143 (4):255–59.

Kluwin, T. 1981. The grammaticality of manual representations of English in classroom settings. *American Annals of the Deaf* 126 (3):417–21.

Luetke-Stahlman, B. 1988. Documenting syntactically and semantically incomplete bimodal input of hearing impaired children. *American Annals of the Deaf* 133 (2):230–34.

Mayer, P., and S. Lowenbraun. 1990. Total communication use among elementary teachers of hearing impaired children. *American Annals of the Deaf* 135 (2):227–33.

McCroskey, R. 1967. Early education of infants with severe auditory impairments. In *Proceedings of International Conference on Oral Education of the Deaf,* 1,891–905. Washington, D.C.: A. G. Bell Association.

Meadow, K. 1967. The effect of early manual communication and family climate on the deaf child's development. Diss., University of California, Berkeley.

Miller, M. 1991. Sign language iconicity and test construction theory for deaf individuals. Diss., Georgetown University, Washington, D.C.

Mitchell, G. 1982. Can deaf children acquire English? An evaluation of manually coded English systems in terms of the principles of language acquisition. *American Annals of the Deaf* 132 (3):331–36.

Moores, D. 1985. Early intervention programs for deaf children. In *Children's language,* vol. 5, ed. K. Nelson, 159–95. Hillsdale, N.J.: Lawrence Erlbaum Associates.

———. 1992. What do we know and when did we know it? In *A free hand,* ed. M. Walworth, D. Moores, and T. J. O'Rourke, 67–88. Silver Spring, Md.: T. J. Publishers.

———. 1996. *Educating the deaf: Psychology, principles and practices.* 4th ed. Boston: Houghton Mifflin.

Philip, M., and M. Kuntze. 1992. Blueprints for the future: Two programs. In *A free hand*, ed. M. Walworth, D. Moores, and T. J. O'Rourke, 3–19. Silver Spring, Md.: T. J. Publishers.

Phillips, W. 1963. Influence of preschool training on language arts, arithmetic concepts, and socialization of young deaf children. Diss., Columbia University, New York.

Pollack, D. 1964. Acoupedics: A unisensory approach to auditory training. *Volta Review* 66 (7):400–409.

Reagan, T. 1990. Cultural considerations in the education of deaf children. In *Developmental and educational aspects of deafness*, ed. D. Moores and K. Meadow-Orlans, 73–84. Washington, D.C.: Gallaudet University Press.

Savage, R. D., J. F. Savage, and J. Potter. 1987. The classroom communication of experienced teachers of the deaf. *Australian Educational and Developmental Psychologist* 4 (1):17–22.

Schick, B., and M. Moeller. 1989. The expressive English language of deaf students exposed to SEE II. Paper presented at the American Speech and Hearing Association annual convention, St. Louis, Missouri.

Schlesinger, H. 1992. The elusive x factor: Parental contributions to literacy. In *A free hand*, ed. M. Walworth, D. Moores, and T. J. O'Rourke, 37–64. Silver Spring, Md.: T. J. Publishers.

Stewart, J., D. Pollack, and M. Downs. 1964. An unisensory approach for the limited hearing child. *ASHA [American Speech and Hearing Association]* 6:151–54.

Stedt, J., and D. Moores. 1990. Manual codes on English and American Sign Language. In *Manual communication: Implications for education*, ed. H. Bornstein, 1–20. Washington, D.C.: Gallaudet University Press.

Stuckless, R., and J. Birch. 1966. The influence of early manual communication on the linguistic development of deaf children. *American Annals of the Deaf* 120 (5):417–21.

Supalla, S. 1992. Equal educational opportunity: The Deaf version. In *A free hand*, ed. M. Walworth, D. Moores, and T. J. O'Rourke, 170–81. Silver Spring, Md.: T. J. Publishers.

Vernon, M., and H. Koh. 1970. Effects of manual communication on deaf children's educational achievement, linguistic competence and psychological development. *American Annals of the Deaf* 115 (5):527–36.

Walworth, M. 1992. ESL/ASL: Unanswered questions, unquestioned answers. In *A free hand*, ed. M. Walworth, D. Moores, and T. J. O'Rourke, 119–39. Silver Spring, Md.: T. J. Publishers.

Walworth, M., D. Moores, and T. J. O'Rourke, eds. 1992. *A free hand*. Silver Spring, Md.: T. J. Publishers.

12

Multicultural Special Education for Increasingly Diverse Societies

Margret A. Winzer   *Kas Mazurek*

The United States and Canada are countries built on immigration and, therefore, have always been multicultural societies. However, during the past three decades, we have witnessed enormous changes in the traditional demographic composition of these two nations. Previously characterized by a predominance of people of European ancestry, Canada and the United States are now societies with prominent and growing populations of minorities. Changing immigration patterns make up one major element that is responsible for accelerating this process.

As of 1997, almost 26 million foreign-born residents lived in the United States out of a total population of approximately 267 million. One out of every two foreign-born residents is a native of Latin America or the Caribbean, with Mexico predominant as the country of origin for fully one-half of this group (U.S. Census Bureau 1997). Immigration statistics reveal that as of 1996, Mexico remained the leading source country with 18 percent of all immigrants, followed by the Philippines with 6 percent, India with 5 percent, Vietnam with 4.6 percent, and China with 4.5 percent. Indeed, for the years 1981–1996, during which more than 13 million persons immigrated to the United States, not one European nation is listed among the ten countries of birth that are most represented. In rank order, those ten countries are Mexico, the Philippines, Vietnam, China, the Dominican Republic, India, Korea, El Salvador, Jamaica, and Cuba. Combined, these ten nations account for 58 percent of the total immigration to the United States during that period (U.S. Immigration and Naturalization Service 1999).

This shift in immigration patterns has significantly added to the tremendous diversity of the population. In 1999, approximately 28 percent of the total 272 million United States residents were members of a racial minority group. In rounded figures, African Americans constituted 12 percent of the total population; Hispanics, 11 percent; Asians and Pacific Islanders, 4 percent; and Native American Indians, Eskimos, and Aleuts, 1 percent (U.S. Census Bureau 1999a).

It is also important to appreciate how quickly the situation is evolving. For example, from 1990 to 1998, the Hispanic population increased by 35 percent while the total population grew by only 8 percent. The projection is that the Hispanic population will grow from 30.4 million in 1998 to 96.5 million in 2050. Then, Hispanics will constitute 24.5 percent of the nation's total population, whereas in 1998, they constituted 11.3 percent. Indeed, projections show that by 2005, Hispanics will surpass non-Hispanic African Americans to become the largest minority group (U.S. Census Bureau 1998).

The case of Asian and Pacific Islander Americans is equally dramatic. Between 1990 and 1998, Asians and Pacific Islanders had the highest rate of population growth (37 percent) of any race or ethnic group in the United States. The 10.4 million Asians and Pacific Islanders constituted 3.8 percent of the United States population in 1998. By 2020, projections show that this group will reach almost 20 million people and will account for a little more than 6 percent of the total population. Recent immigration statistics for this group become even more significant when one considers the related statistics for 1997; that is, 24 percent of foreign-born residents in 1997 were Asians and Pacific Islanders (U.S. Census Bureau 1999b).

Linguistic diversity is the complement to this expanding demographic diversity. The 1990 census reported that some 32 million individuals, ages five years and older—that is, one in seven United States residents or 14 percent of the population—speak a language other than English at home. European languages that are spoken include Spanish, Italian, German, Polish, French, and Yiddish. Other languages include Asian, African, Middle-Eastern, and Native American languages as well as those from Southeast Asia, such as Hmong and Vietnamese. In all, 350 language categories were reported (U.S. Census Bureau 1999a). In addition, current immigration patterns indicate an increase among non-English speakers, especially people from Latin America and Asia, many of whom speak their native language at home (Winzer and Mazurek 1998).

The rich and accelerating diversity evidenced in the United States is also found in Canada. Over the last four decades, the pattern of immigration to Canada has changed greatly. During the 1960s, Europeans accounted for 69 percent of all immigrants to Canada; Asians, 12 percent; and other Americans (excluding the United States, which is a separate category), 12 percent. The relative proportions rapidly changed to 36 percent, 33 percent, and 16 percent in the 1970s; to 26 percent, 47 percent, and 16 percent in the 1980s; and to 19 percent, 57 percent, and 13 percent in the 1990s. Projections show that by the end of the first decade of the new millennium, up to 80 percent of all immigrants to Canada will be visible minorities ("Canada 2005" 1999, 33–41).

The results of these changes in immigration have been dramatic. In 1986, 6.3 percent of Canadians were members of a visible minority. By 1991, this percentage increased to 9.4, and by 1996, to 11.2 (Statistics Canada 1998a). In 2005, the percentage will rise to 16 and, by 2016, it is expected that 20 percent of the Canadian population will be members of a visible minority (Statistics Canada 1996, 3). Of the more than one in ten Canadians who are members of a visible minority, 26.9 percent are Chinese, 21 percent are South Asian, 17.9 percent are African American, 8 percent are Arab or West Asian, 7.7 percent are Filipino, 5.5 percent are Latin American, and 5.4 percent are Southeast Asian (Statistics Canada 1998b).

These demographic realities directly affect schools. Both in the United States and Canada, schools are experiencing high enrollment levels for immigrant and minority students. Indeed, for the United States, projections are that minority students will constitute 46 percent of overall student enrollment by the year 2020 (Banks 1994) and already exceed 25 percent in half of the states. In Canada, as of 1991, 12 percent of all children under the age of 15 were members of a visible minority group; this percentage will double to 25 percent by 2016 (Statistics Canada 1996, 3). Of the approximately 1 million immigrants who came to Canada between 1991 and 1996, almost 80 percent reported a nonofficial language (i.e., not English or French) as their mother tongue. In 1996, one in ten Canadians was speaking a nonofficial language at home (Statistics Canada 1997). As immigration overwhelmingly continues to tilt toward non-European sources, the number of children in U.S. and Canadian schools who do not have English (or French, in the Canadian situation) as a first language or home language and who do not have a European cultural heritage will continue to increase dramatically.

MULTICULTURALISM, SCHOOLING, AND SPECIAL EDUCATION

These mounting cultural and linguistic changes affect the responsibilities that educators have to prepare all children to live in our pluralistic societies, and they bring new challenges to our school systems. These changes have significant implications for general approaches to education, but the challenges that are posed by cultural and linguistic diversity are perhaps even more pervasive and complex within special education. The question of how to teach culturally diverse students who also have disabilities is complex and difficult. Educators must deliver effective instruction and develop evaluation strategies that make instructional sense; that focus on culture, language, and disability; and that comply with legal statutes.

Approaches to provide culturally appropriate education services vary. One approach, broadly encompassed under the term *multicultural education*, describes a perspective and process designed to ensure that all students have the same opportunity to succeed—whatever their ethnic and socioeconomic background, their language or dialect, their geographic location, their gender, or their disability. Multicultural education includes goals such as the movement toward equity; cultural pluralism; intergroup harmony; an expanded multicultural-multiethnic knowledge base; multicultural curricula; a commitment to combating prejudice and discrimination; and the empowerment of teachers, students, and parents.

Advocates often recommend that a multicultural curriculum endorse bilingual education. By extension, multicultural special education should incorporate bilingual special education, a process designed to meet the academic, sociocultural, and psychological needs of non-English speaking (and, in the case of Canada, non-French speaking) pupils with disabilities. However, multicultural education that focuses on the diversity of society is for all students. It exists apart from bilingual education, which serves only those for whom English is not a first language. Multicultural education and bilingual education are not the same thing, and we cannot reduce a multicultural perspective to only an exercise that revolves around teaching a child to speak English or to use a standard dialect. But, even while stressing a separation between multicultural education and bilingual education, we must recognize that language is a critical element of educational programs for linguistically diverse students and, by extension, a component of multicultural education and multicultural special education.

However, in this chapter, we focus only on multicultural education that, in all its varied forms, is influencing what children who receive special education services are learning (Kaplan 1996). The guidelines for a multicultural special education curriculum and program are defined when joined to a specific area of disability. That is, the ingredients of a multicultural special education program need to be combined with instructional techniques that are tailored to each area of disability.

Students with Special Needs from Diverse Backgrounds

To live and develop in two culturally different systems is sufficiently challenging for students without exceptional conditions. The difficulties multiply for students who are also disabled. When special problems in cognitive functioning, sensory use, communication, mobility, or social and behavioral interactions combine with cultural and linguistic diversity, individual differences increase dramatically—as do the chances of school failure, even when special services are provided. So pervasive are the problems that this group has been referred to as "triple threat students" (Rueda and Chan 1979); that is, they are considered to be at risk because of limited English proficiency, disability and, very often, poverty.

Many students of diverse cultural backgrounds may not fit exactly into any of the recognized categories of exceptionality. Conventional definitions do not always apply to these children, particularly for those whose first language is not English. Special factors must be considered when defining a culturally different child who is also disabled: (1) the developmental and cumulative consequences of a disabling condition as they relate to the consequences of limited English, (2) the other consequences of the specific disability condition, (3) the family's expectations, (4) cultural attitudes toward disabilities, and (5) the relationship between the child's cultural community and the larger society. Given these factors, disabled children from different cultures can best be described as children who have diagnosable disabilities that are recognized as such by both the cultural communities of their families and by the larger society.

Demographic information that describes the numbers of children with exceptionalities who have diverse cultural and linguistic backgrounds is difficult to extrapolate from sources because identifying and defining these populations as well as reporting about them has been inconsistent. Likewise, the annual reports to Congress that are required by the Individuals with Disabilities Education Act (IDEA) do not include data on the number of culturally diverse students who are served in special education programs.

Culturally diverse students are represented in all categories of exceptionality. Estimates suggest that the incidence of exceptionality among these children is as high as that for the general population, if not higher. For example, though information about the prevalence of exceptionality among the Native American population is difficult to obtain, conditions such as Fetal Alcohol Syndrome and hemophilus influenza meningitis have been reported to occur at a higher rate than in the general population. In Canada, hearing and visual impairments are widespread among the Native Canadian population; they are endemic throughout the Northwest Territories and are most prevalent in the Eastern and Central Arctic (Watters 1980).

Hardman and colleagues (1993) estimate that among students with disabilities, 41 percent are from culturally diverse backgrounds. Actual numbers are more difficult to verify. Some researchers hypothesize that if disabilities occur at the same percentage rate for students who are limited in English proficiency as for the general population, then about 200,000 children require services (Kaplan 1996). Others (see Baca and Cervantes 1989) estimate that approximately 1 million students in the United States are limited in English proficiency and also have serious learning and behavioral disorders as well as other needs that may qualify them for special services. Still others estimate a minimum of 1.4 million children with disabilities who are also minority group members (Gollnick and Chinn 1990).

The incidence of physical disabilities in some minority groups is related to conditions that are associated with poverty, one of the greatest risk factors in the development of children. "Persistent and concentrated poverty," it is said, "virtually guarantees the presence of a vast collection of risk factors and their continuing destructive impact over time" (Schorr 1988, 30). Berliner claims that we could "reduce special education needs by 50 percent if we reduce poverty in this country" (cited in "OSEP conference...", 9). When families are both poor and culturally different, the deleterious effects of poverty tend to be more pronounced and long lasting (Edelman 1987). Keep in mind that, today, one in four American children lives in poverty, and the gap between the affluent and the poor continues to widen.

Multicultural Education

Multiculturalism includes the many diverse cultural groups of which our society is composed. At the very least, these cultural groupings take into consideration ethnic and linguistic groups, gender differences, differences in family configuration, groups of different socioeconomic status, and differences in ability. The practice of multiculturalism means supporting positive basic commonalities while recognizing and nourishing constructive differences. It takes into account cultural tenacity, ethnic loyalties, and linguistic pride. Multiculturalism also implies that individuals can understand and function comfortably within more than one cultural context.

Multicultural education is often presented as simply an extension of a multicultural society. Of course, multiculturalism and multicultural education are conceptually linked, but they are not the same thing. As an enduring characteristic of American society, multiculturalism is far broader than multicultural education because it subsumes many attitudes and trends in society. Multicultural education is but one part of the solution to questions of diversity, equity, and inclusion. As James Banks explains, multicultural education "suggests a type of education concerned with creating educational environments in which students from a variety of microcultural groups such as race/ethnicity, gender, social class, regional groups, and *people with disabilities* experience educational equality" (1994, 89, emphasis added).

Described as "a significant and sophisticated model of curriculum and instruction" (Davidman and Davidman 1997, 273), multicultural education brings changes to many aspects of a school: classroom climate, teacher expectations, and curricula. Because no single model exists, teachers who are working in multicultural education typically work with an emergent and eclectic conception that is colored by their own values and experiences as well as by the needs of children. They work this way by being knowledgeable about the effect of culture on language and learning, by making efforts to incorporate the language and culture of minority groups into school programs, by helping students to overcome discrimination and bias, by encouraging minority students to participate, and by involving parents and the community (Winzer and Mazurek 1998).

Nevertheless, although many contemporary educators look to multicultural approaches, perspectives, and curricula for direction, the entire conceptualization and practice of multicultural education is still evolving, and a consensus has not been reached. The area is rife with conceptual ambiguity and ideological polarization so that the scope and essence of multicultural education remains ill defined, its meaning misunderstood, and its interpretation open to increasing controversy and criticism.

Multicultural education is contentious because it is a reform movement; it seeks to change the status quo of schools and society. It brings a new vision of a pluralist rather than an assimilated America. It is multifaceted and difficult to understand, and educators have not yet come to common stances on the underlying philosophy and the best practices. At root is the question of whether it is even possible to formulate a theoretical conciliation between pluralism and multiculturalism. On the one hand, pluralism espouses that all people should be treated the same and that we should not accent differences among groups. On the other hand, multiculturalism proposes that although we should treat each person with respect, we should also consider—and even celebrate—the differences among us.

Multicultural education is not a single entity; it has many faces. Varied perceptions of the concept abound, and advocates often disagree about the dimensions that should be included under its rubric. Consequently, we can approach multicultural education in a number of ways. We can view it as the education of culturally different students, education about cultural differences, education for cultural pluralism, and bicultural education. Within these varied approaches, practitioners of multicultural education describe a wide variety of programs and practices that are related to ethnic groups, language minorities, low-income groups, and equity in educational services.

Historical Precedent

In the past, special education was not noted for its responsiveness to cultural differences; the field has demonstrated little recognition or understanding of cultural and linguistic variables. Despite the pervasive literature that culture and language affect learning, most special education teachers were prone to concentrate on a child's disability to the exclusion of cultural and linguistic variables and to plan instruction based on a child's disability only. Children's distinct language genres, behavioral patterns, values, attitudes, and expectations were seen as deficits to be remediated. Even today, the system still fails to reach many at-risk, disadvantaged, disabled, and gifted children. Of these students, those from American backgrounds that are non-European, especially, African Americans, Hispanic Americans, and Native Americans, as well as those with limited English proficiency, are poorly served (Grossman 1995).

Inappropriate Placement

In the past, immigrant and minority-group children were overrepresented in such classifications as slow learner, educable mentally retarded, and learning disabled (Cummins 1984, 1986; Gelb and Mikokawa 1986; Sleeter 1986). A disproportionate representation of culturally diverse students in special education is still an ongoing problem nationwide ("19th Annual Report to Congress" 1998). For example, a high proportion of students served under the category of serious emotional disturbance are from culturally and linguistically diverse groups. Some evidence suggests that teachers are far more likely to refer students for discipline problems when they are from a culture other than that of the teacher

(Bullara 1993). When deciding on the most appropriate placement for students with the exact same behavior and academic problems, special educators and school systems are more likely to choose a special education placement for poor and non-European students, especially if the students are *both* poor and non-European. They are more likely to choose a regular education placement for European American and middle-class students (Grossman 1995). Teachers, for example, are 3.5 times more likely to identify poor African American students as developmentally disabled than their European American peers (Matute-Bianchi 1986).

Students of color are more often classified as special education students than are European American mainstream students. Of all ethnic groups, African Americans are the most represented in programs and in classes for students with behavior disorders and mental retardation (Chinn and Hughes 1987). For example, African Americans account for 16 percent of the overall student population but account for 32 percent of those students in programs for mild mental retardation, 24 percent in programs for serious emotional disturbance or behavioral disorders, and 18 percent of students with specific learning disabilities ("19th Annual Report" 1998). This representation in special education continues to be about twice the rate that would be expected based on the percentage of African Americans in the nation's schools (see Williams 1992).

Native American children are the most likely group to receive special education services after African American students. The number of Hispanic students labeled as mildly mentally retarded or emotionally disturbed has decreased, but a serious overrepresentation of Hispanic children continues in programs for those with learning disabilities. Asian American students tend to be underrepresented in programs for learning disabilities, serious emotional disturbance, and behavioral disorders, and they are overrepresented in programs for speech disorders. In some school districts, as many as 50 percent of Asian children are receiving special education in speech programs (Grossman 1995).

School Failure

Low achievement, school failure, and attrition are more the rule than the exception for both normally developing and exceptional students from diverse cultural backgrounds. Many persuasive explanations have been made to account for the disparate educational outcomes between students from diverse backgrounds and their European American counterparts. These explanations include (but are certainly not limited to) ethnocentric attitudes of racial superiority; low expectations and negative attitudes; assumptions that children from some ethnic groups learn more and faster than children from other groups; the lack of strategies that foster cultural acceptance and diversity; the absence of role models in the schools and the curriculum; the lack of understanding of a child's culture and language; monocultural textbooks and materials; and narrow and limited instructional techniques. Access to learning may be further limited for culturally diverse children with disabilities when the sole focus is on a child's exceptionality.

Learning Styles

The influence of ethnicity on students in both regular and special education is pervasive. Children do not shed their cultural differences at the school door; rather, they bring their socialization patterns, linguistic backgrounds, modes of communication, social mores, learning styles, and the manifestations of their values and culture with them to the classroom. The distinctive work styles, views, values, language, standards, and expectations of culturally diverse children may then affect their reactions to the classroom climate, the classroom structure and routine, classroom discipline, and interactions with teachers and peers.

A culturally diverse student population will reveal significant differences in students' performance and interactions in areas such as verbal and nonverbal communication as well as in orientation modes such as conceptions of time, social values, and cognitive tempo. Cultural differences in learning may be especially apparent in three areas—learning styles, communication styles, and language differences.

Children whose past experiences and whose language and communication, learning styles, and cultural values do not fit into the behavior that is expected in traditional mainstream classrooms may face grave difficulties within the school system. A number of researchers (see Poplin 1988; Tharp 1989) assert that many African American, Hispanic American, and Asian American learners have difficulty with traditional patterns of cognitive functioning because these traditional patterns ignore the effect of culture on language, learning, and thinking. For example, research shows that African American dialect and cognition may require an approach to learning math and science concepts that is at odds with the traditional way in which these subjects are taught (Orr 1987).

Current Realities

Children receiving special education services have the same need that other children have to understand their own culture and that of others, to develop a more positive understanding of their own cultural heritage, to explore similarities and differences, and to confront biases and stereotypes. Regardless of a student's type and degree of disability or of a student's ethnic and linguistic background, he or she should be exposed to multicultural perspectives (although not necessarily exposed to bilingual special education).

Academic Performance

Data suggest that for minority groups who experience disproportionate levels of academic failure, their academic success is predicted by the extent to which their language and culture are incorporated into the school program (Cummins 1985; Willig 1985). Curriculum should be culturally compatible. In essence, cultural compatibility means the use of culturally responsive instruction in which educators employ instructional strategies and curricular adaptations that are consistent with students' experiences, perspectives, and developmental ages (Collier and Kalk 1989; Irvine 1990). That is, ideally, teaching practices should be altered to meet a child's needs. These customized teaching practices require a recognition that

- culture is significant in educational settings,
- specific languages and cultural attitudes influence students' cognitive growth and socialization processes,
- the stereotyping of minorities must be prevented,
- cultural conflicts in the schools must be resolved,
- home and school cultures must be integrated, and
- communication skills must be developed in school (Nel 1993).

Bilingual Special Education

As we pointed out, multicultural education and bilingual education are not synonymous processes and programs. Multicultural education focuses first on culture. The philosophy of bilingual special education is to offer the student the benefit of learning and reinforcing a first language while acquiring a second. The practice in bilingual education is that children learn English but receive basic academic instruction in their first language so that they do not fall behind academically (see Baca and Amato 1989).

Nevertheless, bilingual and multicultural education often proceed hand in hand. As children need culturally compatible instruction, so supporters of bilingual special education argue that when children with limited English proficiency do not receive basic instruction in their native language, at least until they become fully proficient in English, their "chances of succeeding in school are tragically undercut" (First 1988, 207). For students who receive special education services, a school may provide a bilingual special education program, staffed by a bilingual special education teacher, in which students receive individual services that are designed to strengthen their learning and to demonstrate respect for their language and culture (Diaz-Rico and Weed 1995).

MULTICULTURAL SPECIAL EDUCATION

As the nation's public school population becomes more culturally and linguistically diverse, both general and special education must collectively and seriously confront the multitude of issues and challenges surrounding educational equity and academic excellence for all children and youth. Special education can no longer be concerned solely with the nature of a disabling condition and the appropriate intervention strategies tailored for a particular disability. Today and in the future, schools must develop programs, teaching methods, and resources to teach a diverse student body, and they must improve special education service delivery for exceptional learners from a wide variety of cultural and linguistic backgrounds.

Multicultural special education can be defined in this way:

> A set of perspectives and skills that change the climate, curriculum, and interactions in schools and classrooms so that all students, whatever their cultural and linguistic background or type and degree of disability, have equal respect, the opportunity to learn, and are given the skills to develop cross-cultural sensitivity and the competencies necessary to function in a pluralistic society. Multicultural perspectives and skills meld with special education practices, are infused throughout the curriculum, and are tailored to the unique strengths and needs of each child who is exceptional. (Winzer and Mazurek 1998, 104–5)

Rationale

People with disabilities are included within the multicultural rubric. However, appreciating differences is not enough; children who are culturally and linguistically diverse and who also have special needs also require a multicultural curriculum that overarches a supportive environment and climate as well as instruction that is culturally compatible.

The rationales that underlie multicultural special education are diverse and far-reaching. In general, the current demand for multicultural special education is a response to seven factors: historical precedent, inappropriate placement, school failure, learning styles, current realities, academic performance, and bilingual special education.

Program Development

Hard-and-fast formulas to carry out multicultural education are not available because it does not involve a specific way of teaching, a particular approach or technique, or a one-time, one-classroom approach. As a process, multicultural education is ongoing, is continually facing new challenges, and is weathering new priorities. Developing multicultural education in a school takes many years. It is neither a component that is added on nor one that is set apart, separate, or special. Multicultural education is a perspective—a way of viewing schools, students, and the curriculum that infuses cultural sensitivity into everything that is done in classrooms.

When the population to be served is culturally diverse, all educational activities and services must provide for three major characteristics—language, culture, and disability (Garcia and Yates 1994). Multicultural education is an extension of the goals and methods found in regular education; that is, when we add multicultural perspectives, the approaches and methodologies that are used for children from diverse cultures who are also disabled extend in many ways the procedures used with other culturally diverse children. What is effective in classrooms for students who are culturally diverse but normally developing is generally effective in all classrooms because the issues, approaches, and techniques of multicultural education (and bilingual education) cut across educational settings and student characteristics so that, in general, providing a multicultural perspective is simply an application of the principles of good teaching. Competencies, teaching methods, and curriculum are extensions and refinements of core competencies rather than new sets of teaching behaviors and skills.

Therefore, instruction for students who not only are from culturally and linguistically diverse backgrounds but also have disabilities is based on the same principles and purposes as multicultural education that creates supportive learning environments in general education (Garcia and Malkin 1993). This finding means that the curriculum for culturally diverse students is based on a school's knowledge and understanding of each specific minority culture; that a curriculum is based in the students' culture, not on it; that children are given clarified, reflective, and positive ethnic identifications; and that teachers make the effort to incorporate minority students' language and culture into a school program and encourage minority students to participate.

Curriculum

Whether it is for normally developing students or for those with special needs, a multicultural curriculum generally includes goals such as developing an appreciation of the shared national culture, demonstrating the racial and cultural diversity of the country, studying and sharing cultures, respecting other cultures, developing cross-cultural competency, and eliminating stereotypes and biases. To accomplish these goals, children need a meaningful curriculum and developmentally appropriate activities and experiences. They also need carefully selected instructional materials and appropriate instructional resources (Morris 1983).

Teachers, therefore, need to expand their repertoires in a number of areas. They must acquire an appreciation of the differences between and within cultural groups, understand which interactions are effective, and apply multicultural perspectives to special education concerns. Teachers need to modify and then constantly monitor their own attitudes and expectations. Curricula may broaden to encompass pre-referral intervention, English as a second language, bilingual education, appropriate instructional resources, adjustment to and accommodation of different learning styles, the review of assessment practices to ensure that they are as fair as possible, and criterion-referenced or curriculum-based assessment. When planning a curriculum, teachers should examine and include areas related to communication, language experiences and acquisition, the culture of the home, materials and resources, ways to assess capabilities and limitations, management and planning, and modifications for specific disabilities. The instruction offered to culturally and linguistically different students with disabilities should use strategies that address both the disability as well as the cultural and linguistic learning differences. Also, this instruction should be collaborative and involve both general educators and special educators in providing services (Winzer and Mazurek 1998).

Instruction

A multicultural perspective is both an orientation and a set of skills. As a perspective, it is a way of thinking about and looking at the world. As a set of skills, it includes ways of infusing these views into the classroom climate and the curriculum. How the multicultural model is transformed into curricular plans and instructional strategies is up to the teacher who is most in tune with the special needs of the students. Effective multicultural lessons contain the same ingredients as any other lessons, but teachers' responses depend on such factors as the importance of a concept, the language necessary, the degree of disability, and so on. Teachers of special students have to decide how much and what academic work to include, the emphasis to take, the kinds of aids to be used, and the effective use of community resources.

Teachers always must keep in mind that students with disabilities have different levels of maturity and cognitive ability. They must select approaches that match the needs of the individual student, that are relevant to the child's understanding, and that are developmentally as well as age appropriate. Because the type and degree of disability determines the approach, special educators cannot use the same approach with each child. Students' contextual, linguistic, and gender characteristics influence how they learn, and the teaching styles that work with one segment of the population may not work with another. For example, multicultural approaches that are effective with students who have learning and sensory disabilities may not suit the needs of students who have cognitive disabilities.

Although the ways in which multicultural perspectives and skills are put into effect can be complex and encompassing, the general teacher competencies that are required for effective multicultural education fall into three overlapping categories—attitudes, skills, and knowledge.

Attitudes. Attitudes apply specifically to acceptance, tolerance, expectations, and interactions—all of which have a formative effect on the curriculum and on teaching practices. Attitudes have to do with valuing one's own culture and language and appreciating the culture and language of others. Because acceptance and tolerance arise from a teacher's attitudes, the actions that an educator takes regarding the cultures and languages of minority students are critical: They define the extent to which schools either empower or disable students. Educators must not only understand and modify their own values but also should develop empathy with other cultures through both knowledge and experience. Therefore, to become an effective multicultural teacher, an individual must become a multicultural person. First, teachers need to develop self-awareness—an awareness of their own culture—and how that culture affects the teaching and learning process. Second, teachers need cultural sensitivity, which relates to the knowledge of other cultures, to cross-cultural competence, and to the elimination of stereotypes and biases.

Skills. Multicultural skills include the ability to respond to students' learning styles and to adapt classroom organization and grouping. To acknowledge children's heritage without accommodating their instructional needs does little to enhance their performance on school-related tasks. Teachers need to know the characteristics of instructional strategies and materials that are culturally appropriate. They also need to know how to make adaptations to the classroom environment to stress methods such as cooperative learning; how to provide meaningful curriculum activities and experiences; how to effectively coordinate efforts between special education, bilingual education, and regular education; how to work with paraprofessionals; and how to involve parents and the community.

Knowledge. Multicultural knowledge relates to the content of a multicultural curriculum. Because multicultural education does not mean isolated programs or short-term interventions but, rather, changes that permeate the entire school program, multicultural concepts are infused into curriculum, not added on. Two major concepts dominate: (1) basing curriculum in the students' culture, not merely on it, and (2) providing multicultural education so that all children and youth can learn about the processes, contents, and values of the various cultures with which they interact to develop both tolerance and enthusiasm for other cultures.

Strategies For multicultural education to be effective, all of its dimensions must be infused into the classroom environment, the classroom climate, and the curriculum. Teachers should clearly communicate that the classroom is a place where diversity is natural, where each child is respected, and where fairness is modeled and expected.

Curriculum and instruction must be culturally compatible. Cultural compatibility is effected when teachers move away from traditional teaching models that promote the transmission of information through task analysis, structured drills, teacher-directed activities, and independent seatwork and move toward the use of alternate methods. Such a shift may require changes in how teachers interact with students, what they do to teach, the kinds of activities in which students engage, what the teacher views as acceptable outcomes, what responses students make, and the tasks that students undertake to learn. Teachers can make adaptations in instruction, organization, grouping, and materials. Alternative strategies include small-group instruction; peer mediated strategies; different motivational strategies, questioning techniques and wait time; multisensory teaching aids; different reinforcement systems; more "verve" in teaching some groups; cooperative learning; individual learning-center activities; computer-assisted instruction; reciprocal interactive teaching; and pull-in services by special education personnel.

Teachers may particularly stress cooperative learning, which research data suggest is a powerful cross-content, cross-grade-level strategy for accomplishing many multicultural goals such as educational equity, intergroup understanding and harmony, as well as positive collaborative relationships among students (Winzer and Mazurek 1998). For Native American students, for example, cooperative learning complements the values of cooperation and shared learning in the home. Because Native American cultural patterns emphasize the group, harmony with nature, and circularity, children from that culture often respond better to learning approaches that are noncompetitive, holistic, and cooperative (Lustig and Koestner 1996).

Infusion is a key concept and implies that multicultural perspectives are an integral part of every activity in a classroom. Teachers should move away from a tourist curriculum of putting together a special unit or celebration that depicts the cultural heritage of students and understand that multicultural education is not something set apart, separate, or special. Efforts to teach multicultural concepts and processes are an integral part of every subject area and reach all levels of education. A genuinely multicultural approach permeates the curriculum both horizontally and vertically in all subject areas and is supported by high-quality instructional materials.

Although many children with special needs may need such concrete activities as celebrations of special holidays, crafts, and different foods, teachers can modify monocultural routines, objectives, and curricula to incorporate multicultural perspectives. They can ensure that the perspectives, histories, traditions, and contributions of all groups are infused into the curriculum and that all materials are culturally appropriate and relevant.

CONCLUSION

When children arrive in a classroom, they do not come as young people separate from their culture, their backgrounds, or their parents. Every child comes from an environment and a family structure that provide different socialization and experiences. Children bring with them cultural scripts modeled on the material of their social environments and rooted in the values, attitudes, expectations, and behaviors of their family, culture, and community. Every student, therefore, has different experiences and brings different skills and needs to the classroom.

Together with legislators, parents, and the general public, educators in the United States and Canada have a great interest in finding ways to ensure appreciation of the diversity of their populations. Of the many reasons for this rather new-found focus on diversity in our schools, all more or less revolve around the question of equity. When, as is the case, minority students consistently make the lowest achievement scores and make up the majority of underachievers and dropouts, then educational equity within the current system must be examined. If we expect schools to provide citizens with much of the knowledge and skills they need to meet the challenges of life and to profit from the opportunities that life presents them, then all students should be ensured the same opportunity to succeed in school regardless of their country of origin, their English-language proficiency, their ethnic background, their socioeconomic class, the geographic area where they live and study, their gender, or their disability.

In special education, an acknowledgment of the effect that culture and linguistic differences have on learning problems is a relatively recent phenomenon. Today, however, we appreciate that students may not achieve their full potential unless modifications that make education both culturally appropriate and culturally compatible are in place. Just as we adapt the pace and complexity of the instructional format for many students with disabilities, so we further adapt to accommodate cultural and linguistic differences. That is, when instruction and learning are compatible with a child's culture and when minority students' language and culture are incorporated into the school program, more effective learning takes place.

To accommodate the tension between the values of students from diverse cultural backgrounds and a school that is based on the values of the dominant society, many contemporary educators are looking to multicultural education. At its core, multicultural education is a perspective, a way of looking at the world and at classrooms. But although providing a multicultural perspective is simply an application of the principles of good teaching, modifications are needed in what is taught, the manner in which teachers organize and deliver instruction, the way in which teachers assess student learning, and curriculum planning.

Philosophically, teachers need to develop sensitivity to cultural diversity, a recognition of the dynamics of differences, an understanding of the language characteristics of learners, and an awareness of the cultural factors that affect learning. Educationally, they need to be aware of the teaching concepts and strategies that are known to be effective in working with culturally and linguistically diverse children with disabilities. At the classroom level, a multicultural curriculum comes to life when the classroom climate is changed and all participants enter into fair-minded thinking and acting. Teachers stress holistic and cooperative strategies and focus on infusion, not one-time activities. Because multicultural education is a process that is ongoing and dynamic and is not a one-time activity or a one-unit instructional focus, multicultural concepts and attitudes must be infused into learning activities across the curriculum over time if they are to be effective.

REFERENCES

Baca, L. M., and C. Amato. 1989. Bilingual special education: Training issues. *Exceptional Children* 56:168–73.

Baca, L. M., and H. T. Cervantes, eds. 1989. *The bilingual special education interface.* 2d ed. Columbus, Ohio: Merrill.

Banks, J. A. 1994. *Multiethnic education: Theory and practice.* 3d ed. Boston: Allyn and Bacon.

Bullara, D. T. 1993. Classroom management strategies to reduce racially biased treatment of students. *Journal of Education and Psychological Consultation* 4:357–68.

Canada 2005. 1999. *Time* 153 (21):30–59.

Chinn, P. C., and S. Hughes. 1987. Representation of minority students in special education classes. *Remedial and Special Education* 8:41–46.

Collier, C., and M. Kalk. 1989. Bilingual special education curriculum development. In *The bilingual special education interface,* 2d ed., ed. L. M. Baca and H. T. Cervantes, 205–29. Columbus, Ohio: Merrill.

Cummins, J. 1984. *Bilingualism and special education: Issues in assessment and pedagogy.* Clevedon, England: Multilingual Matters.

———. 1985. *Disabling minority students: Power, programs, and pedagogy.* Toronto: OISE [Ontario Institute for Studies in Education] Press.

———. 1986. Empowering minority students: A framework for intervention. *Harvard Educational Review* 56:18–36.

Davidman, L., and P. T. Davidman. 1997. *Teaching with a multicultural perspective: A practical guide.* 2d ed. White Plains, N.Y.: Longman.

Diaz-Rico, L. T., and K. Z. Weed. 1995. *The cross-cultural language and academic development handbook: A complete k–12 reference guide.* Boston: Allyn and Bacon.

Edelman, M. W. 1987. *Families in peril: An agenda for social change.* Cambridge, Mass.: Harvard University Press.

First, J. M. 1988. Immigrant students in the U.S. public schools: Challenges with solutions. *Phi Delta Kappan* 70:205–10.

Garcia, S. B., and D. H. Malkin. 1993. Toward defining programs and services for culturally and linguistically diverse learners in special education. *Teaching Exceptional Children* 26:52–58.

Garcia, S. B., and J. Yates. 1994. Diversity: Teaching a special population. *CEC Today* 1 (1):10.

Gelb, S. A., and D. T. Mikokawa. 1986. Special education and social structure: The commonality of "exceptionality." *American Educational Research Journal* 23:543–57.

Gollnick, D. M., and P. C. Chinn. 1990. *Multicultural education in a pluralistic society.* 3d ed. Columbus, Ohio: Merrill.

Grossman, H. 1995. *Special education in a diverse society.* Boston: Allyn and Bacon.

Hardman, M. L., C. J. Drew, M. W. Egan, and B. Wolf. 1993. *Human exceptionality: Society, school, and family.* 4th ed. Boston: Allyn and Bacon.

Irvine, J. J. 1990. *Black students and school failure. Policies, practices, and prescriptions.* New York: Praeger.

Kaplan, P. S. 1996. *Pathways for exceptional children: School, home, and culture.* Minneapolis–St. Paul, Minn.: West Publishing.

Lustig, M. W., and J. Koestner. 1996. *Intercultural competence: Interpersonal communication across cultures.* 2d ed. New York: Harper Collins.

Matute-Bianchi, M. E. 1986. Ethnic identities and patterns of school success and failure among Mexican-descent and Japanese American students in a California high school: An ethnographic analysis. *American Journal of Education* 95:233–55.

Morris, J. B. 1983. Classroom methods and materials. In *Understanding the multicultural experience in early childhood education*, ed. O. N. Saracho and B. Spodek, 77–90. Washington, D.C.: National Association for the Education of Young Children.

Nel, J. 1993. Preservice teachers' perceptions of the goals of multicultural education: Implications for the empowerment of minority students. *Educational Horizons* 71:120–25.

19th Annual Report to Congress reinforces CEC positions. 1998. *CEC Today* (February/March):1, 9.

Orr, E. W. 1987. *Twice as less: Black English and the performance of black students in math and science.* New York: Norton.

OSEP conference sheds new light on state of education, special education practice. *CEC Today* 5:1, 9, 15.

Poplin, M. S. 1988. Holistic/constructivist principles of the teaching/learning process: Implications for the field of learning disabilities. *Journal of Learning Disabilities* 21:401–16.

Rueda, R., and K. Chan. 1979. Poverty and culture in special education: Separate but equal. *Exceptional Children* 45:422–31.

Schorr, L. B. 1988. *Within our reach.* New York: Doubleday.

Sleeter, C. E. 1986. Learning disabilities: The social construction of a special education category. *Exceptional Children* 53:46–54.

Statistics Canada. 1996. Projections of visible minority groups: 1991–2016. *Canadian Social Trends* 41:3.

———. 1997. 1996 census: Mother tongue, home language and knowledge of languages. Excerpts from *The Daily–Cat.* No. 11-001E (December 2):1–3. Ottawa: Government of Canada.

———. 1998a. 1996 census: Ethnic origin, visible minorities. Excerpts from *The Daily–Cat.* No. 11-001E (February 17):7–10. Ottawa: Government of Canada.

———. 1998b. *Visible minority population by group: 1996 census.* Available: <www.stat can.ca/english/Pgdb/People/Population/demo40a.htm>. Ottawa: Statistics Canada.

Tharp, R. G. 1989. Psychocultural variables and constants: Effects on teaching and learning in schools. *American Psychologist* 44:349–59.

U.S. Census Bureau. 1997. *Current population survey.* Available: <www.bls. census.gov/cps/pub/1997/for_born.htm>. Washington, D.C.: U.S. Census Bureau.

———. 1998. *U.S. Census Bureau facts for features.* Available: <www.census.gov/ PressRelease/cb98-ff.11.html>. Washington, D.C.: U.S. Census Bureau.

———. 1999a. *Resident population estimates of the United States by sex, race, and Hispanic origin.* Available: <www.census.gov/population/estimates/nation/intfile3-1.txt>. Washington, D.C.: U.S. Census Bureau.

———. 1999b. *U.S. Census Bureau facts for features.* Available: <www.census.gov/Press-Release/cb99-ff.06.html>. Washington, D.C.: U.S. Census Bureau.

U.S. Immigration and Naturalization Service. 1999. *Immigration and naturalization statistics.* Available: <www.insusdoj.gov/stat/299.html>. Washington, D.C.: U.S. Immigration and Naturalization Services.

Watters, B. 1980. Special education in the Northwest territories. In *Special education across Canada: Issues and concerns for the '80s*, ed. M. Csapo and L. Goguen. Vancouver: Centre for Human Development and Research.

Williams, B. F. 1992. Changing demographics: Challenges for educators. *Intervention in School and Clinic* 27:157–63.

Willig, A. C. 1985. A meta-analysis of selected studies on the effectiveness of bilingual education. *Review of Educational Research* 55:269–307.

Winzer, M. A., and K. Mazurek. 1998. *Special education in multicultural contexts*. Columbus, Ohio: Merrill.

Contributors

JULIA ELLIS is a professor in the Department of Elementary Education, Faculty of Education, University of Alberta. She teaches courses on qualitative research, models of teaching, and ESL programs and methods. She has a book in press with Garland titled *Teaching from Understanding: Teacher as Interpretive Inquirer.* Her current research focuses on school-based volunteer mentorship programs. A product of her recent research is a video program titled *Listen UP! Kids Talk about Good Teaching.* Earlier in her career, Dr. Ellis taught courses on gifted and enrichment programming and developed materials for using creative problem solving in the classroom. She also conducted program evaluations of three districtwide gifted programs. She was coordinator of the Southern Alberta Gifted and Talented Education Project, based at the University of Lethbridge.

DEBORAH PETERS GOESSLING is an assistant professor of education at Providence College, Providence, Rhode Island. Dr. Goessling received her B.A. and M.Ed. from Boston College, and has more than twelve years of experience teaching students with severe disabilities in segregated and integrated public school settings. In 1994 she received her doctorate in special education from Boston University. Before teaching at Providence College, she was an assistant professor at the University of Maine and coordinator of the graduate studies program in severe disabilities. Her current research interests include inclusion, paraeducators, and beginning teachers.

KELLY HENDERSON is currently a Society for Research in Child Development Policy Fellow at the Office of Special Education Programs, U.S. Department of Education. A former public school special education teacher, Dr. Henderson completed her Ph.D. in special education at the University of Maryland in 1997. Dr. Henderson's research interests include special education and education reform policy as well as programs and services for students identified with emotional and behavioral disorders.

CRAIG H. JONES is a professor of psychology and counseling at Arkansas State University where he has taught since 1977. Current teaching assignments are in educational psychology and research methods. He received a bachelor's degree in psychology from Rutgers University in 1972, a master's degree in social psychology from the University of Kansas in 1975, and an Ed.D. in higher education from the University of Mississippi in 1983. He has published more than fifty articles in peer-reviewed journals in the fields of education and psychology. Current research interests focus on improving the academic achievement of high school and college students.

TIMOTHY J. LANDRUM has been a teacher of students with behavioral disorders in a variety of settings. He received his doctorate in special education from the University of Virginia. He is currently a faculty member in special education at Cleveland State University, where he teaches courses to prepare teachers to work with students who have mild and moderate disabilities.

CLEBORNE D. MADDUX taught for ten years in the public schools of Oregon and Arizona before earning his Ph.D. in learning disabilities from the University of Arizona in 1978. Since that time, he has been an assistant, associate, and a full professor at four institutions, most recently at the University of Nevada, Reno, where he is a professor in the Department of Counseling and Educational Psychology and teaches classes in statistics and in information technology in education. He has written fourteen books and more than one hundred scholarly articles in the areas of special education and in information technology in education. His current interests focus on the use of the Internet and the World Wide Web in education.

KAS MAZUREK is professor of education at the University of Lethbridge, Alberta, Canada. His research interests overlap the fields of comparative education; multiculturalism and minority group relations; the social contexts of educational ideas, policies, and practices; and the logic of inquiry.

MARGARET McFADDEN is a doctoral student in gifted education in the Department of Educational Psychology, Faculty of Education, University of Alberta. She has several years of teaching experience in both special education and regular education settings in grades k–9 in Alberta and in Saskatchewan.

MARGARET J. McLAUGHLIN is the associate director of the Institute for the Study of Exceptional Children and Youth, College of Education, University of Maryland, College Park. She specializes in the area of disability policy with a particular focus on special education. Her recent research has been concerned with how current educational reform initiatives are affecting students with disabilities.

MARGERY MILLER is a professor of psychology at Gallaudet University. In her tenure at Gallaudet, Dr. Miller has been director of Family Learning Vacations, coordinator of the Family Life Program at the National Academy, and director of the Counseling and Development Center at the former Northwest Campus. Her graduate degrees include a Ph.D. in psychology from Georgetown University and an M.A. in school psychology. Dr. Miller has published extensively and presented widely in the United States and abroad. Research interests and activities include signed test adaptations for deaf children; assessment of verbal intelligence and expressive and receptive language development; language and literacy issues; and family and cultural issues.

DONALD MOORES is a professor of education at Gallaudet University and has been editor of the *American Annals of the Deaf* since 1990. He was director of the Gallaudet Center for Studies in Education and Human Development during its existence from 1981 to 1996. He has a Ph.D. in educational psychology from the University of Illinois and an M.A. in education from Gallaudet. Dr. Moores is the author of *Educating the Deaf: Psychology, Principles, and Practices*, with the fifth edition in production. He has been involved in research in the acquisition of ASL, evaluation of preschool programs, public school education, mathematics achievement, literacy, and vocational adjustment of deaf individuals.

MARY ANNE PRATER is a professor in and chair of the Department of Special Education at the University of Hawaii at Manoa. She earned her doctorate in special education from Utah State University. Her current research and professional interests include self-management strategies for students with mild disabilities and for students at risk for educational failure, instructional design, general and special education teacher preparation, multicultural education, and the depiction of youth with disabilities in children's literature.

THOMAS W. SILEO is a professor in the Department of Special Education and NCATE Coordinator in the College of Education at the University of Hawaii at Manoa. He earned his doctorate in special education from the University of Northern Colorado. His current research and professional interests concern multicultural education, higher education instructional strategies, working with youth who are at risk for educational failure, family involvement programs, as well as innovations in general and special education teacher preparation.

JOHN R. SLATE received his Ph.D. in psychology from the University of Tennessee in 1984. He began his academic career as an assistant professor of psychology at Western Carolina University, moved to Arkansas State University where he was promoted to full professor and awarded tenure, and currently is a full professor of educational leadership at Valdosta State University in Georgia. Research interests involve special education assessment as well as study skills and related attitudinal variables. He also collaborates with faculty and students on myriad research topics.

SUSAN BRAY STAINBACK received her doctorate from the University of Virginia. Her professional experiences involve elementary, secondary, and university teaching and research. She has authored and edited numerous publications including books, monographs, chapters in books, and articles in professional journals. She has served as a visiting scholar to several universities and on the editorial-consulting boards of many national journals and organizations. Dr. Stainback was recently selected to fill the Matthew J. Guglielmo Endowed Chair Professorship for Distinguished Scholars at California State University. Her current professional interests involve how to address the educational needs of all students in regular schools and classrooms.

MELODY TANKERSLEY earned her doctorate in special education from the University of Virginia and completed a postdoctoral fellowship at the University of Kansas, Juniper Gardens Children's Project. She is currently an associate professor of special education at Kent State University, where she conducts research and teaches courses in the area of behavior disorders.

SHAVAUN M. WALL is an associate professor of education at Catholic University of America in Washington, D.C. Dr. Wall is the principal investigator in Catholic University's Early Head Start local research project conducted with the Early Head Start program, which is administered by United Cerebral Palsy of Washington and Northern Virginia. A licensed psychologist, Dr. Wall has worked with children with disabilities and their families for more than twenty years.

MARGRET A. WINZER is a professor at the University of Lethbridge in Alberta, Canada, where she teaches courses on special education, early childhood education, and educational psychology. She has written extensively in the area of special education, particularly on the history of early childhood special education, comparative studies in special education, and multicultural special education.

Index